HOW TO BECOME
--A--
SUCCESSFUL MOTORMAN

This book contains information regarding the Dynamo, the Motors, Systems of Control, Trolley and Third Rail Lines, Rolling Stock, Air Compressors, Multiple Unit Control, Automatic Air Brake, Rules and Regulations and Examination Questions for Motormen.

BY

SIDNEY AYLMER-SMALL, M. A. I. E. E.

FULLY ILLUSTRATED

©2008-2010 Periscope Film LLC
All Rights Reserved
ISBN #978-1-935700-24-1
www.PeriscopeFilm.com

PREFACE.

The seeker after knowledge pertaining to electrical power and all the term implies will find this a book of instruction, written in a clear, simple and thorough manner.

It begins at the base of electrical force—the Dynamo—and, step by step, shows the evolution of electricity as applied to motive force and the correct results that are or should be obtained.

No man is so thoroughly posted on electric power but he can learn much from this book. He will find it corroborates his practical experience, and suggests new ideas and improvements.

It points the way to the operator of motor rolling stock which will make his duties lighter and more agreeable, for it places within his reach at all times a knowledge of motors which he could not obtain without years of experience as a motorman.

To the man of limited experience as a motorman it supplies information of the most useful character. It shortens the way for him to become an expert and saves him time and money.

It is educational and illustrates the things essential to motors and their appliances and, through a series of questions, ascertains the amount of knowledge one actually has of the matters disclosed in the book. It is a work needed for a long time and it fulfills the need in every way.

CONTENTS.

The Dynamo 1
The Alternator 10
Drum Windings 21
Classes of Dynamos 29
Motors 32
Starting Motors 34
Counter E. M. F. 37
Railway Motors 41
The Series Motor 50
The Induction Motor 51
Transmission Lines, Feeders, Trolley and Third Rail. 58
Over Head Trolley Line 65
Third Rail 73
Systems of Control 81
The Sprague General Electric Type M. Control 93
Rolling Stock 107
Trucks 125
Car Equipment 134
Contact Devices 137
Heaters 138
Air Brake 141
Air Brake Equipment on Motor Cars 149
Air Compressor on Electric Locomotives 152
Suburban Motor Car Catechism 158
Instruction for the Operation of Multiple Unit Control 163

CONTENTS.

Motor Control	164
Master Control	182
The Emergency Air Brake Attachment	196
Train Operation	198
Train Failure	201
Failure of Power	202
Defect in Motor Control Circuit	204
General Directions	206
Automatic Air Brake Catechism	208
The Air Compressor	210
Electric Pump Governor	213
Main Reservoirs	215
Safety Valve	216
Slide-Valve, Feed-Valve	216
Control Pipe	220
Motorman's Brake Valve	221
Brake Pipe	224
Triple Valve	226
Auxiliary Reservoir	227
Brake Cylinder	227
Levers	228
General Operation	230
General Rules	241
Definitions	244
Train Rules	247
Standard Times	247
Time Tables	248
Signal Rules	249
Visible Signals	250
Audible Signals	252
Bell Cord Signals	253
Train Signals	254

CONTENTS.

Use of Signals..................................255
Classifications of Trains.......................256
Movement of Trains..............................257
Rules for Movement by Train Orders............260
Forms of Train Orders...........................265
Examples 266
Fixed Signals 281
Semaphore Signals 281
Bulletin Orders 282
Train Dispatchers 282
Conductors and Motormen.........................283
Conductors 285
Motormen......................................288
Markers 292
Examination Questions 298
Questions on Air Brake........................310

The Dynamo.

The dynamo is a machine for transforming mechanical energy into electrical energy, by use of the principles of electro-magnetic induction. These principles were discovered by Faraday. You may repeat his experiments for yourself.

Direction of the Induced E. M. F. In front of you on the table lay a magnet with its N-end projecting over the edge. Take a copper wire and connect its two ends to a galvanometer or pressure meter; usually called a *Voltmeter*. Stretch a portion of this wire between the right and left hands, and move the wire rapidly down in front of the N-end of the magnet at right angles to lines of its action. There will be induced in the wire a pressure or *Electro-motive force* which will send current through the wire from your right hand to your left. The galvanometer will give a deflection showing the flow of current.

This deflection is not a permanent one, the needle instantly dropping back to zero, proving that only a momentary current was produced.

If the experiment is tried moving the wire upwards the direction of the momentary circuit is reversed.

With a downward motion in front of a S-pole we get a left to right current.

Hence, starting with a certain polarity and direction of motion, changing one changes the direction of the induced current, while changing both the polarity and the direction of the motion does not reverse the current.

Now hold the wire a foot away from the magnet and directly opposite it, moving the wire up to the magnet and back again, keeping the distance from the wire to the floor the same, so that the motion shall be parallel to the flux. No E. M. F. is generated in this case.

An electromagnet would do as well and probably better as they are usually stronger than permanent magnets.

The value of the Induced E. M. F. depends on the following:—

1. The greater the strength of the magnet the greater the E. M. F.

2. The more rapidly the wire is moved, the greater the induction.

3. The larger the number of turns in a coil of wire the greater is the E. M. F. induced in it.

The induced E. M. F. therefore depends on the *flux*, the *speed of cutting* this flux, and the *number of wires* cutting this flux.

A dynamo reduced to its simplest form is a coil of wire arranged so as to cut the magnetic flux of an electro magnet, thus producing an induced electromotive force.

A dynamo therefore does not generate electricity, but pumps up a pressure as does a water pump, thus causing the electricity to flow through the circuit, which is called a current.

The current flows through the dynamo and the external circuit in *series,* hence the greater the current the larger must be the dynamo and the heavier the wires of the external circuit.

Since the E. M. F. (electromotive force) can be produced almost entirely by speed of the machine, the voltage at which the current is delivered does not affect the weight of the machine very much.

It is also evident that the faster a machine is driven the smaller the magnets can be and yet the same E. M. F. be produced. This is why high speed generators weigh less than low speed machines. The usual 600 volt railway generator weighs 11, 13, or 16 pounds per ampere of current capacity.

The railway generator whose voltage is 600 and whose resistance is 0.025 of an ohm, would give a current which can be calculated by Ohms law.

$$\text{Amperes} = \frac{\text{E. M. F.}}{\text{Resistance of generator plus resistance of the external circuit.}}$$

If we allowed the external resistance to fall too low by attempting to operate too many locomotives at the same time, the current drawn would generate a great amount of heat while passing through the machine. The amount of this heat can be calculated by the rule.

Heat in Watts is equal to the Square of the current multiplied by the resistance of the generator.

If we build an 11-ton generator and load it too heavily, that is, put 4000 amperes on it; it will have C^2R

watts of heat or 16,000,000 x 0.025 equal to 40 K. W. (kilo watts) to dissipate. Now a machine like this has such a small surface that it cannot radiate 40 K. W. of heat to the air, whereas if a heavier machine had been built, one of 22 tons, it could have gotten rid of the heat. Moreover the copper wires of the 22-ton machine being larger than those of the light machine, the resistance they offer is less, and there will be less heat generated. Thus the heavier machine will run cooler than even the light machine properly loaded.

The danger in overheating of generators is the damage done to the cotton insulation of the wires, due to scorching, and the melting of the shellac varnish between the layers of mica. The mica itself stands the heat very nicely. Any overheating of the armature and the commutator is at once conducted to the bearings.

To prevent the generation and retention of too much heat it is customary to allow 700 C. M. (circular mils) of copper for each ampere of current and to design the shape of the coils of wire so that they will have one square inch of surface for every two watts of heat to be gotten rid of.

The generator must be protected by fuses (which will melt) or by circuit breakers (automatic switches opening at a definite current) which will open the circuit and prevent the further flow of current in case of an accidental low resistance or *short circuit,* as it is called, which would otherwise draw a very heavy current and *burn out* the dynamo. The armature is the part that suffers first.

In talking about dynamos or generators (the two names are used for the same machine) we use the words

E. M. F. and *voltage*. By the E. M. F. of a dynamo is meant *the total pressure generated by the armature*. As the current flows through the armature and field circuits of a railway generator it encounters the *internal resistance* of the generator and pressure is lost according to the rule: Drop in pressure is equal to the product of the current and the resistance. Hence the current as it flows out of the generator is at a reduced pressure; and this pressure at which current is delivered to the switch board, is called the terminal voltage or simply the *Voltage* of the machine. For the generator like above Drop=C x R=2000 x 0.025=50 volts.

If we intend to deliver power at 600 volts it will be necessary to design the speed and the magnetic flux to produce a pressure of about 650 volts.

If a voltmeter be applied to the brushes of a generator just ready to go into service, but not yet carrying any load, the reading obtained is called the E. M. F. When the switches are closed and the generator furnishes power to the line the reading of the voltmeter will drop and its reading is called the *Voltage* of the machine.

We often speak of current being drawn from the dynamo. The generator keeps a steady pressure on the line of 600 volts and the flow of current is regulated by the load in the following way:

One locomotive hauling a train at speed will have a resistance of 0.3 ohm and will draw 600 divided by 0.3 or 2000 amperes.

It would be more accurate to say 2000 amperes are allowed to flow. This locomotive is the only path for current to pass from the feeder (third rail) to the return (rails). When two locomotives are in use there are two paths between the feeder and the return. The conducttivity between conductors has been doubled and the resistance halved. Double the previous current now flows.

In this way we get the current desired by lowering the resistance, and as the current passes it performs the work.

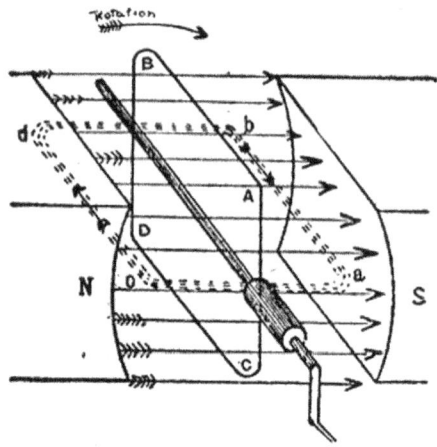

Fig. 179. Direction of Induced E. M. F. in Dynamo.

Two locomotives draw twice the current of one, hence their conductivity is double that of one, and their combined resistance is half of one.

The conductivity of three locomotives is treble, so their combined resistance or Joint Resistance is one-third that of one.

In the usual type of railroad generator, the revolving part is the armature and the stationary part the field magnets. Fig. 179 shows the elements of a dynamo, and as the loop is rotated there is an E. M. F. generated in it.

While the loop is coming into and passing away from the position ABCD, there is no E. M. F. generated, for the motion is parallel to the flux. As the loop moves towards the position ABCD by a uniform rotative speed it cuts the lines of force faster and faster, for first it cuts in an oblique manner but as the loop comes into the position of abcd the loop is moving straight across the flux. Hence the actual number of lines cut per second is least at ABCD and gradually increasing becomes greatest at abcd; thus producing an E. M. F. of varying value.

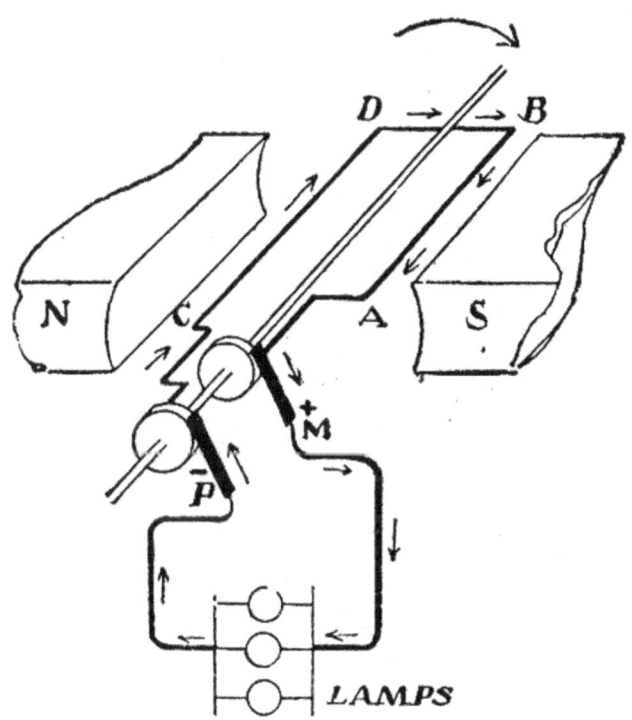

Fig. 180. The Simple Alternating Current Dynamo. Brush M Is Positive.

During this quarter of a revolution the wire BA has moved down in front of a S-pole inducing an E. M. F. tending to send current from B towards A. The other part of the loop CD has moved upward in front of an N-pole inducing an E. M. F. tending to send current from C towards D.

These results are in accordance with the experiments described at the beginning of the lesson. Remember that in applying the rule you must *face* the pole.

This action is repeated during the next quarter of a revolution, and when finally the coil is in the position ABCD with AB at the bottom the pressure is again at zero.

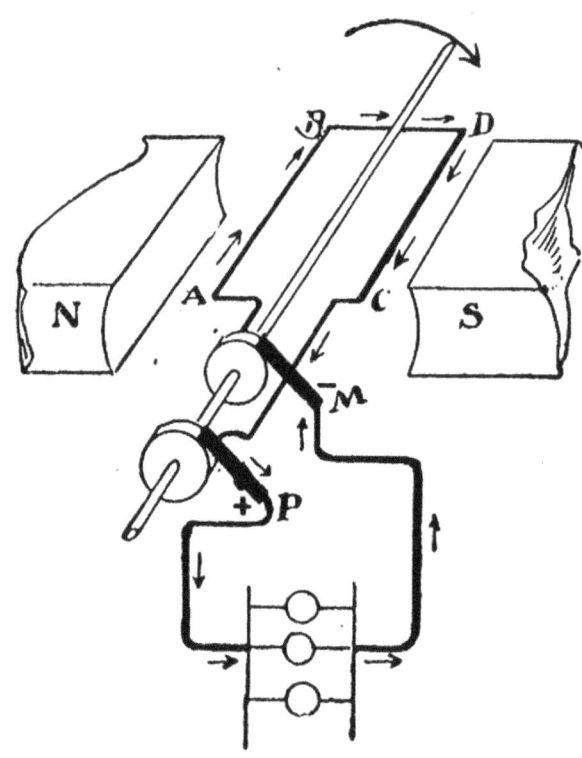

Fig. 181. The Simple Alternator, Shows Coil at One-half a Revolution from Fig. 180. Brush M is Now Negative.

The value of the E. M. F. has started at zero, risen to a maximum, and decreased to zero again. This gives a fluctuating current or pulsating current in the external circuit.

When AB rises in front of the N-pole the E. M. F. will be in the direction of from A to B, while before it was from B to A. During each revolution of the loop the current flows one way half the time and then is reversed and flows the other way.

This is what happens in the armatures of all dynamos whether alternating (A.C.) or direct (D.C.) current types.

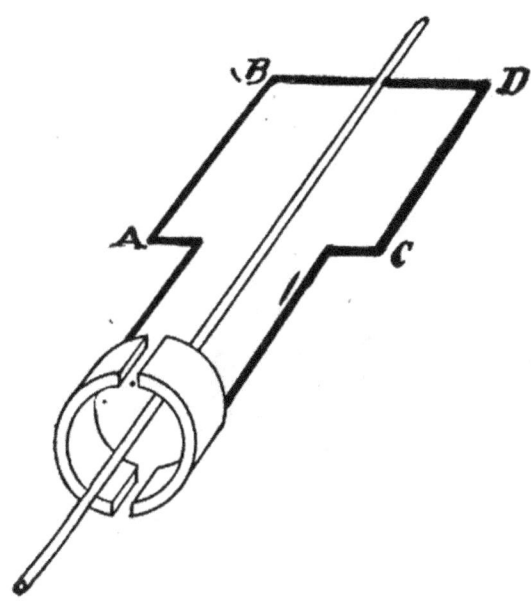

Fig. 182. An Armature Coil Connected to a Two-part Commutator, so as to Deliver Direct Current.

When we wish to utilize the current flowing in the loop of Fig. 179, we attach two collector rings as shown in Figs. 180 and 181, which gives us an A. C. generator or an *Alternator*. For a D. C. generator or simply *Generator*, the ends of the loop are connected to one ring split as shown in Fig. 182, whose halves are insulated from each other and from the shaft. Two brushes are placed as in Fig. 183. In this case the alternating E. M. F. will be *reversed* or *commuted* at the proper instant and there will be a one direction E. M. F. impressed on the external circuit. The split ring is called a *Commutator.*

THE ALTERNATOR.

In Figs. 180 and 181 are shown two positions of the loop on the armature of an alternator. The collector rings are insulated from the shaft and each other by mica. The terminals of the loop are soldered or riveted (sometimes both) to the rings and current is led to the external circuit containing the lamps by stationary strips of copper which form a sliding contact with the rings.

Fig. 183. Cross Section of Simple Commutator. Black Represents Copper; White Space Is Mica Insulation.

Look at Fig. 180 and notice that during the first half of the revolution of the loop ABCD, the direction of the E. M. F. in AB is from B to A, and in CD is from C to D.

The current flows from the brush M to the lamps so that M is positive.

Looking at Fig. 181 note that the wire in front of the S-pole is still positive, but that it is now the wire CD instead of AB, so P is the positive brush for the second half of the revolution. There are two reversals of the current per revolution.

The number of *alterations per minute* is the speed in revolutions per minute multiplied by the number of poles.

The number of *cycles* is found by multiplying the speed in revolutions per second by the number of pairs of poles. The number of cycles is usually spoken of as the *Frequency* of the alternator.

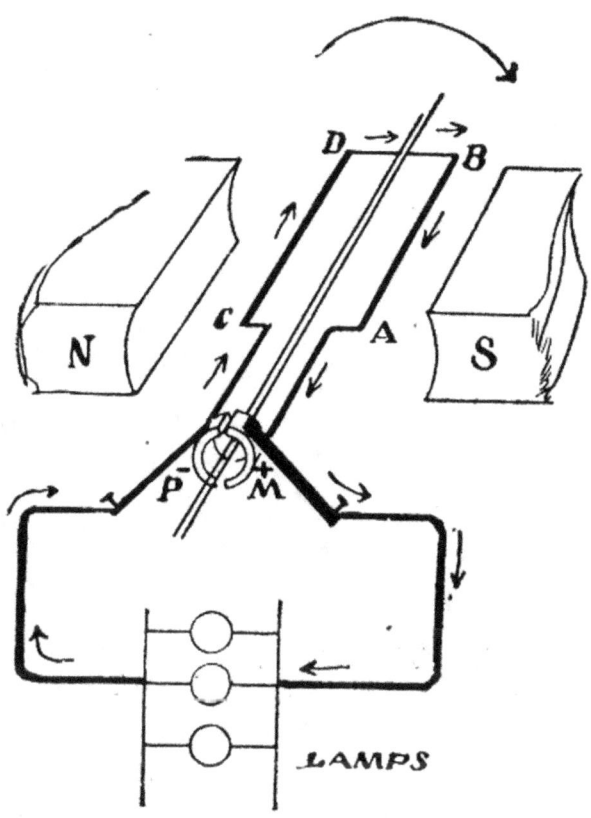

Fig. 184. Simple D. C. Generator. At This Instant the Brush M Is Positive.

The usual frequencies are for power 25, for motor circuits, and arc lamps 66, and for incandescent lighting 133.

THE DIRECT CURRENT GENERATOR.

In Fig. 184 is shown a loop and a two part commutator of a D.C. generator.

Since the wire AB is moving down past a S-pole, the current flows from B to A and out of the brush M, which is called the positive brush. In wire CD the current flows from C to D, making P the negative brush.

After half a revolution the wire CD is over where AB was, and is now delivering current towards the external circuit instead of away from it; *but CD is now connected through its commutator bar to brush M instead of to P so that the brush M is still positive.* (See Fig. 185.)

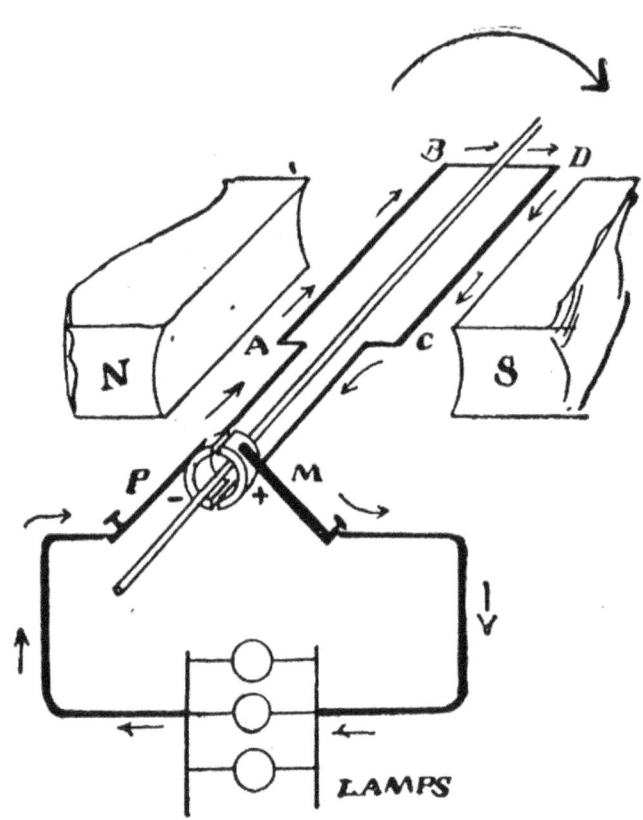

Fig. 185. Simple D. C. Generator. The Armature Has Made Half a Revolution, but Brush M Is Still Positive.

This arrangement of commutator bars and brushes performs the duty of connecting the brush M to that part of the winding, and only that part which is moving down in front of a S-pole. As long as the wire AB moves up in front of a N-pole the commutator connects it to brush P, but as soon as it begins to move down in front of a S-pole it is immediately disconnected from P and a connection made with M.

To increase the E.M.F. The greater the field strength the greater the E.F.M. and the higher the speed the greater the E.M.F.

When the speed has been raised until the surface of the armature is traveling at the rate of 3000 ft. a minute* no further increase is made, lest the bursting stresses become too great.

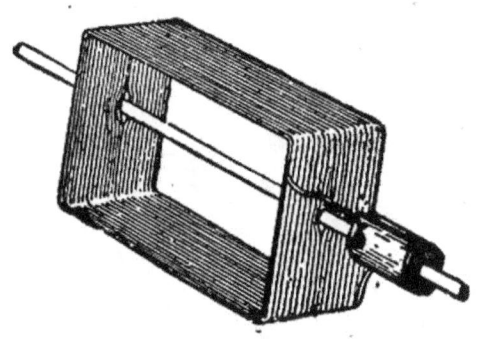

Fig. 186. A Single Coil Armature of Many Turns.

In order to further increase the E.M.F. more *turns* or *loops* of wire must be wound on the armature. A coil of 16 turns as in Fig. 186 will give an E.M.F. 16 times as great as a coil like Fig. 182. Looking at Fig. 187 will convince you of this.

Suppose the direction of rotation to be the same as the hands of a watch (or as we say, *clockwise*) when viewed from the commutator end of machine; then the

---

*This is called the Peripheral Speed of the armature and is calculated by this rule:

P. S. equals 3.1416 x D x R. P. M. where D is the diameter of armature in feet and **R. P. M. is the revolutions of the armature per minute.**

E. M. F.'s induced in the successive portions of the wire will be as shown by the arrows, and will add to each other, impressing a high E.M.F. on the brushes. We say that these turns of wire are all in *series*.

Any betterment of the magnetic conductivity of the frame of the machine will increase the E.M.F.; by producing a greater flux per pound of copper on the field magnets. Hence the winding of the armature inductors (wires) on a core of very softest iron is an economic necessity, resulting in either a higher E.M.F. or a reduction of the expense for copper in the field coils.

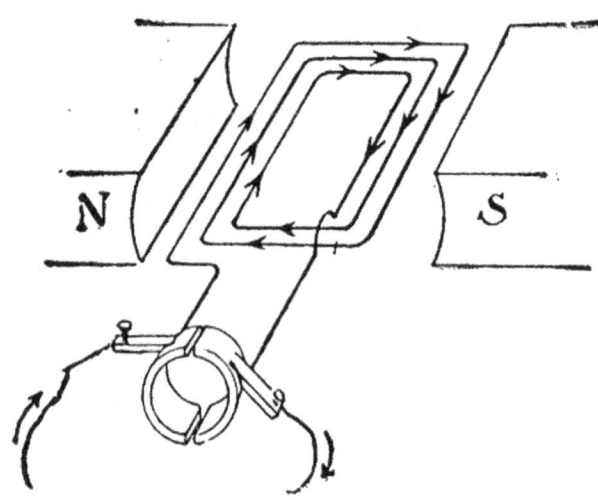

Fig. 187. An Armature Coil of Many Turns Showing How the Induced E. M. F. of Each Turn Adds Itself to That of Other Turns.

These cores are called *Drum cores* when the central hole is just large enough for the shaft and the insulation around it (Fig. 188); and are named *Ring cores* when the internal diameter of the ring is much larger than the shaft. (Fig. 190.) The armature in Fig. 191 has a ring core, but the end plates being in position, the large hole is concealed.

These cores are built up of a great many punchings of soft iron from 15 to 40 mils thick, pickled so as to rust them a little. Every tenth one is varnished or tissue

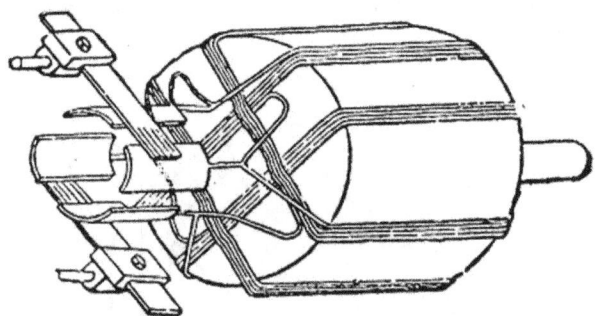

Fig. 188. Drum Winding on a Drum Core. Four Coils and Four Commutator Bars. For Direct Current.

paper pasted on. The rust, varnish and paper are all insulators and when the punchings are assembled in a

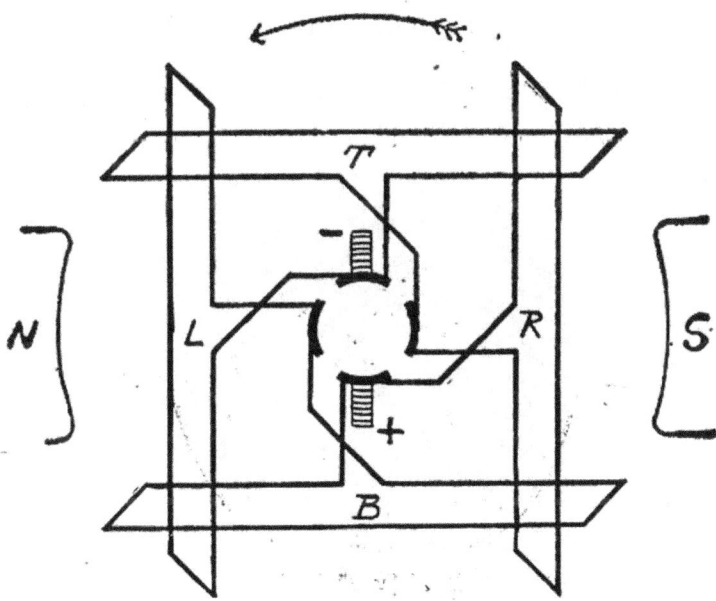

Fig. 189. Diagram of Fig. 188.

core prevent currents called *Eddy currents* from flowing from one end of the armature to the other and heating it.

These cores are sometimes *smooth* but more frequently are *slotted* with the wires laid in the slots.

About 10 to 15% of the length of the core is insulation, and about 50% of the surface is slots containing the inductors.

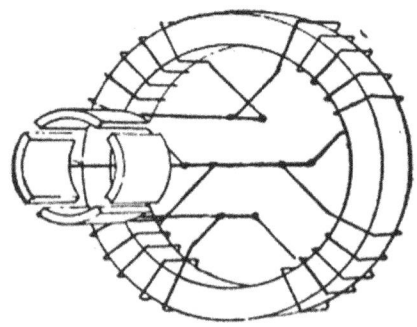

Fig. 190. Simple Gramme Ring Winding.

To get a Continuous E.M.F. While a single coil of many turns produces a high E.M.F., which by a two part commutator is always applied to the external circuit

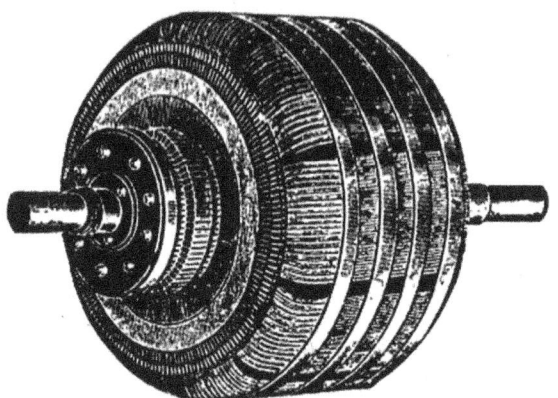

Fig. 191. Eight Section Eighty Coil Ring Winding on a Smooth Ring Core, with Eighty Bar Commutator. For Direct Current.

in the same direction, yet this coil passes through all the changes in voltage mentioned in connection with Fig. 179.

Examine the ring winding (invented by Gramme) of Fig. 190, which is wound on a ring core made up of soft iron punchings 25 mils thick.

The wires on the outer surface are *active,* having E.M.F. induced in them, and are called *armature inductors.* The rest of the wire is *dead* wire and only useful to complete the circuits between inductors.

Notice the connections between commutator bars and winding. Number the coils and commutator bars with a pencil, sketch in the two magnetic poles and the two brushes. Imagine the armature to rotate clockwise and figure out the value of the voltage at the brushes during different parts of a revolution.

In Fig. 192 we have the same windings with eight coils and eight commutator bars. In Fig. 191 the armature as diagrammed in Fig. 192 is shown completed with its four bands. These bands are from 12 to 25 convolutions of phosphor-bronze wire in sizes varying from No. 20 up to 14 laid on tightly over a mica insulation and sweated with solder all the way round.

In Fig. 192 you will notice that the complete winding can be divided into two parts, one influenced by the N-pole, the other by the S-pole standing at the commutator end. The N-pole side moving upwards has its E.M.F. in direction from back to front of armature *through the inductors;* the S-pole side has E.M.F. in direction from back to front of armature *through the dead wire.*

In winding the armature the wire is laid on in a continuous spiral as shown. This makes the E.M.F. in each half of the armature in series, and allows the current to flow from one coil to another, except at the points where the N-half and S-half of the armature meet. Here the E.M.F.'s oppose and if wires were connected for an instant to the winding, as shown in the picture, the two opposing E.M.F.'s would both force electricity out into the wire at the top of the armature and draw it in at the bottom as shown by the arrows on these wires. This will cause a current to flow in the external circuit.

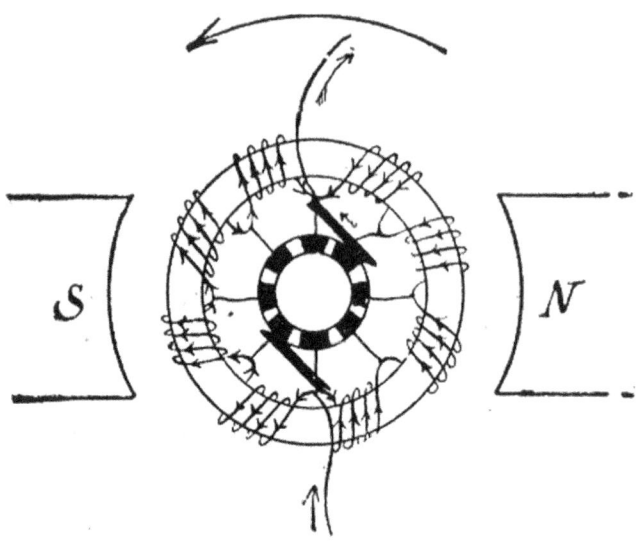

Fig. 192. Eight Coil Gramme Ring Winding, with Eight Part Commutator.

If the junctions of the coils are connected to eight commutator bars (one bar per coil) and connect the ends of the external circuit by brushes to the commutator bars which are midway between the N- and S-poles, then each half of the armature separately generates an E.M.F. and delivers current to the external circuit.

Suppose the armature to be revolving at the highest safe speed. Each inductor will move past the magnet poles at a speed of 3000 ft. a minute. With pole pieces 5 x 8 inches and a *flux density* of 90,000 lines per square inch, the *total flux* will be 5 x 8 x 90,000 or 3.6 million lines.

The armature may be 9 inches in diameter, which gives its rotative speed 1270 (nearly).

For R.P.M.*=P.S.†÷(3.1416 × diameter).

$$= \frac{3000 \times 12}{3.1416 \times 9}$$

$$= 1270 \text{ nearly.}$$

which R.P.S.‡=21 nearly.

An inductor therefore cuts 3.6 million lines of magnetism twenty-one times a second, which is equivalent to cutting 75.6 millions once per second.

Since the cutting of 100 million lines per second by an inductor induces 1 volt pressure, each inductor on this armature revolving in this field will produce 75.6÷100 or ¾ of a volt (aprox.).

The 4 coils of 4 inductors each (Fig. 192) on the N-half of armature being in series produces 3 volts per coil or a total of 12 volts *which is the E.M.F. of the generator.*

The S-half of the armature also generates a pressure of 12 volts, which is not added to the pressure of the N-half, being in parallel with it. An inspection of Fig. 192 shows that they oppose rather than add to each other; but an outlet being provided they turn aside through it, and send current separately and independently towards the outside circuit.

If the armature is wound with No. 10 A. W. G.,§ the

---

*Revolutions per minute.
†Peripheral speed.
‡Revolutions per second.

§American Wire Gauge. A table of sizes and properties of the sizes of wire according to the Brown & Sharp or American Gauge will be found in Lesson 18.

diameter of which is 0.102 inch or 102 mils, its area is 102 squared equal to 10,404 c.m. Allowing 700 c.m. per ampere, it will carry 15 amperes, without too much heating.

Since each side of the armature delivers its own current to the brushes, the safe current output of this generator is 30 amperes.

Suppose there are 250 ft. of this No. 10 wire on this armature. The resistance of the wire from the wire table is 1.02 ohms per 1000 ft.

The resistance of *all the wire* on armature is 0.255 ohm, and the resistance of the wire on each *half* of the armature is 0.128 ohm.

But the two halves are in parallel so *the resistance of the armature as measured from brush to brush* will be half of 0.128 or 0.064 ohms.

The drop or loss of pressure in armature will be $C \times R$ or 30×0.064, equal to 1.92 or say 2 volts.

This machine being a *shunt generator,* the main current does *not* pass through the fields, and there is no further voltage loss.

The E.M.F. of this dynamo is 12 volts and its *voltage* 10 volts. Its output in watts will be $10 \times 30 = 300$ watts or 0.3 kw. This is the *rating* of the generator.

The generator will carry this load 22 hours a day without getting more than 90° Fah. hotter than the surrounding air.

A properly proportioned machine will stand a 25% overload for half an hour rising an extra 30° in temperature, and it will stand a 50% overload for one minute without being damaged by the heat.

Drum Windings.

The extra labor involved in passing the dead wire through the bore of a ring core is avoided by going back to first principles again and placing on the core (either drum or ring) a number of coils shaped as in Fig. 186, producing a winding as in Fig. 188.

It is to be noted that the inductors lie entirely on the outer surface of the core and that the percentage of dead wire is less than in Fig. 190.

For a long, small diameter armature drum winding uses the least wire; while for a short, large diameter core the ring winding will require fewer pounds of copper.

Take Fig. 188 and mark in pencil as directed, using Fig. 189 as a guide. In order to make the diagram in Fig. 189 clear, it has its proportions wrong. The dead part of the wire is drawn very long and the active part very short. The reverse is true of an actual winding.

Mark the top horizontal coil of Fig. 188 T, the bottom one B. Mark the right and left hand vertical coils L and R. Mark the upper brush negative and the lower one positive.

The left side of the armature is the N-pole side and the right the S-pole side; then we know that the armature is revolving anti-clockwise (else the upper brush would be positive).

The E.M.F.'s on the N-side and S-side of coil T, just as in Fig. 187, are in series and add producing a current flow towards the lower (positive) brush. The current passes through the inactive (dead) coil R in order to get to positive brush.

At the same time the E.M.F.'s in coil B add up and passing through the dead coil L drive current out of lower brush.

The value of the E.M.F. is eight times that which one inductor can produce. For the active coil T has 4 loops, i. e., 8 inductors in series, as also has the coil B. Suppose T produces 8 volts, the two coils T and B are in parallel and do not add their E.M.F.'s.

The coils L and R are dead, L being in series with B and R in series with T, but they produce no E.M.F. At the present instant they are but a wasteful resistance, their value, however, will be soon seen.

When the armature has moved about $\frac{1}{8}$ of a revolution, you will find that T is cutting flux slantingly and that R, which is in series with it, is beginnng to cut flux also. T is only $\frac{3}{4}$ active, producing say 6 volts, and R is not totally dead but $\frac{1}{4}$ active, producing 2 volts. Hence the voltage of the machine is still 8.

At $\frac{1}{4}$ revolution R is doing full work and B is dead and in series with it, while T is dead and L in series with it is at full activity. Now R and L produce the E.M.F.

The student must revolve Fig. 189, using slips of paper as brushes to gain a full understanding of these actions.

The current enters the armature through the upper brush, splits and passes through the armature by two parallel circuits, one containing T and R in series and the other containing L and B. During a revolution these coils interchange places, but two coils are always in each circuit.

When 6 amperes flow in the external circuit, the No. 16 wire of the armature is not overheated, as it only has to carry 3 amperes (half of 6), which it is well able to do. It has 2583 C.M., and which is more than 3×700 C.M.

Self exciting of a Dynamo. When a dynamo is standing idle the field magnets are weakly magnetic due to residual magnetism.

Let the armature revolve and in a shunt or compound machine open, in a series generator close the external circuit.

A few volts will be generated and cause a current to flow through the fields, hence the magnetism will increase and more voltage will be induced. This voltage will send increased current through the shunt field and cause more volts to be induced.

The machine is now *"building up."*

As more and more magnetism is put into the fields, it becomes harder to get any more in as the iron is approaching *saturation* and there is more and more *leakage*.

Hence at a certain point, depending on the design of the machine, the difficulty of increasing the magnetism being added to the effect of the leakage just balances the tendency of the voltage to be increased. If nothing else is done the voltage of the dynamo will remain constant.

In the series field is passing all the current drawn from the machine and the field strength and voltage tend to increase. This increase is opposed by the C. R. loss in armature and field, and the effect of the increasing field density. The net result is a *building up* of the voltage and if the load is not changed the voltage of the machine will **remain constant**.

Regulation. If now in the shunt generator you **close** the external circuit an extra current (very large in proportion to the field current) is drawn from the armature and causes a C R loss.

A lower voltage is thus impressed on the external circuit and to make matters worse, also on the field. Hence the field weakens and the added results of C R loss and weaker field is a considerable drop in voltage for each increase in load.

Resistance must be cut out of field as load increases.

When in the series generator the load increases a shunt should be placed around the field to weaken it, if a constant potential is desired.

Position of the Brushes. In order that one set of brushes may take away from and the other set deliver current to the generator in a bipolar machine these sets are on opposite sides of the commutator.

In some dynamos when the inductors come out of the slots, one goes straight on to a commutator bar and the other is bent over to its proper bar. This puts the brushes in line with part of the coil and they will be found half way between the pole tips.

It is usual to bend both inductors as they leave the slots and connect to bars half way between the slots. Then the brushes will be found opposite the middle of the pole piece.

In dynamos and non-reversing motors the brushes are a little distance away from the points mentioned, but in reversing motors are exactly at these points.

If you will consider that a multipolar dynamo or motor is merely a lot of bipolar fields which for economy of material are working on one large armature, the placing of the brushes on such machines will be clear to you.

The alternate brushes are of the same polarity and there is usually a set of brushes for each field magnet.

The placing of the brushes on the commutator with a certain relation to the winding is necessary as a reference to Fig. 193 or to the diagram of any winding will show you that the brush while collecting current is at the same time *short circuiting* one of the coils.

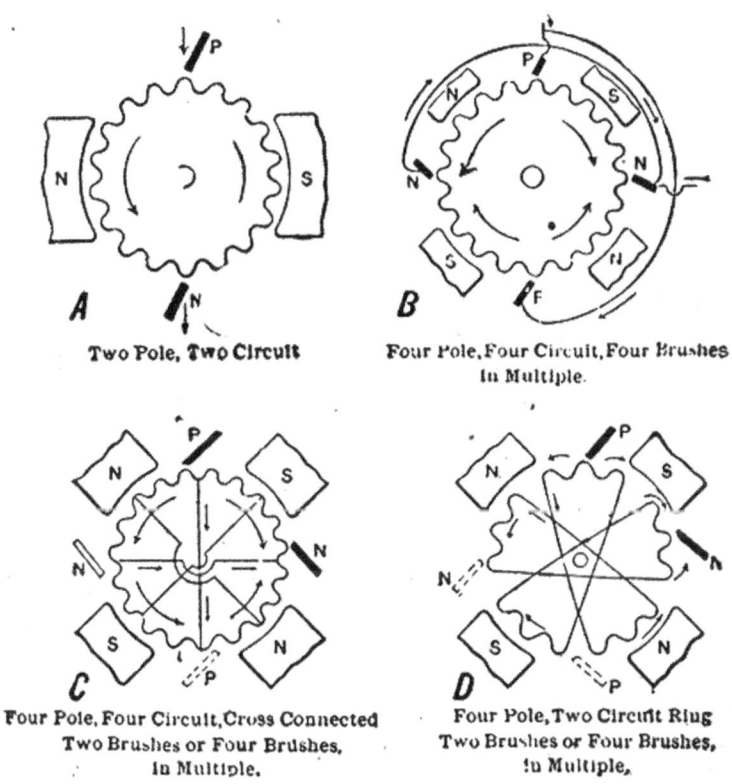

Fig. 193. Showing the Number and Position of Brushes on Different Armature Windings.

The black brushes are the ones actually used, the dotted ones being dispensed with on account of the particular winding.

In order that an excessive current may not be generated in this short circuited coil it must be out in the interpolar space at the time the brush touches the two bars belonging to it.

Sparking. When a current is broken there is always a spark, which is greater the more turns in the wire and the more iron within these turns. That is, the more *inductive* the current the worse the spark.

The conditions are right for excessive sparking in a machine, for the circuit is *inductive* and although the circuit is not actually broken, the current being merely shifted, yet the result is equivalent to it.

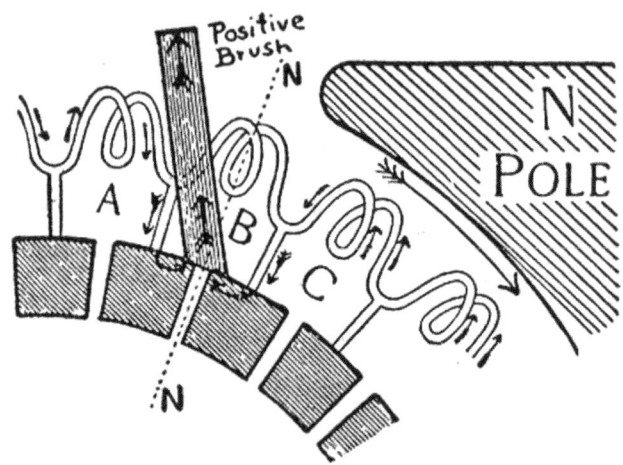

Fig. 194. Showing Position of Brush for Sparklers. Collection of Current.

Looking at Fig. 194 and considering the line N N to be about midway between the pole pieces. The coil B is short circuited but has no current in it because

1st. The field is very weak and the coil is moving parallel to it, so no E.M.F. is generated in the coil.

2d. The currents from the N and S-side of winding enter the brush without going through the coil B.

Coil B has therefore no *current* in it, but being connected to A and C whose potential is high B is *charged* with electricity, and it is full of *coulombs,** which are at rest.

When the armature revolves as shown and the toe of a copper brush leaves bar 3 the current from C must instantly change over going through B to reach the brush. The coulombs in B which are at rest should instantly move at full speed becoming a part of the armature current.

It being impossible to set the coulombs in B into motion instantaneously it is evident that the current from C encounters *more* than the *ohmic resistance* of the coil B. This extra opposition being called *reactance*.

The path through B being momentarily practically nonconducting the circuit is broken by the brush moving away from the bar, and a spark or arc formed.

The circuit being *inductive* (having turns containing iron) the spark is persistent and holds until the *reactance* of coil B decreasing, it begins to conduct and diverts enough current into the proper path and the arc goes out for lack of current to maintain it.

This *sparking* is avoided in the following way:

1st. Carbon brushes of high resistance are used which, as the part of the brush touching a bar gets narrower, due to the high resistance, throttles the current, gradually forcing it over to the coil B. Hence B does not have to instantly carry *all* the current.

2d. Move the brushes of a dynamo in direction of rotation until they are nearer the pole shoe, exactly as is shown in Fig. 194.

---

*A coulomb is a certain quantity of electricity. When a coulomb passes a given point every second a current of one ampere is said to flow.

The short circuited coil B is now under the *fringe* from the pole piece; and is moving obliquely through a stronger field. A small E.M.F. is generated in it.

From the illustration it will be seen that a current in the same, as in C (for B and C are under influence of same pole piece) flows around through B, the bars 2 and 3 and the brush.

By *shifting* the brushes a little to and fro the correct strength of field can be selected and the obliquity at which it is cut adjusted, so that a current will be made to flow in B not only of *the same direction as that in C* but also of exactly the *same value*.

Hence when the toe of the brush slips from bar 3 the current in C instead of running against the *impedance* (the sum of the resistance and reactance) of coil B, finds itself merely falling in behind the flow already established, and there is no tendency to spark.

In a motor the brushes are shifted in opposite direction to the rotation to get to the no sparking position. Hence the positions for sparkless forward or backward running are some distance apart.

It is a mere matter of first cost to produce a machine with absolutely *sparkless commutation* under any conditions. It is the skill of the designers which has (without prohibitive cost) so reduced the distance between these two points that it may be spanned by a thick carbon brush.

The railroad motor of to-day operates in either direction, without shift of brushes, under all loads, and some overloads, without serious sparking. What little occurs is of such small volume and such low temperature that no great harm is done.

Classes of Dynamos.

Dynamos are divided into classes with reference to the manner in which their fields and armature are inter-connected.

The series dynamo. Fig. 195. The same current traverses the field, armature and main or external circuits. The conductors in these circuits are about the same size. The circuits are all in *series*.

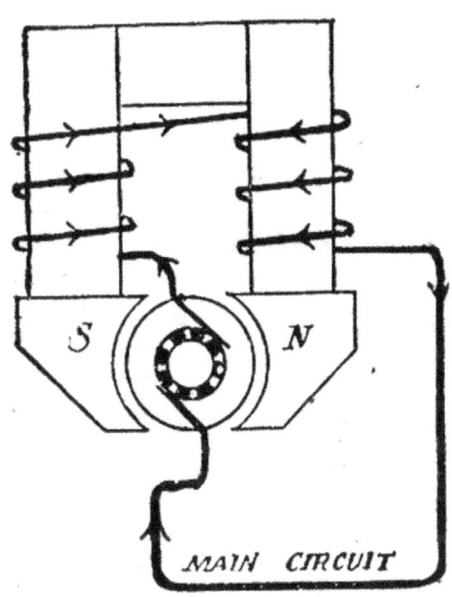

Fig. 195. Circuits in a Series Dynamo or Motor.

This dynamo is used for arc lighting and as boosters for increasing the pressure on a *feeder* carrying current furnished by some other generator.

The characteristic of this type is to furnish power at an increased voltage as the load increases. If sufficient current is drawn to overload the machine the voltage will fall.

The shunt dynamo. Fig. 196. Here the field circuit is arranged as a shunt circuit. The armature and external circuits are in series. The armature current is the sum of the external and field currents. The conductors on the field are very much smaller than those on armature, as they only carry 2 to 5 per cent as much current.

Used for incandescent lamp lighting, mill and factory power.

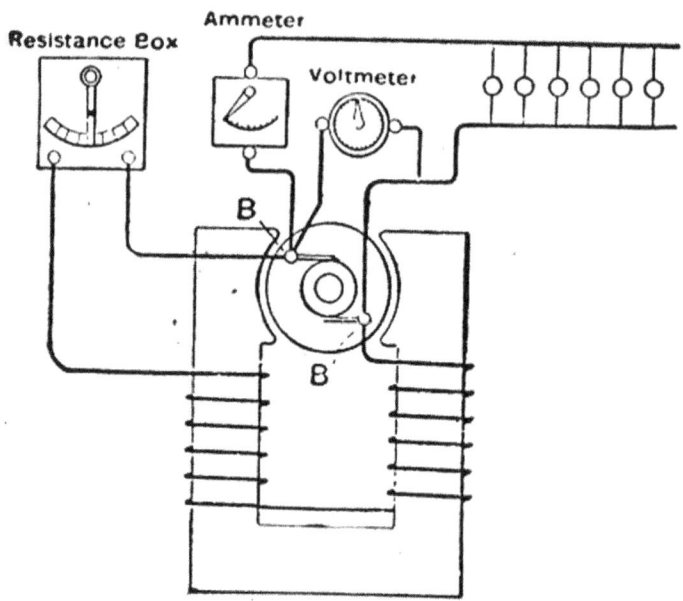

Fig. 196. Circuits of a Shunt Dynamo with Instruments and a Load of Lamps.

The characteristic of the shunt generator is to allow the voltage to fall as the load is increased.

It is evident that only by a combination of these two into a *compound dynamo*, Fig. 197, can a generator be produced which will deliver any power within its rated capacity and yet hold a steady voltage.

The armature is the same as a shunt dynamo, but the fields have **two distinct windings, one shunt and the other series.**

The series dynamo is often called a *constant current* generator because its tendency is that way, and with a regulator it will furnish a constant current.

The shunt dynamo is similarly termed a *constant potential* generator. For with a regulator it will keep to a constant voltage.

The compound generator will of its own accord, without any regulator, furnish at its terminals or at any distant point on the line steady power, at an absolutely constant voltage.

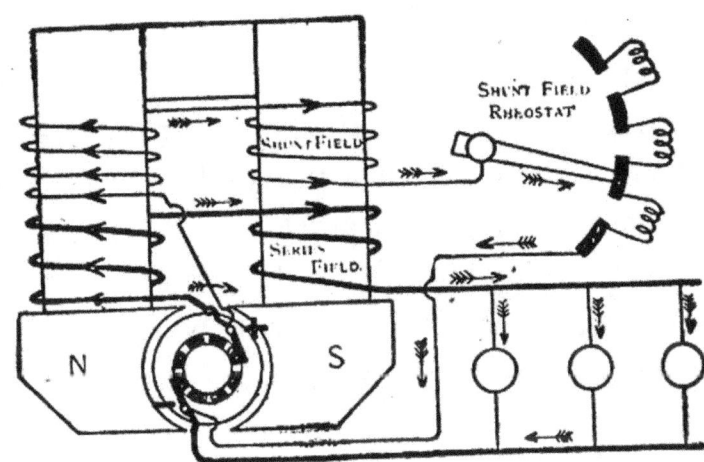

Fig. 197. Circuits in a Compound Dynamo.

In railway service where the amount of power required fluctuates violently, the voltage will vary somewhat, for the generator scarcely has time to adjust itself to the present conditions before the condition no longer exists and a new demand arises.

It is not necessary that the pressure on the third-rail should be absolutely constant, and for this kind of service the compound generator, with the series characteristic predominating, so as to keep a steady pressure *out on the line* is good and plenty.

Motors.

It might be said that another class of dynamos is *motors*.

Any of the D. C. dynamos and many of the A. C. machines in power houses would revolve and produce mechanical power if they were supplied with the proper kind of current at proper voltage. In fact, one of the troubles that may occur in a power house is to have one out of a set of generators start to act as a motor, thus placing heavier load on all the other machines.

The same electrical machines can be used as a dynamo or a motor; but as most dynamos are *compound* or *shunt* and built for power houses, where there is sufficient, if not plenty of room, and as all railroad motors are *series wound* and placed where there is very little room, it is natural that the dynamos and motors a railroad man sees should not look alike.

The similarity of their electrical action must be remembered so that one may understand that the parts of a dynamo and motor, though a little different in shape, act alike electrically and have the same names.

Comparison between Dynamo and Motor. Since it takes power to force a dynamo armature to revolve while generating current, and none when not generating (field and armature circuits open) we conclude that it is the action between field and armature magnetisms which causes the dynamo to resist rotation.

To test truth of this remove the armature from the fields and pass current through its conductors *in same direction as the flow was before*. You will find that the armature is a large, strong electro-magnet.

Testing the polarity of the field magnets and of the armature poles you will find that where using as a dynamo, we are forcing a N-armature pole towards a N-field pole. These poles repel each other and power is absorbed by the rotation of the dynamo.

The repulsion of these poles would make the armature rotate if current were supplied to it and the fields, and the steam engine removed.

The difference between ordinary and railway motors is the extreme simplicity of the latter.

Many of the refinements of design and construction which theoretically are necessary, are in railway motors omitted. It being found that for successful operation they are *not* necessary, and by their omission much is gained, i. e., saving in weight, cost, number of parts, absence of complication and ease of repair.

It is not needful to say that parts of a railway motor are put together so as to "stay put."

That motor is best, which with the fewest pounds of material, will with reliability and low cost of repairs propel the greatest number of tons of pay load.

The main differences between all motors and dynamos are the method of starting and the effect of the E.M.F. produced.

Starting Motors.

We can not turn on steam to an engine instantaneously, for it takes time to open the throttle. We do, however, turn it on more slowly than the opening of the throttle compels us, for we wish to give the engine and its dynamo time to get up to speed.

In the same way we must give current to a motor easily, in order to start it. On the closing of a switch the current jumps up to full value so quickly that the motor armature would be brought up to such a temperature as would char the cotton insulation on the winding.

In starting a motor an extra resistance is used, and it is placed either in the main or armature circuit. It is only in use for a few seconds at a time and if well ventilated can be made very small and light in proportion to the current passing.

When applied to small motors where the starting is at infrequent intervals this starting rheostat and its operating drum and handle is combined with two automatic protective devices and contained partly in a latticed iron box and partly on its cover. It is called a *starting box*.

For larger motors doing similar work and for traction or railway work, each of the parts becomes so large that the four pieces are mounted separately. The operating drum, the resistances, the overload release and the no voltage release.

The operating drum is familiar to us all as the *controller* of the street cars.

The *resistance* in the form of cast iron girds held in skeleton frames are fastened under the sills of the cars.

The *overload release* or *circuit breaker* automatically

opens the circuit when a current large enough to damage the motors is accidentally drawn. In street cars this device is usually fastened under the hood over the motorman's head.

No voltage release, a magnetically operated switch or series of switches kept closed by the magnet, thus giving the current access to the motors circuits or the circuits controlling them.

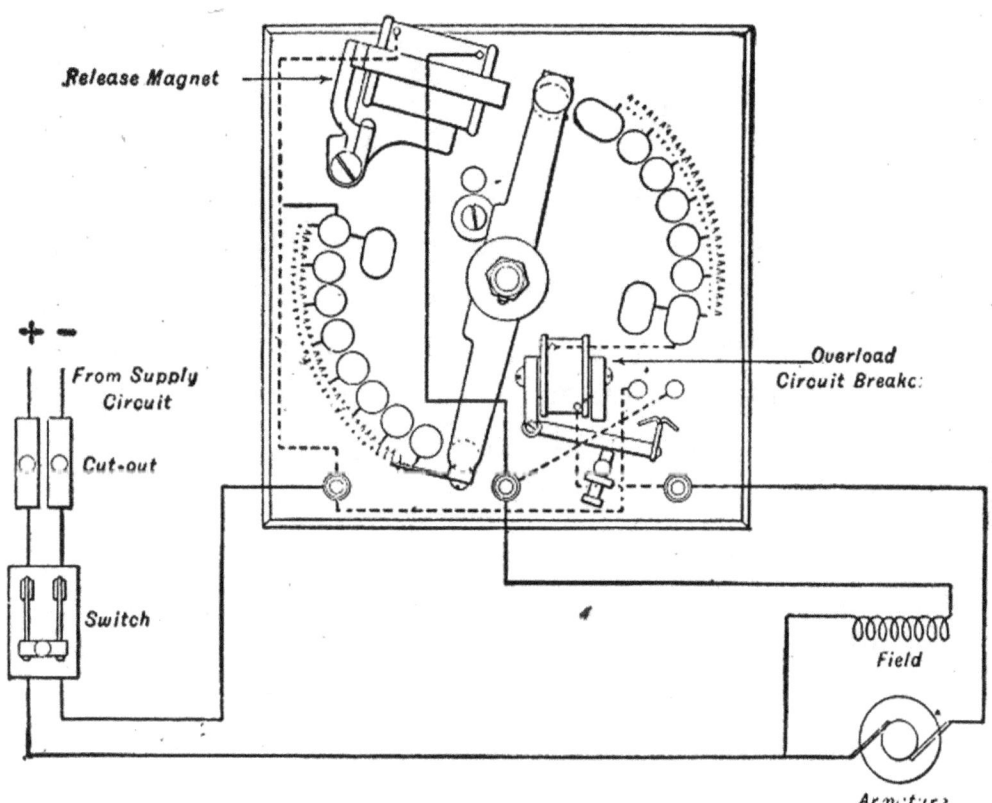

Fig. 198. Starting Box and Connections for Shunt Motor.

If the power is cut off the line the device operates, opening all the circuits leading to the motors, thus protecting the motors from the damage done by applying full voltage suddenly to a motor while standing still.

Fig. 198 shows a starting box with the proper connections ready to start a *shunt motor*. (Off position.)

As soon as the switch is closed there is full voltage on the field, but no voltage on the armature, as the circuit is open at each end of the starting arm.

As the arm is swung clockwise, current flows to armature through a resistance which gradually grows less, until when at right angles to its original position the full voltage is on the armature and the motor operating at full speed.

The hook on the left end of the arm catches on the knuckle at the lower left side of the release magnet and holds the arm in spite of the effort of a coiled spring (not shown) to return arm to *off* position.

Tracing the circuits will show that the release magnet is always energized if the supply circuit is *alive* and switch closed. Should the supply be interrupted the release magnet becomes demagnetized and the upper end of the knuckle is no longer held. The knuckle turns on the pin (with screw head) releasing the hook, and the spring returns the arm to the *off* position.

The motor would have stopped itself, but now it can only be restarted in the proper way.

Consider the arm in the "running position," the *overload circuit breaker* magnet in energized, but the armature* being a considerable distance away the magnet is too weak to draw it up.

Should the motor be overloaded and too much current pass the strength of this magnet is increased so that the armature swings up and jams the jumper in between the two studs shown on the right of the magnet. This completes a *shunt* or by-pass circuit around the release magnet, diverting enough current from it that it weakens and releases the knuckle. The arm then flies back

---
*Armature or keeper of a magnet; not of a dynamo.

to the *off* position and the circuit to the armature is opened.

The motor is stopped, which may be inconvenient, but it is to be preferred to a *burnt out* armature.

In a railway motor this heavy current would also pass through the fields, but they are better adapted to stand heat and the armature usually suffers first.

To start a motor with this *box*, close the switch and swing the starting arm from *off* to *running* position and let go. The overload circuit breaker may have danced up and down while this is being done. If so, next time swing arm more slowly.

To stop the motor *open the switch*. The motor will slow down and stop. Just before stopping, the release magnet will allow the starting arm to return to the *off* position.

The cutout shown consists of a fuse enclosed in a cardboard tube and designed to melt or *blow* at a current a little higher than that for which the circuit breaker is adjusted.

COUNTER E. M. F.

Counter E. M. F. When the motor is operating all the parts and conditions of a dynamo are present, hence there is a dynamo action which produces an E. M. F. in opposite direction to the *impressed E. M. F.* supplied by the line.*

This is a most important and useful action.

---

*This I know by using the rule: Place the thumb, first and second fingers of the right hand all at right angles to each other.

1st Thumb in direction of the motion.

2d First finger pointing from a N-pole to a S-pole.

3d Second finger shows direction of induced. E. M. F.

You will see that when we are starting a motor that the faster it moves the more C. E. M. F. it generates. This is why we can not throw full voltage on a motor until it is nearly up to its full speed.

The actual voltage sending current through a motor is the difference between the impressed and counter E. M. F.'s.

The working of this in actual practice is best shown as follows:

Suppose a set of four motors are on a 600-volt line making 460 revolutions per minute with 44-inch wheels. The locomotive they are a part of weighs 100 tons and pulls 350 tons behind it at 60 miles per hour.

It is on a level track and must exert a pull of 17½ pounds for each ton pulled or 6,125 pounds in all.

It must exert through its drivers at the rail head 6,125 pounds for the train behind and 1,750 pounds for its own weight. The total tractive effort is therefore 7,900 pounds (7,875 to be exact).*

At 60 miles per hour a train moves 5,280 feet per minute; so the motors move 7,900 pounds 5,280 feet a minute which is 41,700,000 foot pounds per minute. Since 33,000 foot pounds per minute is a *Horse Power*, we get the H. P. of the motors as 1,264.

The efficiency of the locomotive is 80%, *i. e.*, the motors waste 20% of the intake. Hence 1,580 H. P. is taken from the line.

This is expressed in *Kilo Watts* by multiplying by **746** and dividing by 1,000 giving us 1,185 K. W.†

---

*With certain problems a foolish amount of accuracy in figuring is a waste of time. Since the condition of the rails is a variable quality in traction work, figuring on the *safe side* is the only sensible way to work.

†There are 746 watts in 1 H. P., and 1000 watts in a K. W

This being supplied at 600 volts needs 2,000 amperes (1,975).

An ammeter placed in the main conductor of one of the New York Central locomotives will read about 2,000 amperes when pulling train No. 51 or No. 41 along the Hudson River towards Croton, N. Y.

What is it that limits the current in this case to 2,000 amperes, *i. e.*, to 500 amperes per motor? Certainly not the ohmic resistance of them.‡

The resistance of *each* motor is only 0.1 ohm or all four in parallel or multiple is 0.025. The current is limited by the dynamo action of the motors, *i. e.*, by the counter E. M. F.

Each of the motors generates about 1.2 volts per revolution per minute, hence at 460 revolutions per minute the C.E.M.F. of each motor is 550 volts. This neutralizes all but 50 of the 600 volts on the line, and leaves that 50 to send current through the resistance of the motor. Fifty volts on 0.1 ohm gives 500 amperes or 2,000 amperes for all four motors.

Now let the train strike a grade. It will slow down in speed and drawing more current develop in its motors the H. P. required to pull the train.

How can motors whose resistance is fixed draw more current when the line voltage is constant? By means of the C.E.M.F.

---

‡By ohmic resistance I mean the actual resistance of the material the conductors are made of. There is another resistance which depends on the rate at which a current *changes*, and has nothing to do with the material. Counter E. M. F. acts like resistance, as it opposes the flow of current. The *apparent resistance* of a locomotive drawing 2000 amperes is 0.3 ohm for 600÷0.3=2000. The actual ohmic resistance is 0.025 ohms.

If the speed drops to 55 M.P.H. then the R.P.M. of the drivers (and armature) change to 422, and the C.E.M.F. to 510 volts. Hence 90 volts acting on each 0.1 ohm motor passes 900 amperes, or 3,600 for the whole locomotive.

Railway Motors.

The main difference between ordinary and railway motors is compactness and inclosure.

The space that can be given to a motor on a truck is limited by the gauge of the rails and the size of the wheels. The gauge being fixed makes this dimension of the motor absolutely fixed; so that more room can only

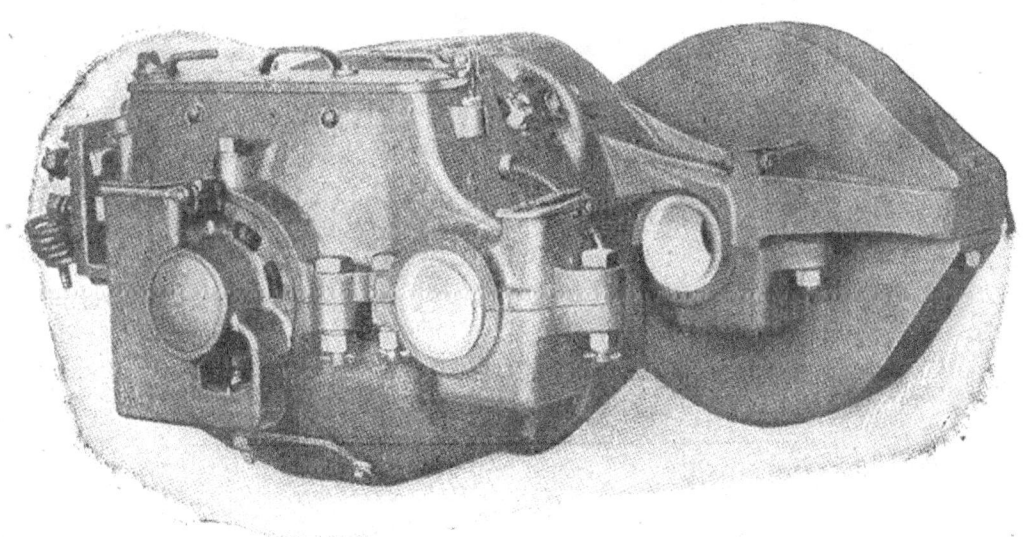

Fig. 221. D. C. Railway Motor, 40 H. P.

be obtained by using larger wheels. A 36 inch wheel gives none too much room to instal motors which are to be called on at times to give 200 H. P. The usual car wheel is 33 inches in diameter.

A railway motor must be completely inclosed to protect it from dust and flying stones.

Figs. 221 and 222 show inclosure of the motor and the gear case. The cast steel box which protects the motor also serves as the field yoke.

This motor has an armature 14 inches in diameter, the commutator is 10¼ inches in diameter and is composed of 111 bars. Motor with gears and gear case weighs 2730 pounds.

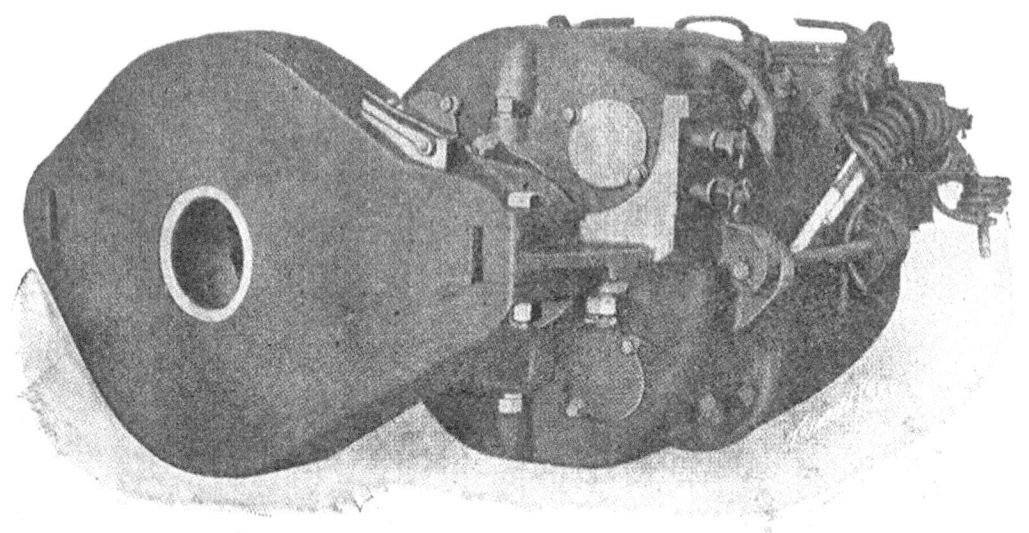

Fig. 222. Gear Case end of D. C. Railway Motor, 40 H. P.

The motor in Figs. 223 and 224 is a 60 H. P. motor built for A. C. work. The armature is 16 inches in diameter and commutator 12 inches in diameter, having 117 bars.

As shown it weighs 4000 lbs. and the gears and gear case weigh 500 lbs. more.

When mounted on 33 inch wheels there is 4⅜ inches clearance between bottom of motor and top of rail.

On account of the almost complete inclosure the armature must be designed to ventilate itself as much as is possible.

Fig. 223. Commutator end of A. C. Railway Motor, 60 H. P.

Fig. 224. Pinion end of Fig. 223.

The air is usually drawn in at the rear end (Fig. 225) and forced through windings and core by the shape of the spider, being discharged between commutator leads and against the pole pieces.

The case of a railway motor is usually split so that the lower half swings down or in a few instances the upper part of case can be swung up.

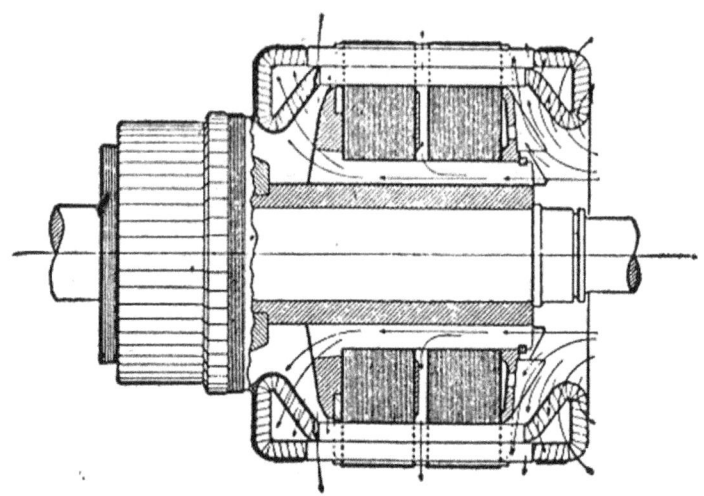

Fig. 225. Method of Ventilating Armature.

Fig. 226 shows the 40 H. P. motor of Fig. 221 with lower part of case down. By loosening the bearing bolts the armature can now be lowered into the pit and removed.

The pole piece and its field coil surrounding it are shown in the upper half of case.

The 60 H. P. motor of Fig. 223 is shown with upper part of case removed in Fig. 227. This is a four pole motor, two of them showing in the part removed. The brush holders also show in top part of upper case.

The four pole pieces are built up of soft steel punchings, riveted together between end plates of wrought iron and are held to the motor frame by bolts. The poles project radially inward at angles of 45° with the

Fig. 226. Lower part of Case let down. Same motor as Fig. 221.

horizontal. Two bolts, secured by lock washers, hold each pole piece in place. They do not penetrate the pole face but terminate in heavy rivets inside the pole made for this purpose. A smooth and unbroken pole face is thus presented to the armature.

The poles are made with projecting tips, which properly distribute the magnetic field, and also serve to retain the field coils, which are held firmly in place by spring washers. The coils are wound with asbestos-covered wire. They are heavily taped and are treated with specially-prepared insulating compounds which render them practically moisture proof.

Fig. 227. Upper part of Case on Motor shown in Fig. 223 taken off.

Fig. 228 shows a 50 H. P. motor for A. C. with upper part of case raised.

There is in railway use to-day in this country practically only one motor, the series motor. This is used or D. C. or A. C. with very little difference in construction.

The armature winding for A. C. use being slightly different, for a separate winding is connected to the commutator bars called a preventive winding which prevents sparking.

In Europe the induction motor supplied with polyphase current is used considerably. The necessity for two or three line wires and double or triple trolleys, while not so very objectionable, has prevented its use in this country.

Fig. 228. Upper part of Case Raised on 50 H. P. A. C. Motor.

Box Frame Type of Motor. The rapid development of inter-urban railways created a demand for a motor of large capacity, which could be mounted under a car in a limited space. To meet this contingency was devel-

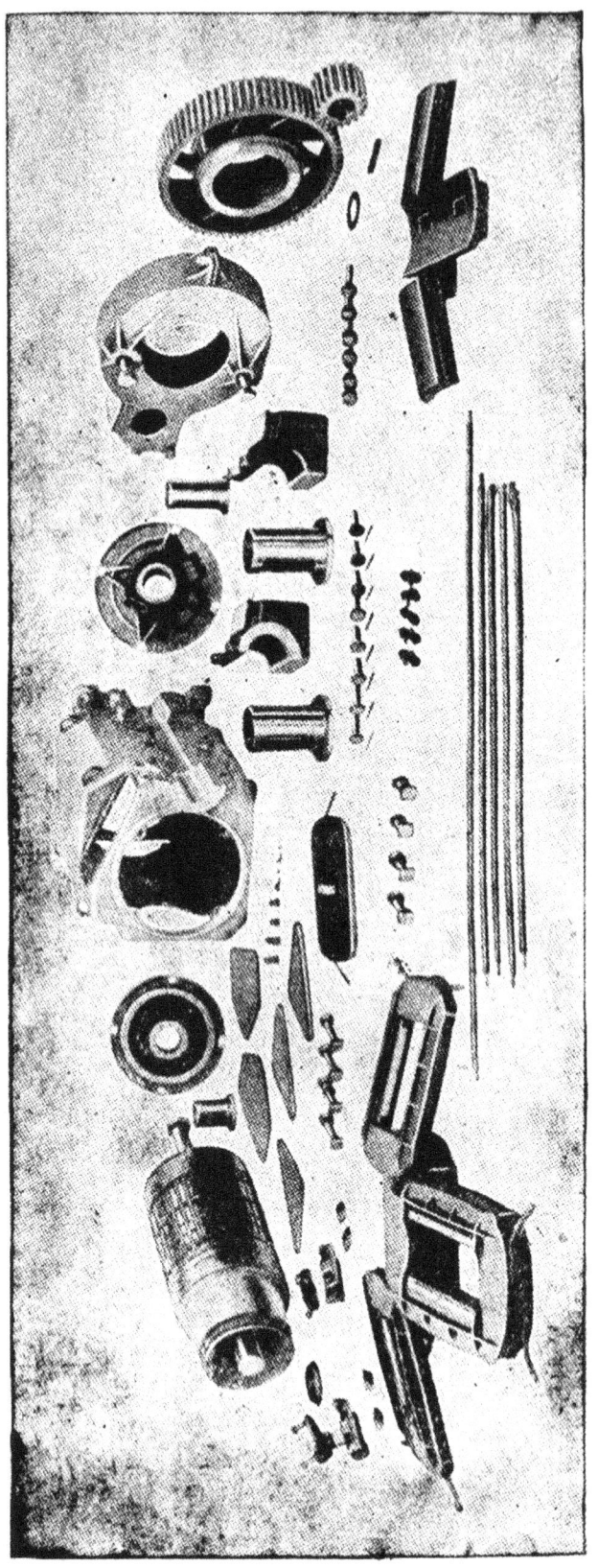

Fig. 229. Parts of a Box Frame Motor.

oped the box frame type of railway motor. This type of motor differs from the ordinary split frame motor, in that the magnet frame consists of a one-piece hollow casting, open at both ends. The armature is inserted in position from the side, being retained in place by end plates, which fasten to the field frame. One of the advantages of the box frame motor is the continuous mag-

Fig. 230. 125 H. P. Box Frame Motor.

netic circuit which exists throughout the frame. Additional advantages consist of a long commutator, ample room for ventilation, and absence of leakage of oil and water into the motor body. The armature may be removed from the motor frame at one side, obviating the necessity of employing a pit. Fig. 229 illustrates the various parts of the box frame type of motor ready for assembling. Fig. 230 shows a 125 H. P. motor of the box type.

The Series Motor.

The series motor is a motor in which the same current goes through field and armature. It is usually a four pole motor only two of which have field coils, the other two being magnets because they are a part of the magnetic circuit. The poles are short and the coils broad and flat. The armatures are drum wound. When used on D. C. the magnet cores may be solid metal, but for A. C. they must be of sheet iron, as is also the *yoke*.

The only difficulty in operating such a series motor on A. C. circuits is the sparking. This is prevented by a resistance placed between each commutator bar and the one next to it, and lowering the voltage applied.

These resistances are wound in the armature slots and are called the preventive winding.

However, to make the motor operate with good efficiency on A. C. the field coils are actually imbedded in the iron of the magnet core, and the armature is made about 10% greater in diameter, revolving also at a greater number of revolutions per minute.

Such a motor takes only 250 volts A. C. against 500 volts D. C. It is larger and heavier than its mate designed to run on D. C.

If you will notice the air gap between pole pieces and armature it is less on the A. C. motor.

The D. C. series motor can exert a greater H. P. to start a train than the A. C. series motor; and the D. C. motor will get the train up to full speed quicker than the A. C.

It is a peculiar thing that all additions to the D. C. series motor in order to make it equally good as an A. C. motor also make it a better D. C. motor.

If a 200 H. P. motor giving 80% efficiency at 500 volts increased in size and weight by the additions and then run on 300 volts A. C. it will develop nearly 200 H. P., but if put back on D. C. again it will develop 275 H. P.

The fact is that a cheap, light D. C. series motor develops the same horse power as a more expensive heavier A. C. series motor.

Further an A. C. and D. C. motor of the same size and weight operate respectively on 225 and 550 volts and give 125 and 240 horse power.

The Induction Motor.

It has been known for a long time that there was a strong repulsion between the coils of a transformer, so that it was hardly a novelty when a transformer was made with the secondary built on the inside of a ring yoke and the primary on the outside of an armature core.

This transformer acted like a motor—in fact it was a motor. In order to give the motor good starting power it was wound for and served with three phase currents, and a resistance wound in with the primary so arranged as to be cut out after machine was up to speed.

The names armature and field will hardly apply to such a motor, so that the names Stator and Rotor have been adopted.

The Stator is the stationary winding whether connected to outside power or not.

The Rotor is the rotating part.

As usually built the stator consists of a winding producing a large number of poles, six and upwards, for the more poles the slower the rate of speed. The induction motor having an inherent tendency to revolve at tremendous speeds according to formula,

Velocity in rev. per min. $= 60 \times$ frequency $\div$ number of pairs of poles,

it will be seen that many poles and low frequency are necessities.

The stator being served with two or three phase currents each pole is caused by the action of two or three coils. As the current rises and falls in these coils the magnetism grows and fades away. Hence the point of the stator where magnetism is greatest is continually moving around the stator.

Hence we say that it is a revolving field.

The stator winding is continuous and has no connection with rotor or outside power. The current in it is induced by the transformer actions of the rotor.

The rotor is usually a slotted core of sheet iron in each of which is part of a single conductor coil. These coils are all connected together at one end and in groups of two or three; are connected to slip rings through which current is carried to the rotor windings.

Sometimes the ends of the windings project out of the slots and have German silver pieces attached to them, a ring being arranged to slide along the German silver pieces. To start motor the ring is slid out so that the winding has a high resistance. When up to speed the ring is slid in and cuts out the resistance, leaving only the regular winding in circuit.

For railway work the coils are usually connected directly to the slip rings and the resistances inserted in the lead going to the brush. Care must be taken to have these resistances exactly equal and to have them reduced simultaneously until cut out altogether.

These motors are doing excellent work in Europe, but to an American the induction motor equipped locomotive or car seems a huge joke.

In the first place an induction motor runs at one speed and only one speed. After train is started it runs at 20, 30 or 40 miles per hour as steady as a clock, up hills, down hills.

In order to get different speeds four motors are often used, all being used at low speeds and only two of them for high speeds. This is so because if the current from one stator is fed into next rotor, the result is the same as if one motor of many poles was being used and the speed is slow, when each motor is being worked independently the result is same as one motor of few poles and the speed is high.

In certain cases two motors having a different number of poles are used. For slow speed, the rotor of one feeds stator of second. For next highest speed the motor with larger number of poles is used alone; and for highest speed the motor with fewest poles is used alone.

Induction motors have the peculiar property on down grades of feeding power back into the trolley and thus assisting the power house to run other trains up the hills.

Relation of Flux in Armature and Field of Motor.

It has caused much surprise to the unthinking that a series motor should continue to revolve when switched from D. C. to A. C.

Consider the diagram in Fig. 231. Suppose the current

to flow so that the field polarities are as marked. The armature polarities will be such that near the upper brush is a N-pole and near the under brush a S-pole, these poles being directly opposite each other. The top pole of armature being N, the N-field magnet will push and the S-field magnet pull, so that armature will begin to rotate in clock-wise direction.

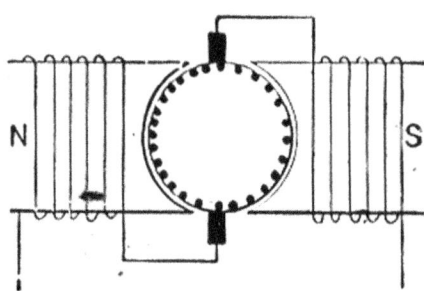

Fig. 231. Diagram of Circuits in Series Motor.

Suddenly reverse the current. All the polarities will change, but motor will continue to revolve in same direction.

The left magnet is now S, the top of armature S, and the right field magnet is N; hence the push and pull of fields on armature is same as before. Hence a series motor will run on A. C. circuits, for while the polarities keep changing the turning effort or torque is always exerted in some direction.

Reversing a Motor. To reverse the direction of a motor, you must change the direction of the current through the fields or through the armature, but not through both. Interchanging the two main leads to a motor will not affect its direction of rotation. Remember that reversing the current reverses the polarity.

Direction of Rotation of a Motor. In Figs. 232, 233 and 234, A represents the armature core and S. N. the pole faces. The windings of armature and fields are indicated by circles, being marked $+$ when current flows toward observer, and $-$ when it flows away from him. The blank circles carry no current.

In Fig. 232 the flux is due to the field coils alone and the polarity is indicated by the letters S. and N.

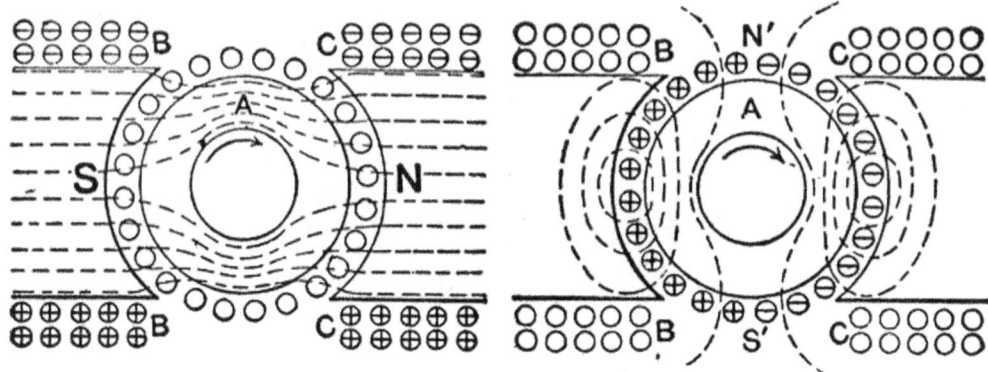

Fig. 232. Field Flux Alone.   Fig. 233. Armature Flux Alone.

In Fig. 233 we have the flux due to the armature current alone, when the machine is driven as a generator in direction as shown by arrow, producing poles at N′ and S′.

Instead of letting the machine supply electricity, furnish current to it; flowing through armature and fields at the same time and in the same direction as before. The polarities will remain unchanged and the armature will begin to revolve as *a series motor, in the opposite direction to that in which it was driven as a series dynamo.*

A shunt motor will rotate in same direction as a motor or as a generator because when current is supplied to terminals of machine it runs through field in same direction as before, but through armature in opposite direction. Refer to Fig. 196.

Sparkless Reversing. The conditions when current flows through an ordinary series motor ready to operate in a direction opposite to the indication of the arrow are shown in Fig. 234.

The brushes are, of course, at N' and S' but since they should be in a line at a right angle to the general direction of the flux, it is evident that they are *not* at the place for sparkless operation.

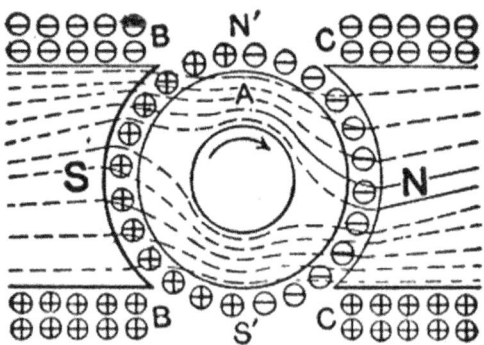

Fig. 234. Combined Field and Armature Fluxes.

The magnetic flux takes the peculiar direction shown in Fig. 234 due to the interaction of the field and armature fluxes.

Looking back at Figs. 134 and 135 you will see that it is natural that when these fluxes occur at the same time, the N' would attract the S flux, and the S' pull the N flux so that the resultant or machine flux would be as in Fig. 234.

The stronger the armature flux and the weaker the field flux the more the machine flux is twisted.

If the armature is weak and the field very strong the effect of the armature will be very slight, or as we say "the *armature reaction* is small," and the machine flux will look like Fig. 232.

In this case the brushes at N' and S' are in the proper place for sparkless operation.

If the flux were like Fig. 234 upon reversal of the armature current the flux would twist in the other direction, but if the flux were like Fig. 232 the reversal has no effect.

The machine flux of all railroad motors is like Fig. 232, so that they may be reversed without any change of brushes.

Transmission Lines, Feeders, Trolley and Third Rail.

The transmission line from power house to sub-station or point of feeding into trolley or third rail is usually a pole line.

With high voltages the use of iron poles along the right of way is becoming standard practice. Such a pole is shown in Fig. 330.

From the thickly settled parts of cities and at terminal stations the transmission line should be excluded; but the feeders must be carried underground.

This is done by running insulated cables in ducts. Fig. 331 shows cables supported on side wall of tunnel; Fig. 332 shows ducts for cables in side wall of tunnel or a station; Fig. 333 showing these same ducts arranged under platform of station.

The pole line is of bare wire, copper or aluminum, supported on porcelain or earthen ware insulators.

Fig. 334 shows a 50,000 volt insulator of three separate pieces of porcelain cemented together. It is 11 inches high and weighs 27 pounds. The distance the voltage would have to jump to get to pin or cross arm is 8½ inches.

A 60,000 volt porcelain insulator of four pieces is shown in Fig. 335, while Fig. 336 shows a 75,000 volt three piece porcelain insulator, 15 inches high, weight 40 pounds, with a sparking distance of 11 inches.

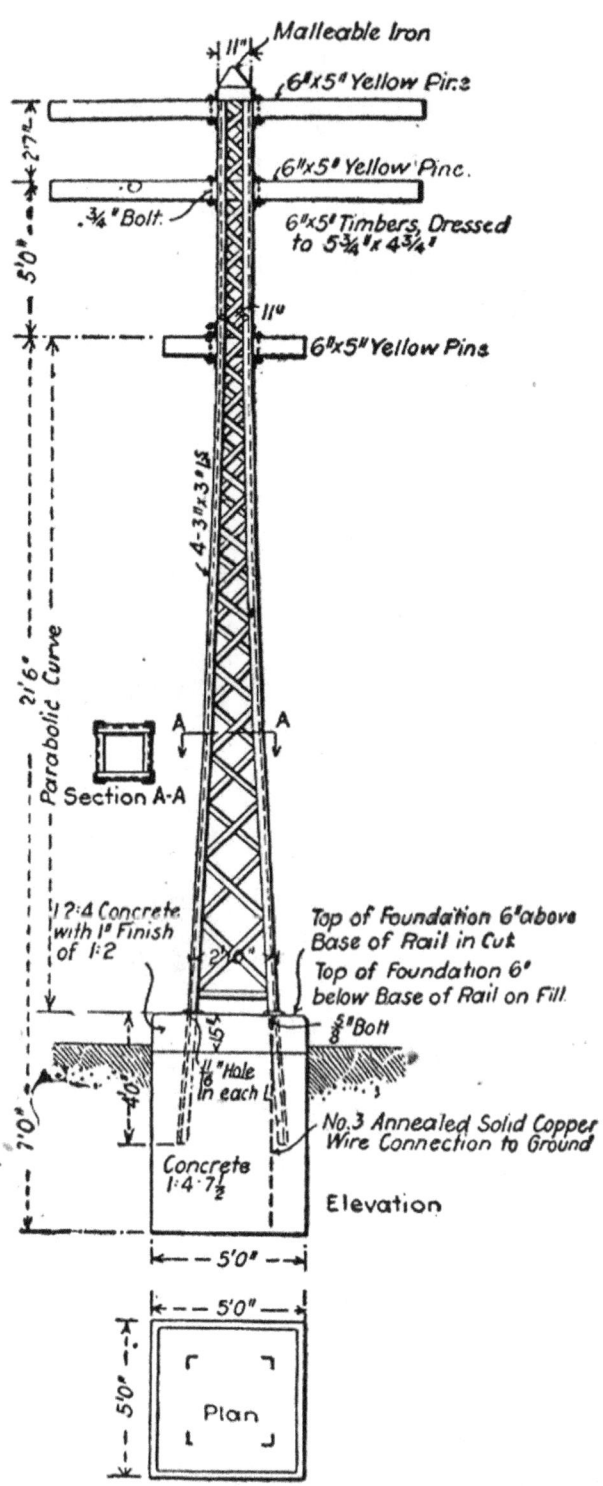

Fig. 330. Transmission Line Pole. New York Central R. R.

When cables are used the voltage is usually lower and glass may be used. Fig. 337 is a glass insulator for cables carrying a pressure of not over 10,000 volts.

Iron pins are used now, as shown in Fig. 338, because the distance the arc must jump is increased by use of a porcelain covered iron pin. Fig. 339 shows the sparking distance with wood pin, and Fig. 340 the increase with porcelain covered iron pin.

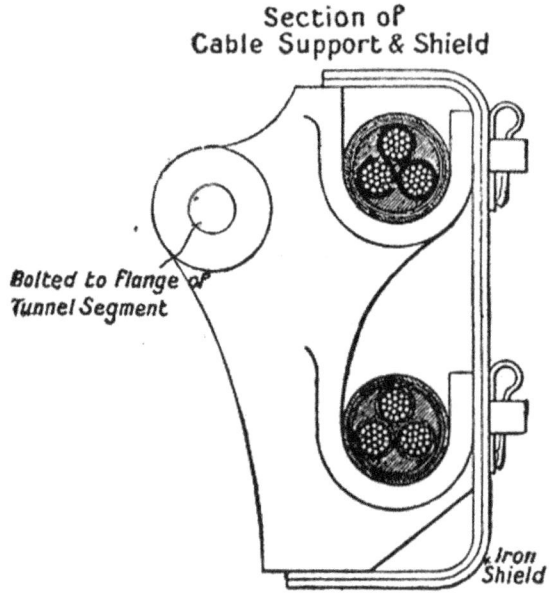

Fig. 331. Cables Supported on Side of Tunnel.

Fig. 341 shows a pin ready to be put straddle of a pole top and Fig. 342 shows an iron pin adapted to bolt on the side of the pole. The porcelain cover has not yet been attached to this pin.

The sparking or arcing distance on an insulator is estimated by imagining a rain storm coming at an angle of 45° and thus conducting the electricity from top umbrella or petticoat to the pin sleeve as in A, Fig. 343.

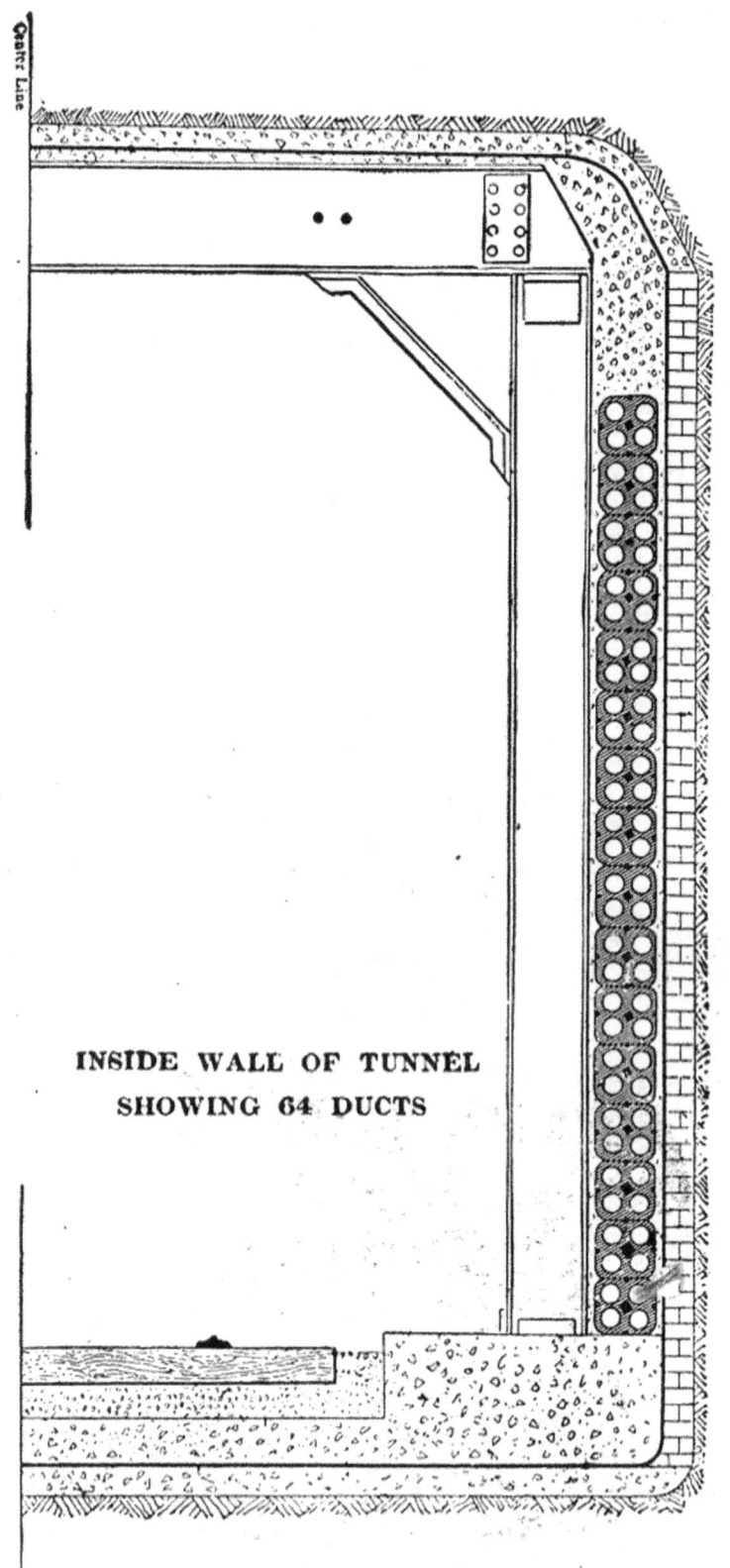

Fig. 332. Ducts Inside of Wall of Tunnel.

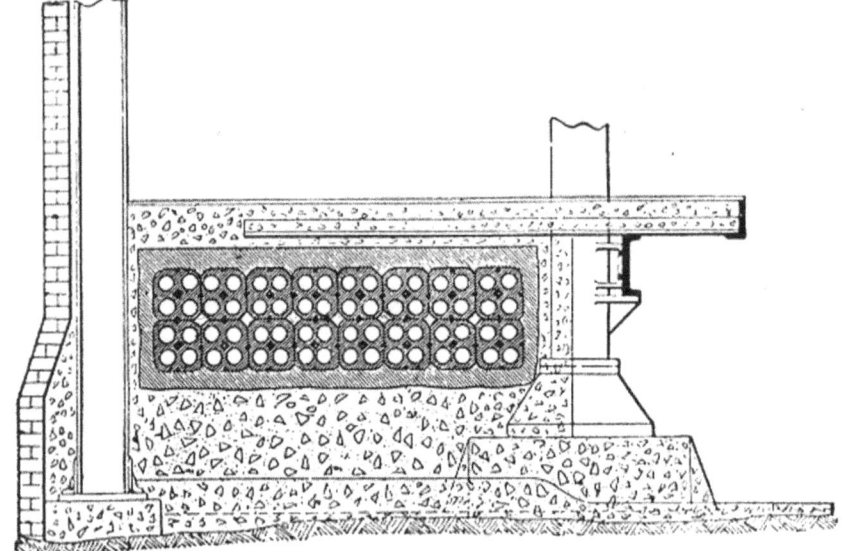
Fig. 333. Ducts Under Passenger Station Platform.

Fig. 334. 50,000 Volt Insulator.

This distance plus the distance B across which the spark would have to jump gives total sparking distance.

When the high tension wires enter a sub-station the arrangement of Fig. 344 is a good one. A large square of slate holds a tube of porcelain, while the shed keeps

Fig. 335. 60,000 Volt Insulator.

whole dry. A sectional view of the porcelain tube is given in Fig. 345.

When the line drops from pole to sub-station a set of strain insulators must be put in to hold the end of line taut. Fig. 346 shows a complete one for moderate pres-

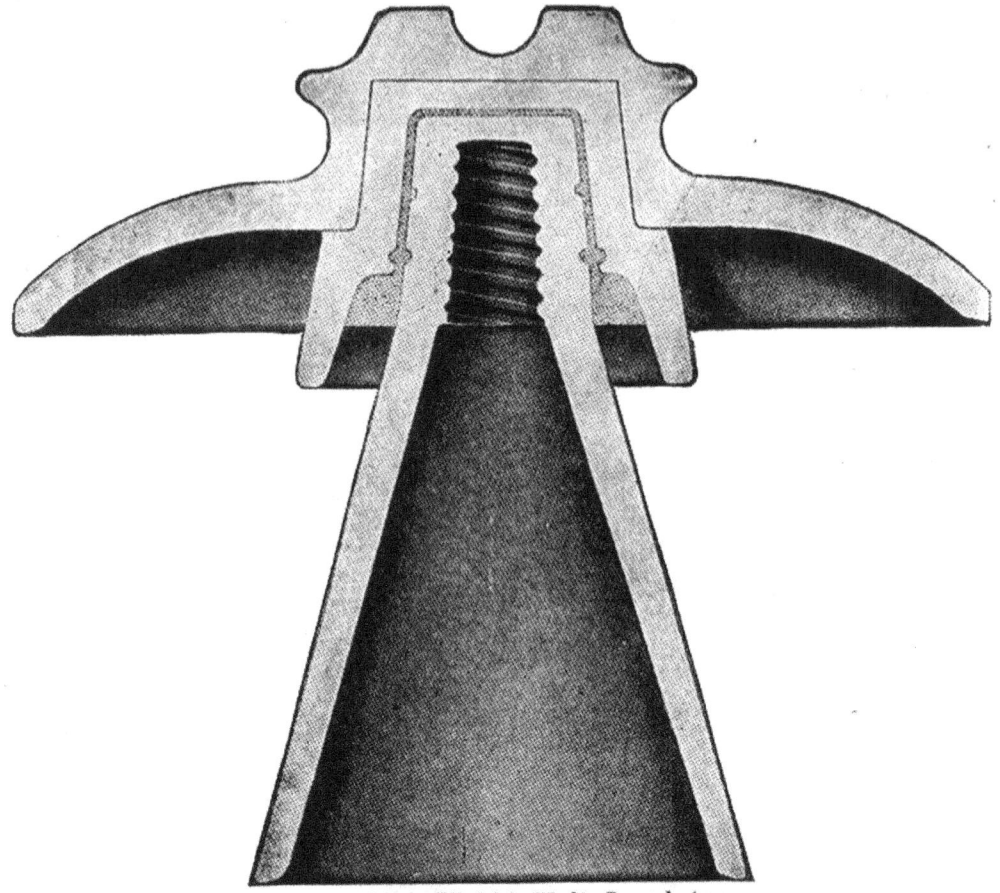

Fig. 336. 75,000 Volt Insulator.

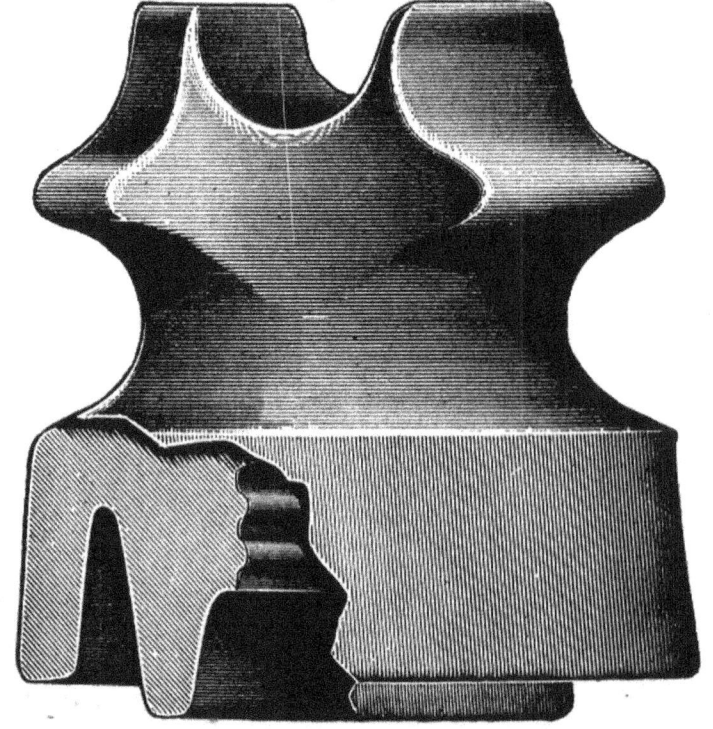

Fig. 337. 10,000 Volt Insulator.

sures and one end of a triple one when the line is very heavy.

The testing of insulators is shown in Fig. 347, but in addition to this insulators are also tested when complete in their natural position, with regular voltage, while a stream of water, at a downward angle of 45°, is being played on them from a hose.

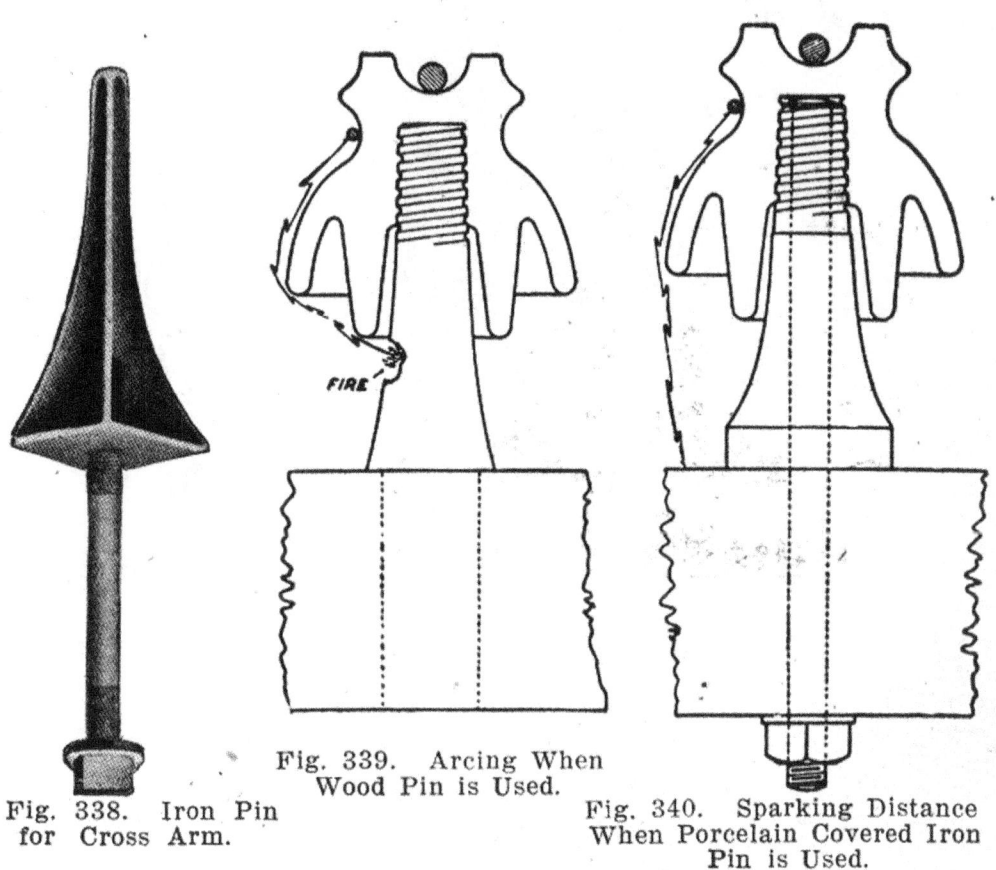

Fig. 338. Iron Pin for Cross Arm.

Fig. 339. Arcing When Wood Pin is Used.

Fig. 340. Sparking Distance When Porcelain Covered Iron Pin is Used.

Overhead Trolley Line.

The old-fashioned single trolley wire with trolley wheel collecting current is unsuitable for high speeds. Its place is taken by the catenary line and bow trolley.

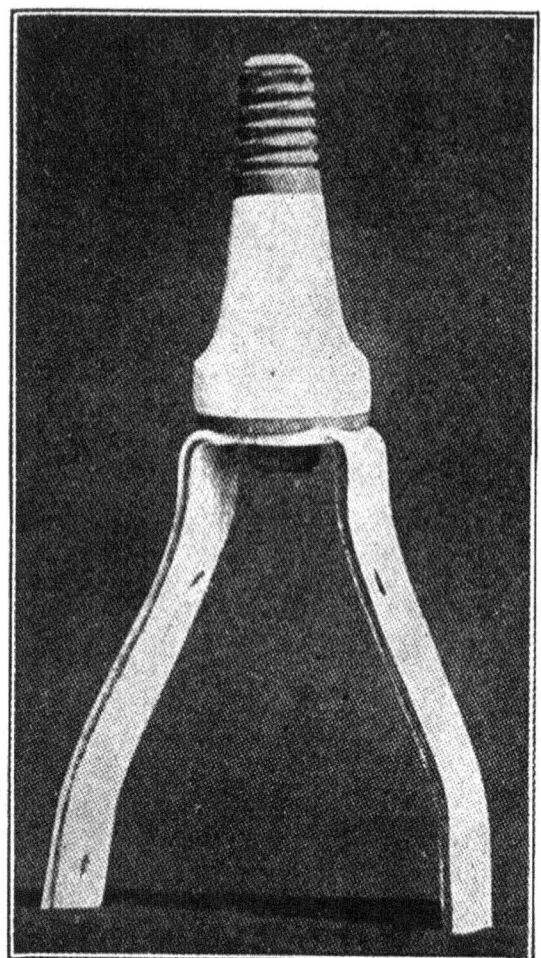
Fig. 341. Pin for Top of Pole.

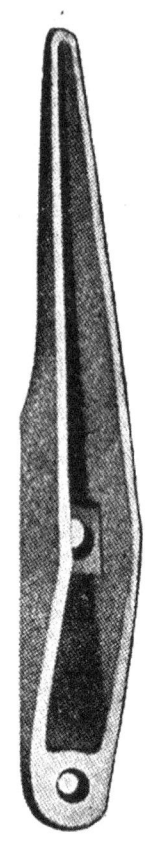
Fig. 342. Pin for Side of Top of Pole.

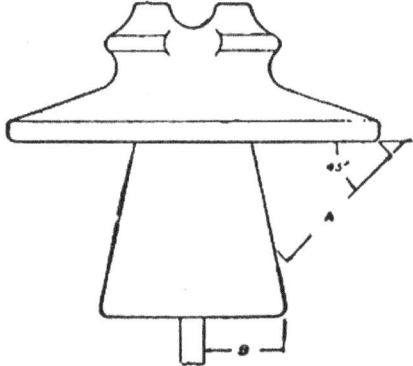

$A + B = 4\tfrac{1}{2}'' =$ Arcing Distance Wet

Fig. 343. Measurement of Arcing or Sparking Distance.

sures and one end of a triple one when the line is very heavy.

The testing of insulators is shown in Fig. 347, but in addition to this insulators are also tested when complete in their natural position, with regular voltage, while a stream of water, at a downward angle of 45°, is being played on them from a hose.

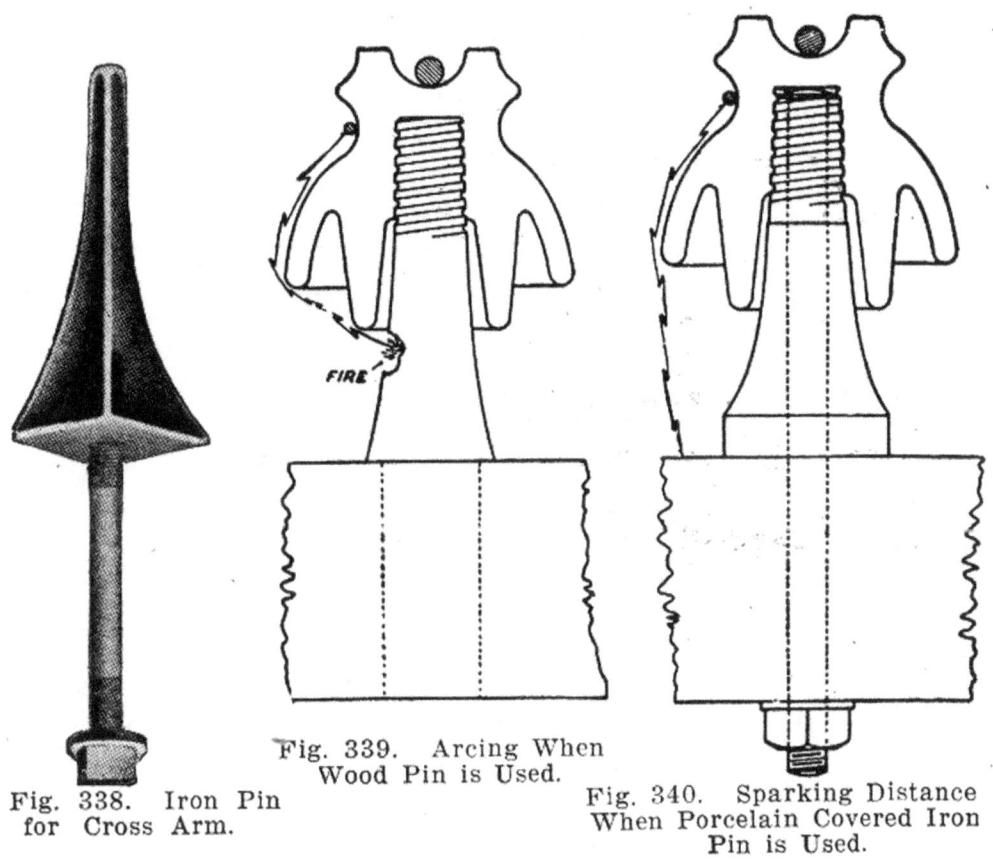

Fig. 338. Iron Pin for Cross Arm.

Fig. 339. Arcing When Wood Pin is Used.

Fig. 340. Sparking Distance When Porcelain Covered Iron Pin is Used.

Overhead Trolley Line.

The old-fashioned single trolley wire with trolley wheel collecting current is unsuitable for high speeds. Its place is taken by the catenary line and bow trolley.

These triangles are fastened to the two steel cables at their corners. This brings the cables in near each other at centers of spans. They therefore, starting from the cross bridges or gantries curve in and down.

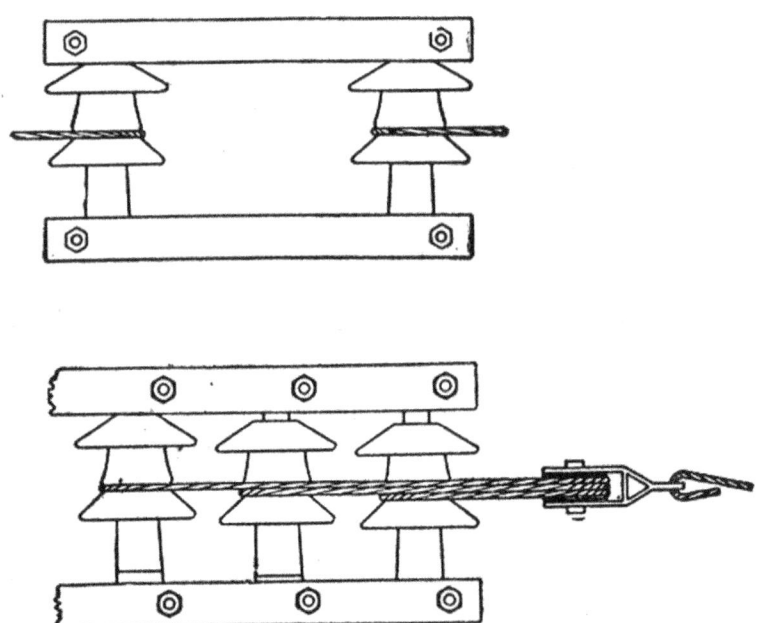

Fig. 346. Single Pin Strain Insulator and one end of a Triple Pin Strain Insulator.

The other corners of the triangles all fall in a straight line 22 feet above the level of track. The copper trolley wire is soldered into the ears which the lower corners of triangles carry.

Fig. 349 shows the curve of the supporting catenary construction and the straight line of the trolley wire.

Fig. 350 shows a gantry with section switches and transformers for operating switches and lights. These gantries occur every two miles. Fig. 351 gives a diagram of such a gantry, also carrying signals. Fig. 352 gives a diagram of a whole span showing curving of cables,

ELECTRIC RAILROADING

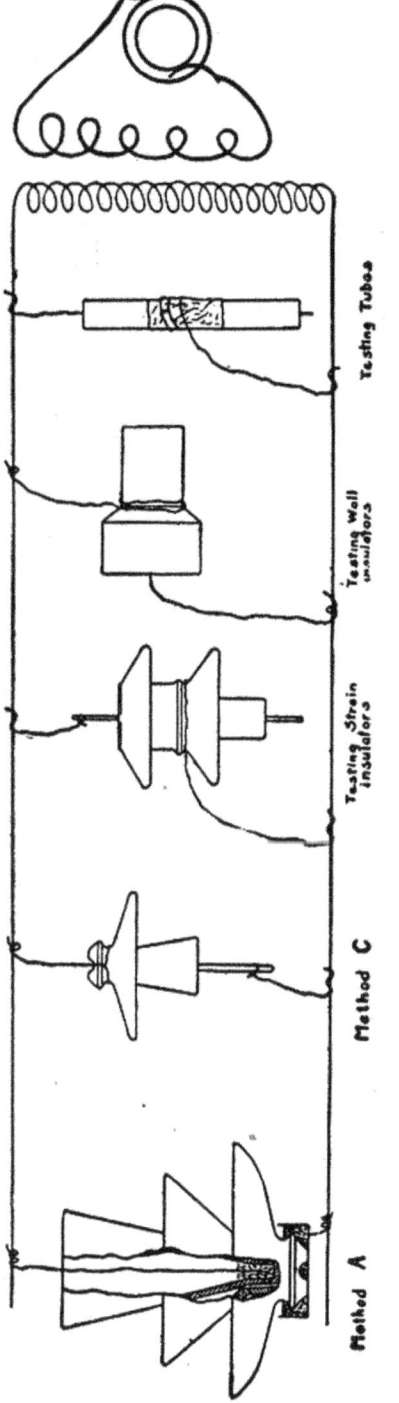

Fig. 347. Method of Testing Insulators.

Fig. 348. Four Track Catenary Line, N. Y. N. H. & H. R. R.

Fig. 349. Catenary Line.

Fig. 350. Gantry with Section Switches, N. Y. N. H. & H. R. R.

Third Rail.

The third rail is usually a 70 pound ordinary steel rail, but lately rails with a certain percentage of copper in them are being used. The rail of the New York Central is copper alloyed.

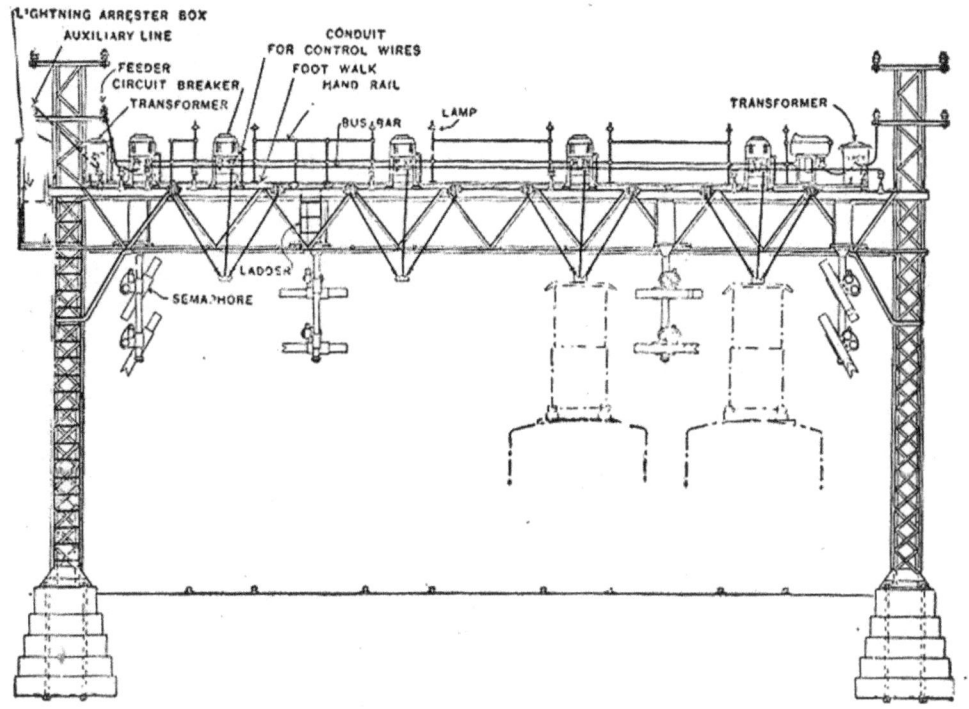

Fig. 351. Gantry with Full Equipment Showing Clearance of Two Locomotives with Trolleys Raised.

Some of the methods of installing the third rail are shown in Fig. 353, while Fig. 354 shows the New York Central under contact type. Heavy snow and sleet storms have shown the under contact to be the most reliable under such conditions.

74 TRANSMISSION LINES

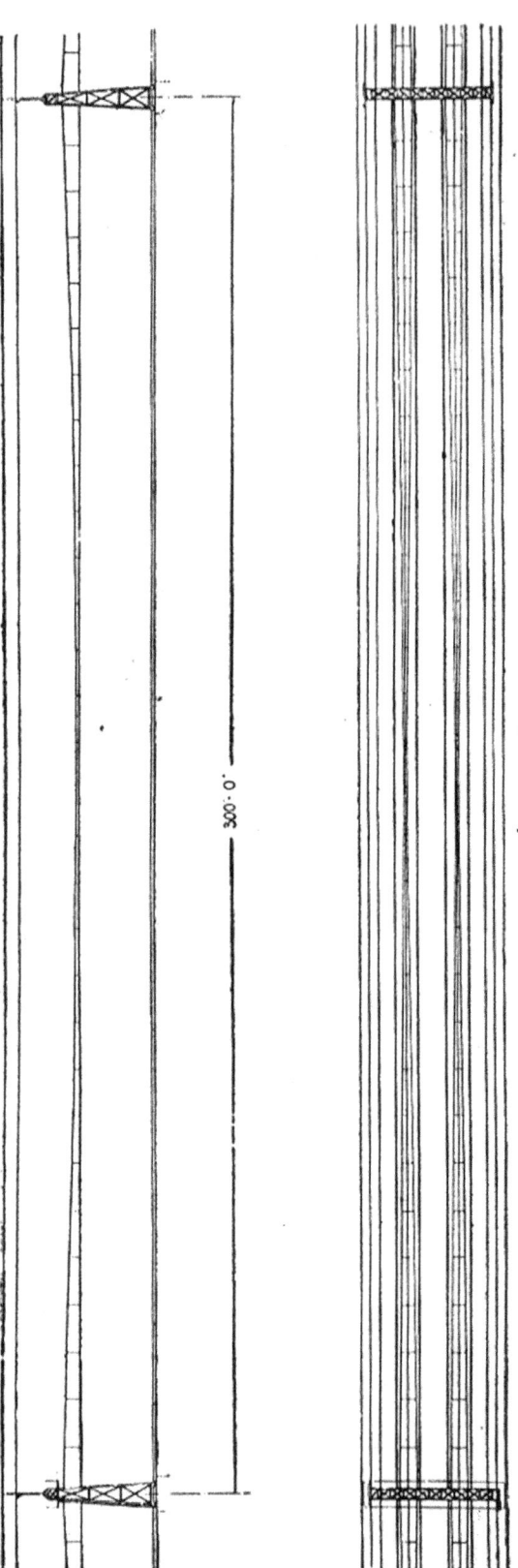

Fig. 352. Side View and Plan of Catenary Span.

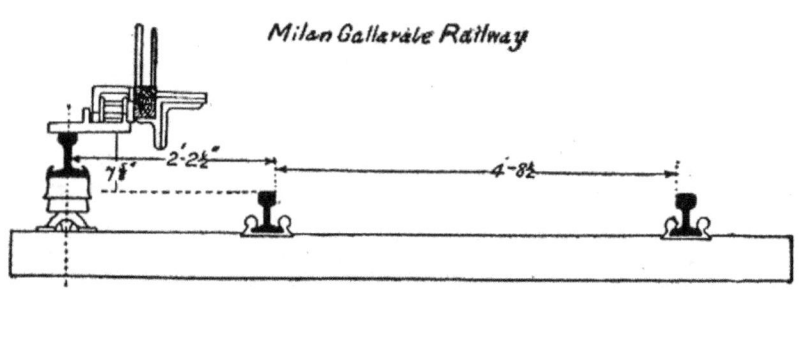
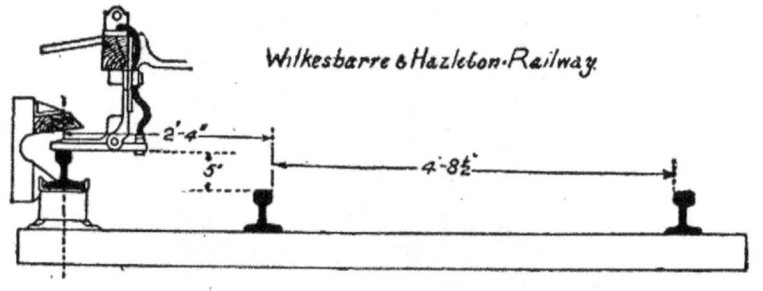
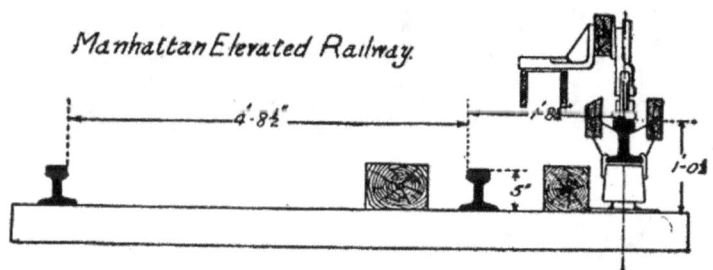
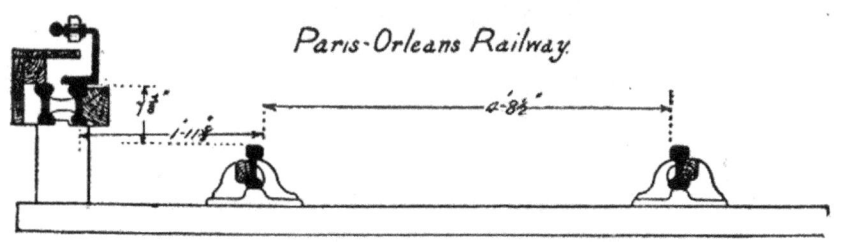

Fig. 353. Third Rail Constructions.

76 TRANSMISSION LINES

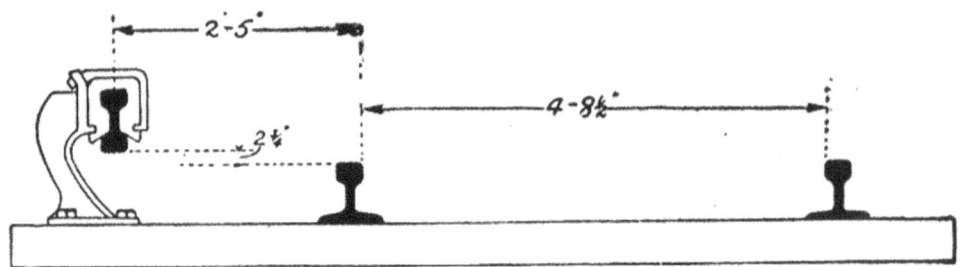

Fig. 354. New York Central Third Rail Construction.

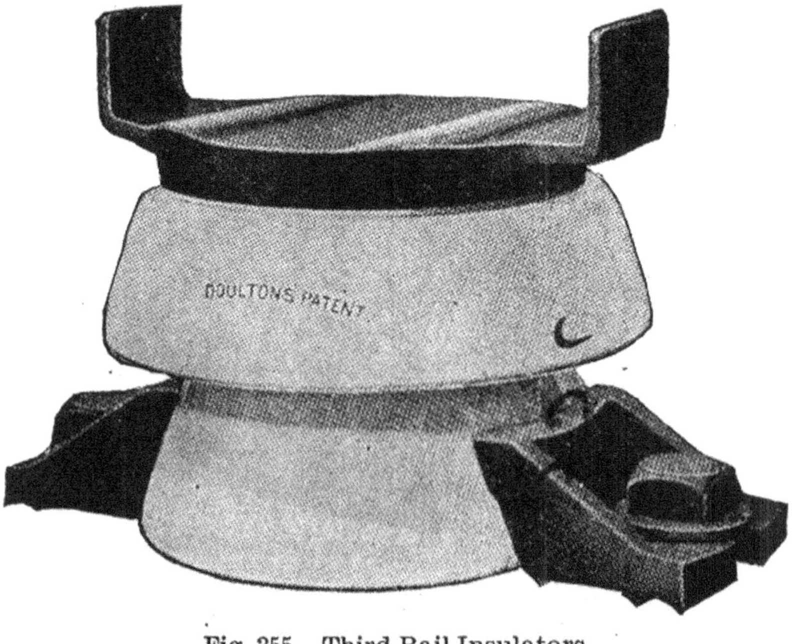

Fig. 355. Third Rail Insulators.

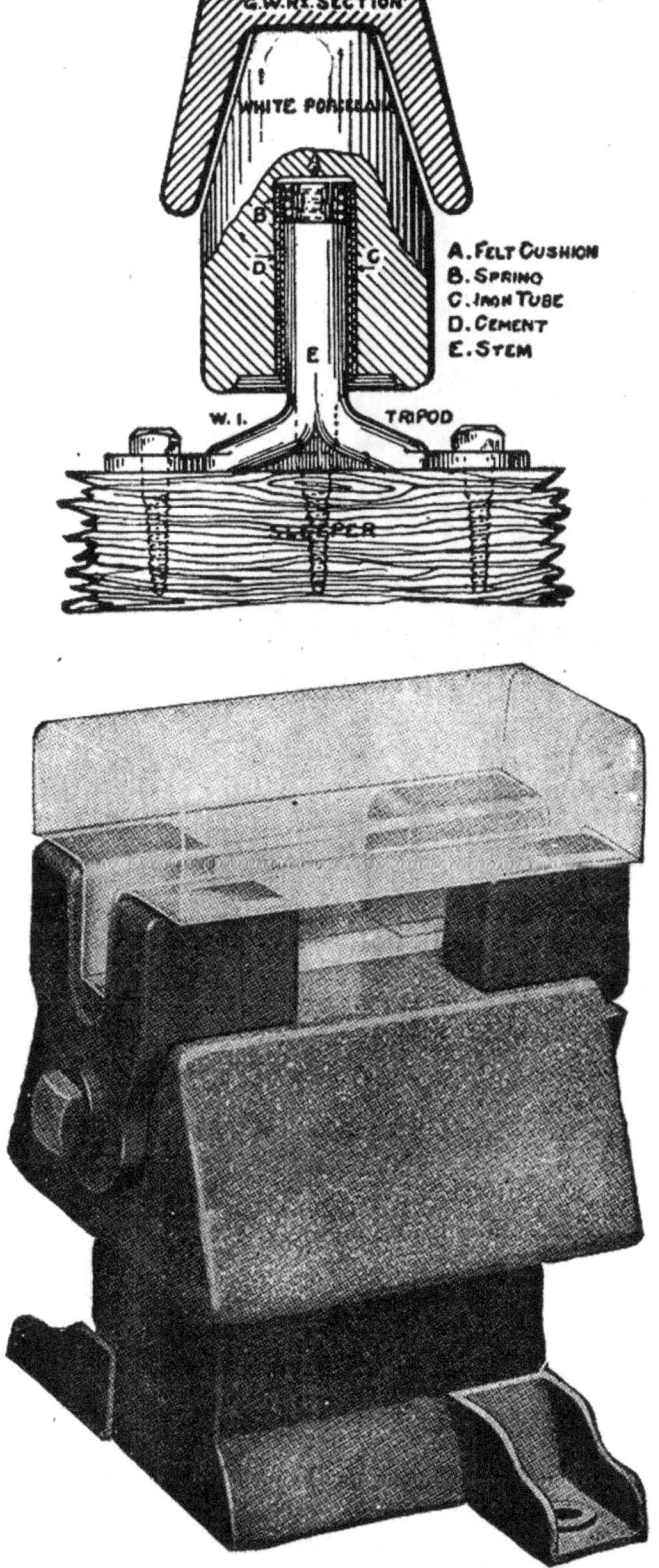

Fig. 356. Two English Third Rails and Insulators.

Insulators for third rail are made of earthen ware and stones such as soap stone. Figs. 355 and 356 show such insulators.

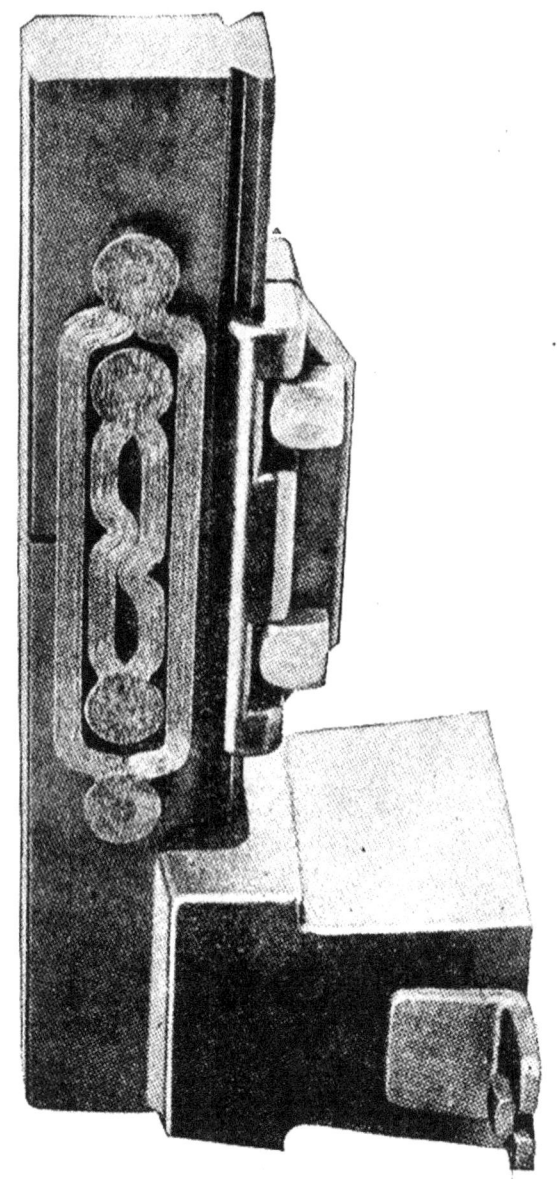

Fig. 357. Third Rail, Insulator, Connector and Riveted Bond.

Bonding.

The resistance of the joints in the third rail or track rails (which return current to power house) is so great that they are shunted by copper conductors called bonds.

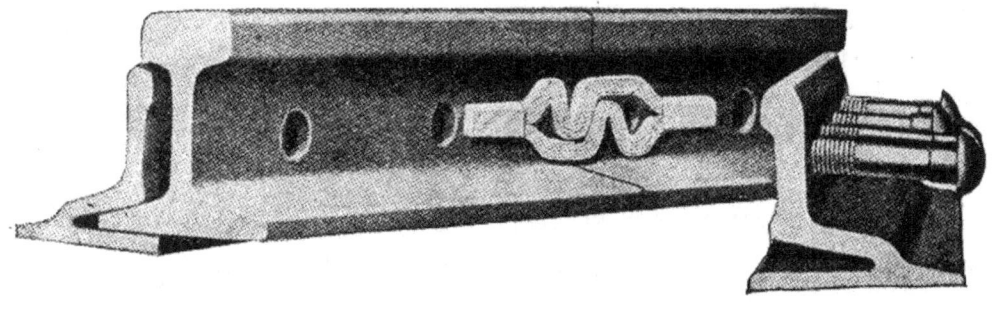
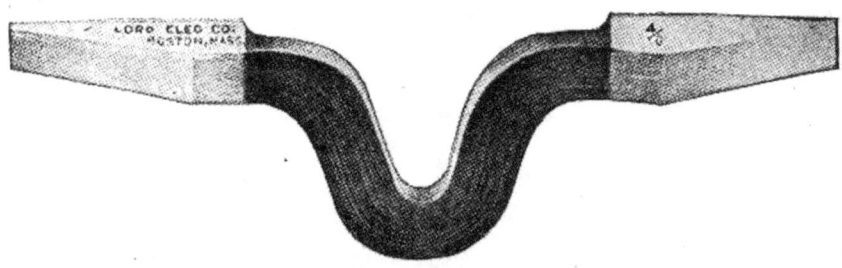

Fig. 358. Bond Protected by Fish-Plate. Soldered to Rail.

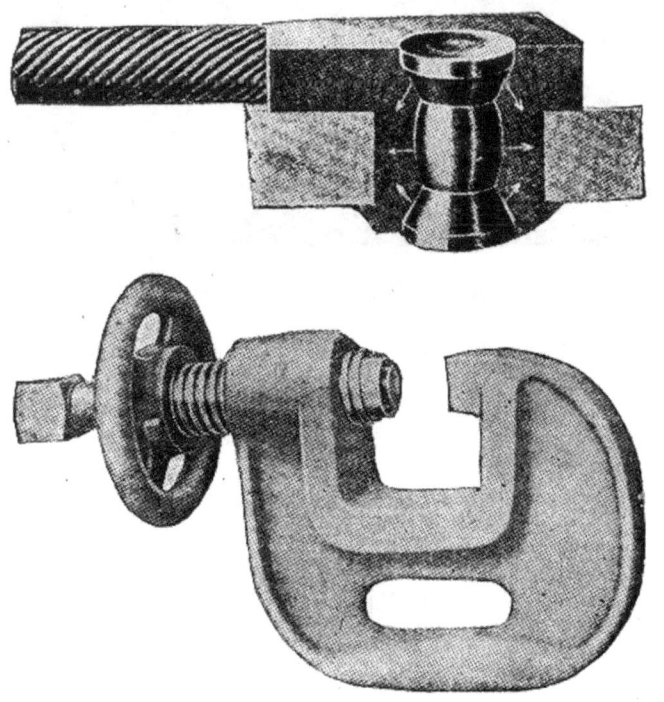

Fig. 359. Riveted Bond and Screw Compressor.

Fig. 357 shows a bond whose conductivity is as good as that of the rail itself.

To prevent theft of bonds, for the value of the copper, they are generally installed under the fish plates as in Fig. 358. They may be soldered on rail as in this case or may be inserted in drilled holes and riveted in by screw press. Fig. 359 shows the riveted end and the screw press.

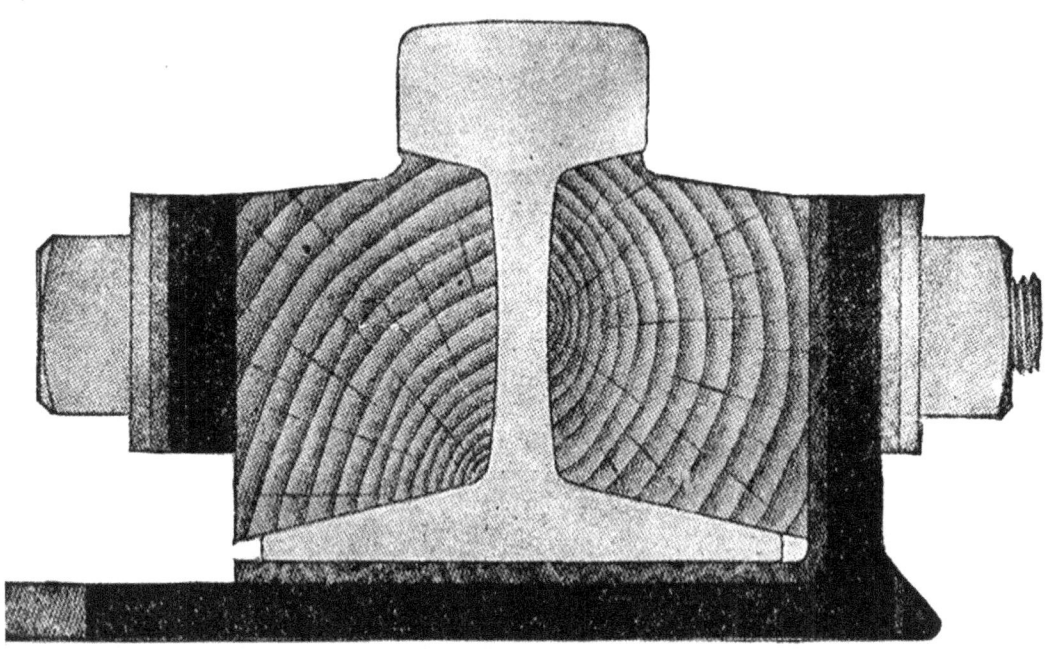

Fig. 360. Insulated Joint.

Insulated Joints.

If for signalling reasons it is desired to cut the track rails into sections, raw hide is placed between ends of rails and wood insulators under fish plates. See Fig. 360.

Systems of Control.

The control of speed of train is by means of a controller, which throws grids of resistance in or out of motor circuits for D. C. motors; connects motor to different taps of the transformer for A. C. motors; and interchanges the relations of armature and field terminals for either A. C. or D. C. motors.

A control with resistances alone must be used when there is bu one motor, as in some mine and factory locomotives. This is called *rheostatic control.*

When there are two motors we may place both in series, giving each motor 250 volts, for half speed, and both in parallel, giving each motor full voltage for full speed.

Acceleration is controlled by use of grid resistances, made of cast iron, shown in Fig. 366. These are cut in the circuit at start by controller and cut out one by one while accelerating to full series; they are then cut into the circuit with the two motors in parallel and again cut out one by one until motors are in full parallel. Thus at the two free running speeds there are no resistances in circuit.

This is called the *series-parallel control.*

When A. C. is used the voltage applied to the motors is varied by connecting more or less of the secondary turns of the step down transformer to the motor. This is called *potential control.*

The series-parallel control is the most familiar to us, for the two K controllers shown in Figs. 367 and 368 are regular equipment on many interurban lines.

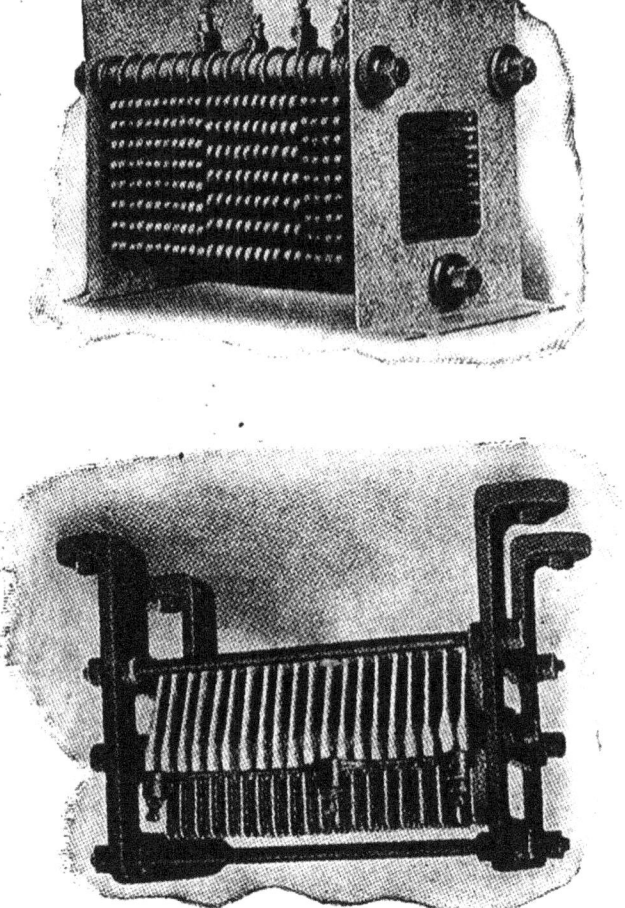

Fig. 366. Cast Iron Grid Resistances.

The letter K designates a controller which never opens the circuit from time motors are started till they are in full parallel or multiple (two names for same thing).

For very heavy equipments the K controller takes the form of Fig. 369, where the cylinder is gear driven.

The letter L used in connection with controllers means

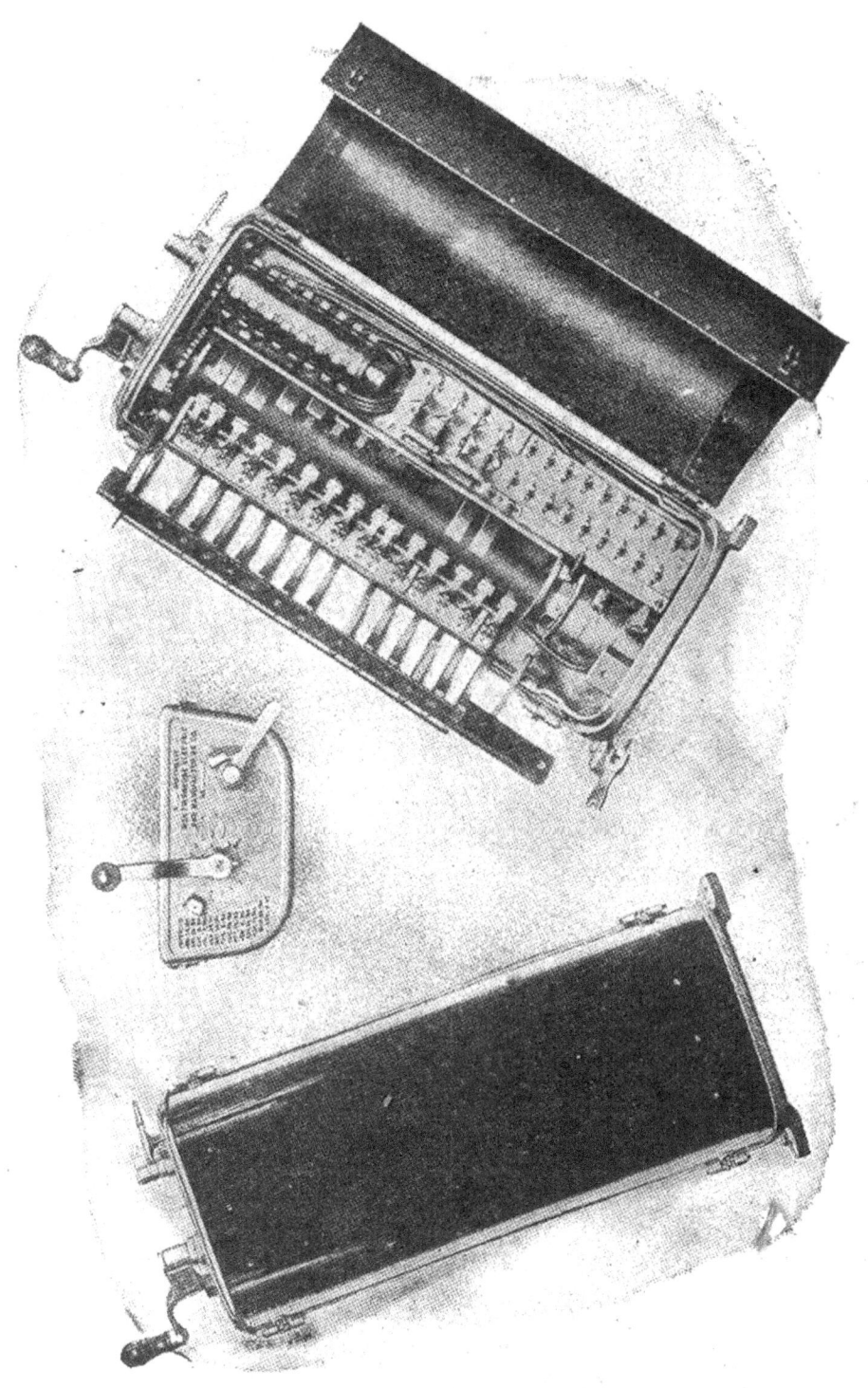

Fig. 367. K Controller.

84 SYSTEMS OF CONTROL

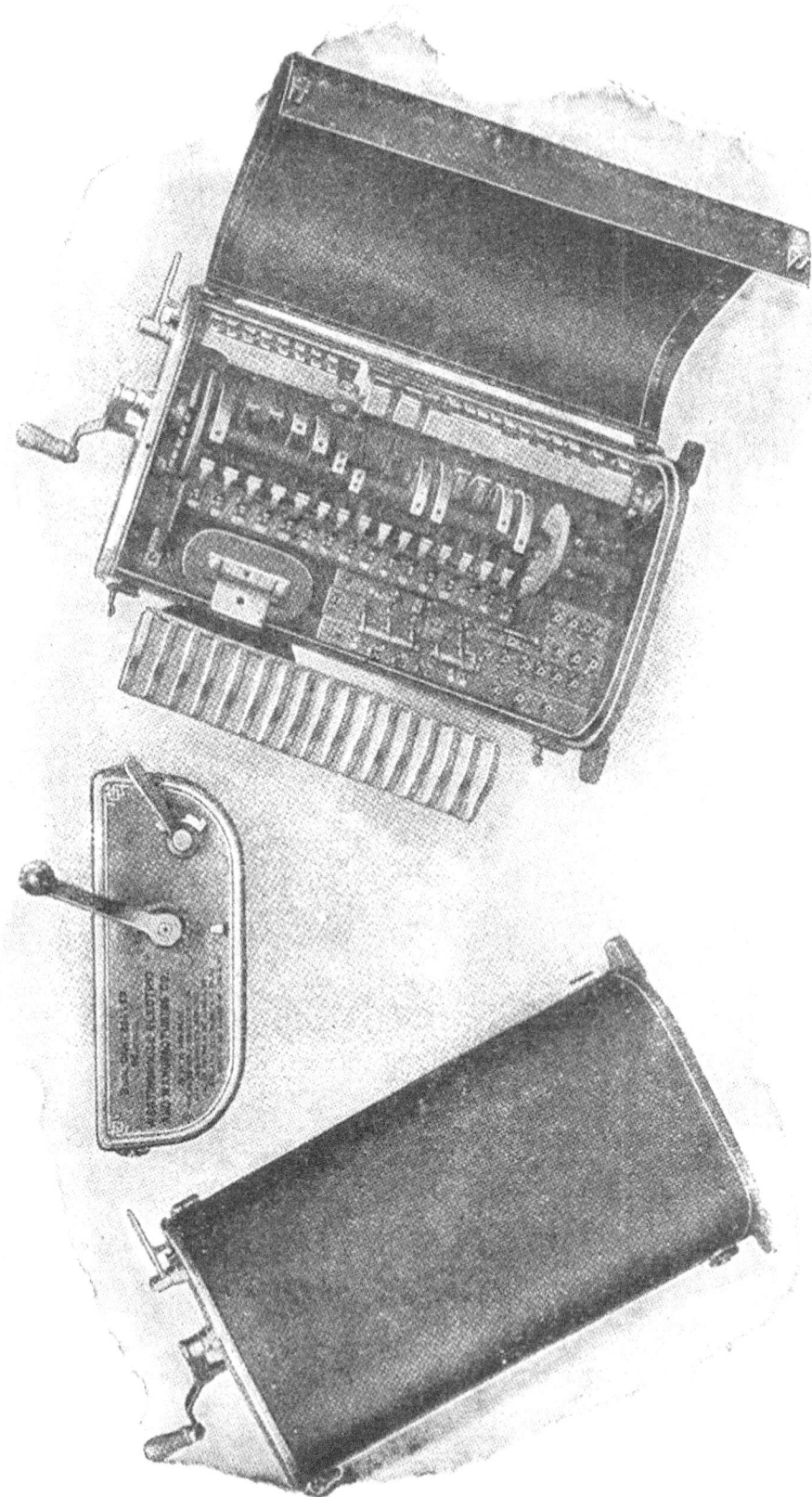

Fig. 368. K Controller.

that when changing motors from full series to parallel with resistance the circuit is momentarily opened. Fig. 370 shows such a controller.

When fitted for electrical braking the letter B is used to designate the type of controller. See Fig. 371.

Fig. 372 shows the electrical connections made by a K controller with two motors.

The notches of a controller are the positions of handle where a spring pawl drops into notches on a plate so as to hold the handle against vibration or slight pressure. The notches are named resistance, running and transition notches.

A resistance notch is one where some resistance is in circuit. These should only be used for very short periods of running. It not only wastes power to use them, but by getting the resistance grid red hot may warp it or might even start a fire.

The running notches are those where there is no resistance in circuit and the motors are in an arrangement suitable for continued use.

A transition notch is where the motors are in some combination so unsuitable for delivering power, that the notch should be passed over quickly.

All notches except transition ones are indicated on top of controller.

Fig. 373 shows connections made by a K controller with four motors.

Fig. 374 shows connections made by an L controller with two motors. The points to be noticed are: The gradual decrease of the resistance* in circuit, it taking

---

*The decrease of resistance is shown in a novel way by placing more of them in parallel. In diagram the wider the resistance, the lower it is.

86 SYSTEMS OF CONTROL

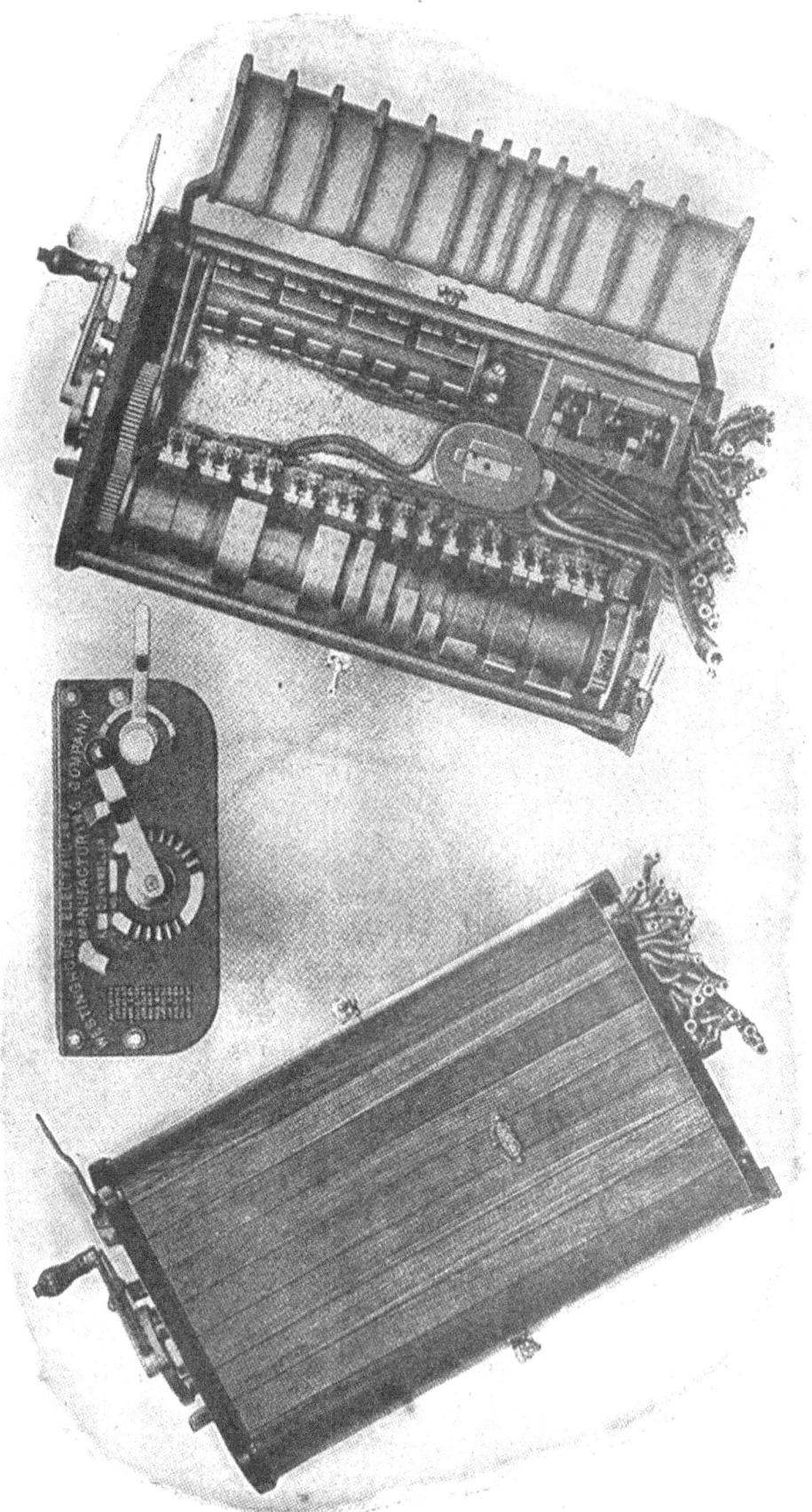

Fig. 369. K-B Controller.

12 notches to get a full series. There are a lot of resistance notches called transition notches simply because there are no marks on top on controller to indicate them. Note the opening of circuit at notch 12½.

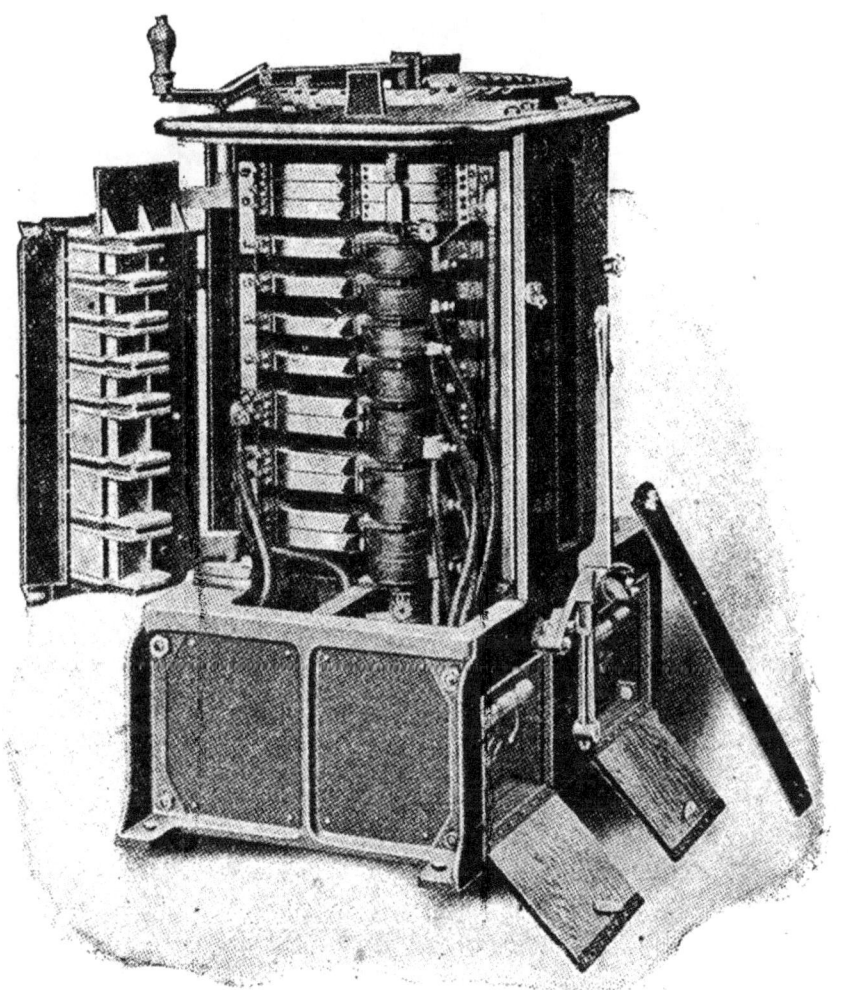

Fig. 370. L Controller.

The student should number the multiple notches up to 24 himself.

Fig. 375 shows the connections made for electrical braking when two and four motors are used.

Fig. 371. B Controller.

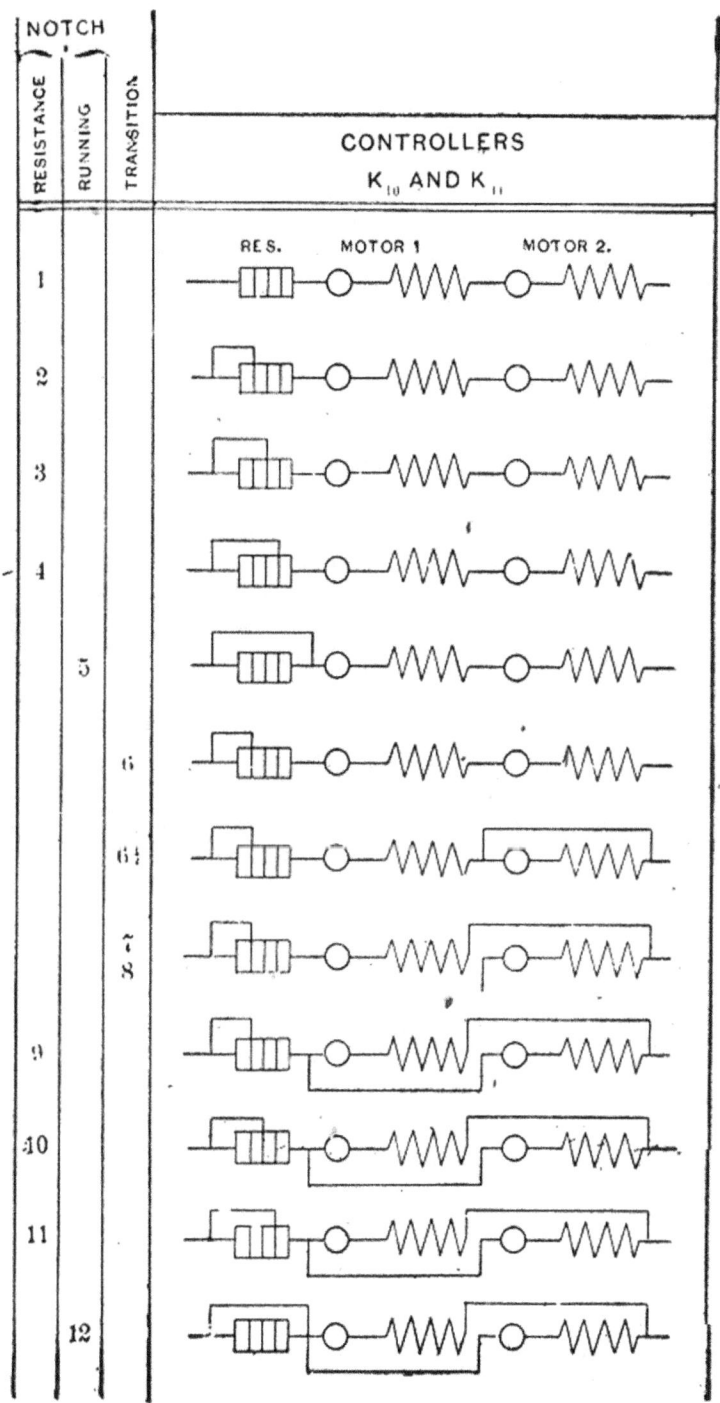

Fig. 372. Scheme of K Control with Two Motors.

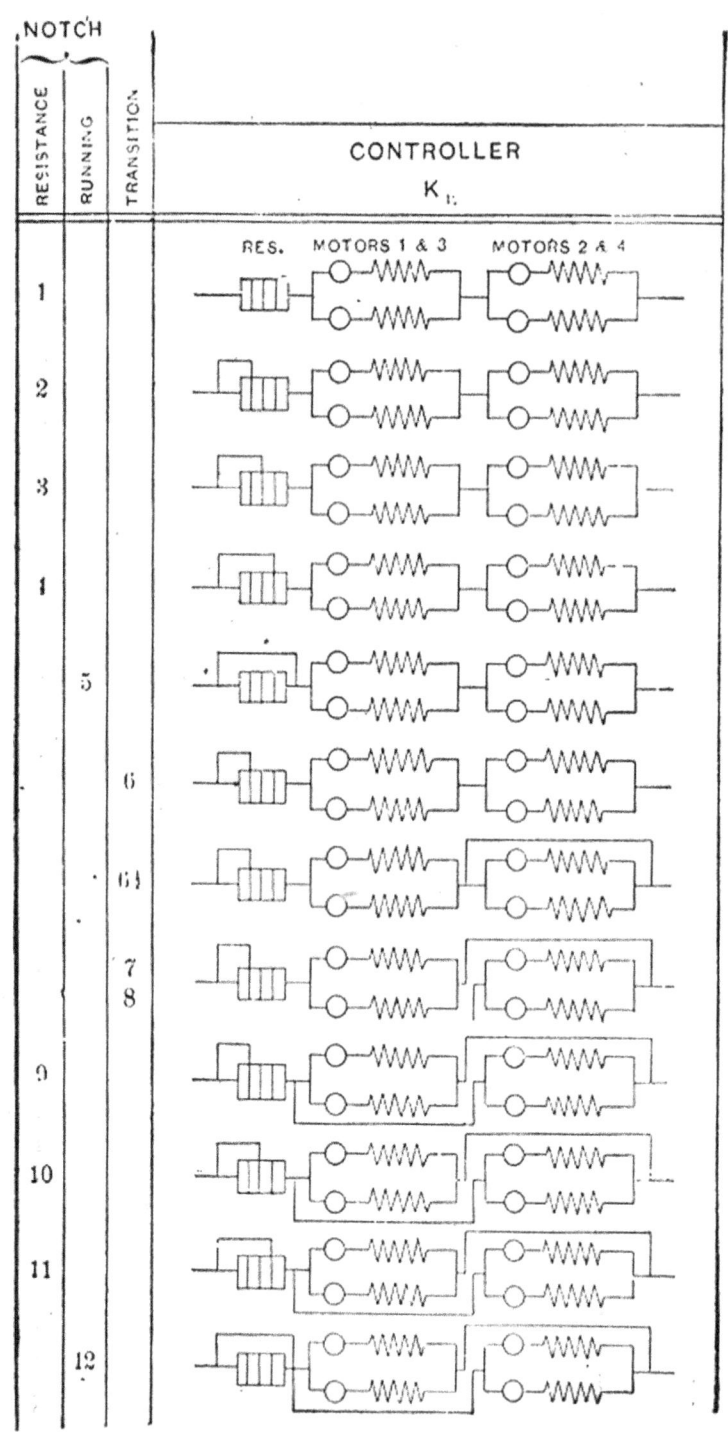

Fig. 373. Scheme of K Control with Four Motors.

Electrical braking uses the motors more than simply running the car, and so they heat more. This means a larger motor for the same schedule speed.

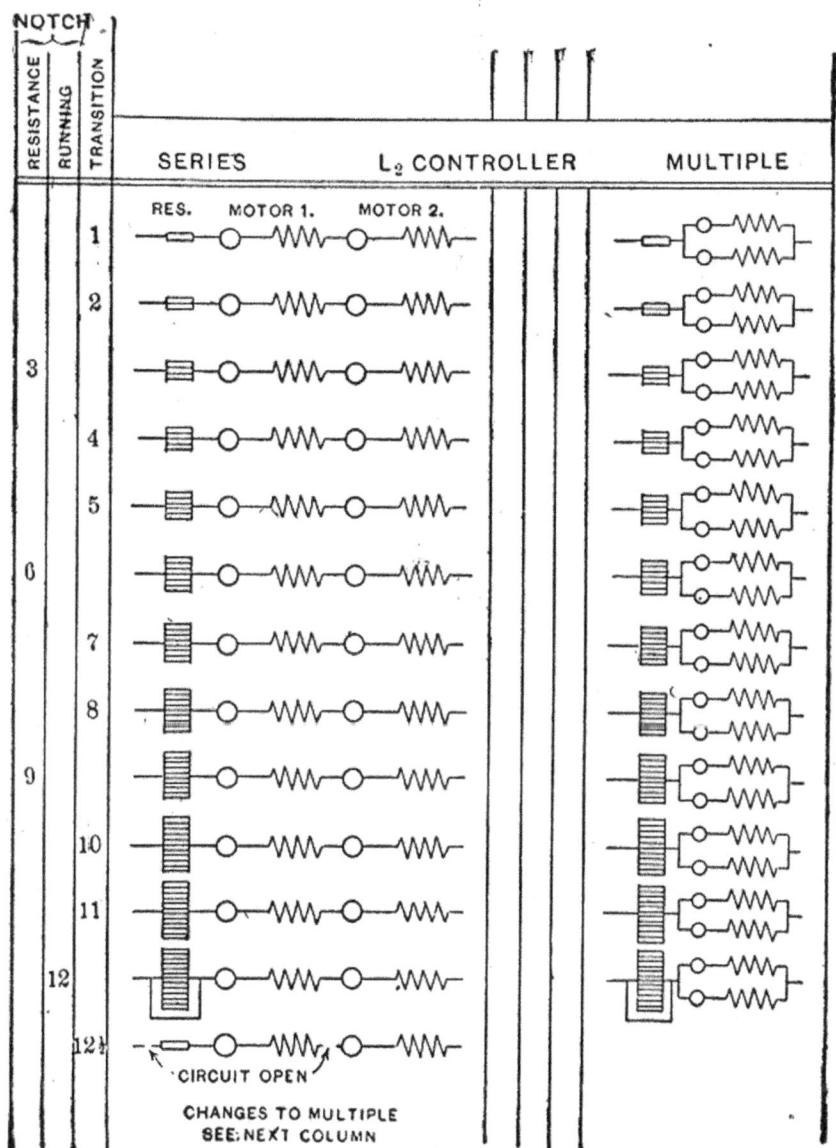

Fig. 374. Scheme of L Control.

In some controllers the movement of the hand is mechanically connected to the cylinder. Such a control is a *manual* control.

92 SYSTEMS OF CONTROL

In other cases the controller merely arranges contacts which energize circuits to electro-magnetically operated switches called contactors; or electro-magnetic valves

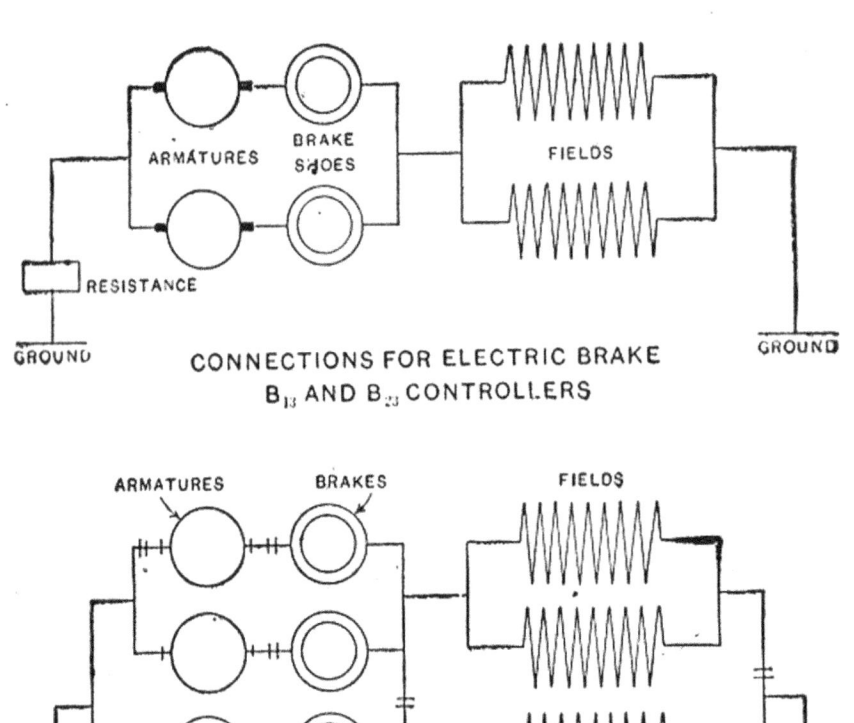

Fig. 375. Scheme of Electrical Braking Connections.

are operated which in turn operate pneumatic cylinders. The push rods from these cylinders open and close the switches. Controllers of this class are called *master controllers.*

The Sprague General Electric Type M Control.

The Sprague-General Electric Type M Control is designed primarily for the operation of a train of motor and trail cars, coupled in any combination and the whole operated as a single unit from any controller on the train. The system may also be used to advantage on individual equipments and locomotives.

The control apparatus for each motor car may be considered as consisting essentially of a motor controller and a master controller.

The motor controller comprises a set of apparatus (Fig. 376) usually located underneath the car (Fig. 377), which handles directly the power circuits for the motors, connecting them in series and parallel and commutating the starting resistance in series with them. This motor controller is operated electrically, and its operation in establishing the desired motor connections is controlled by the motorman by means of the master controller, Fig. 378, which is similar in construction to the ordinary cylinder controller and is handled in the same manner. Instead of effecting the motor combinations directly, however, this controller merely governs the operation of the motor controller.

The master controller operates a number of electrically operated switches, or "contactors," which close and open the various motor and resistance circuits, and an electrically operated "reverser" that connects the field

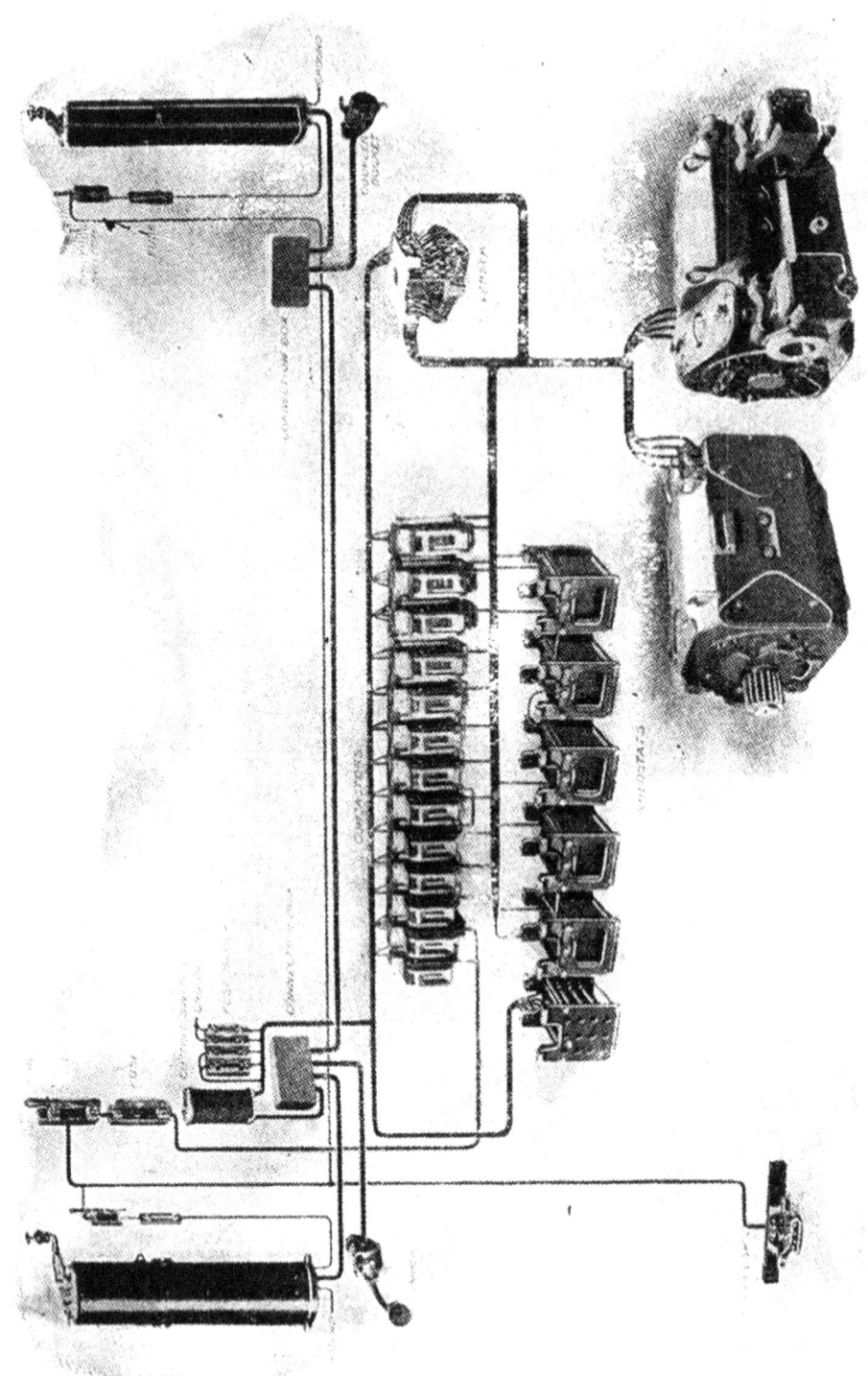

Fig. 376. General View of Apparatus Type M Control.

Fig. 377. Arrangement of Control Apparatus Under Car.

and armature leads of the motors to give the desired direction of movement to the car. Both the contactors and reverser are operated by solenoids, the operating current for which is admitted to them by the master controller.

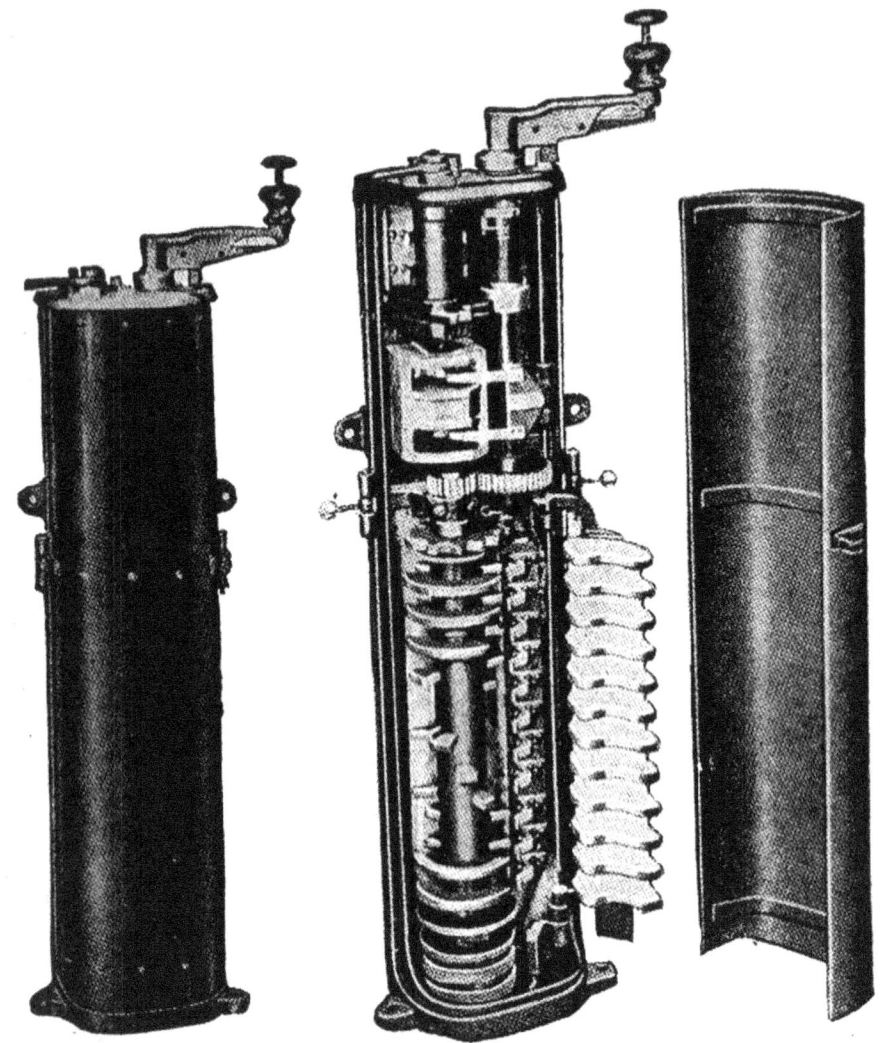

Fig. 378. Master Controller for Sprague-General Electric Control.

Each motor and trail car is equipped with train cable, consisting of nine or ten individually insulated conductors connected to corresponding contacts in coupler sockets located at each end of the car. This train cable is connected identically on each motor car to the master controller fingers and the contactor and reverser operating coils, and is made continuous throughout the train by couplers between cars, connecting corresponding terminals in the coupler sockets.

All wires carrying current supplied directly from the master controller form the "control circuit"; those carrying current for the motors form the "motor" or "power circuit."

Inasmuch as the motor controller operating coils are connected to this control train line, it will be appreciated that energizing the proper wires by means of any master controller on the train will simultaneously operate corresponding contactors on all the motor cars, and simultaneously establish similar motor connections on all cars.

Advantages.

The Sprague-General Electric Type M Control permits a train of motor cars and trailers to be operated as a single unit from any master controller on the train. If desired, a master controller can be placed on each platform of trail cars, thereby providing for the operation of the train from any platform. With this arrangement, the motorman can be always at the head of the train, regardless of the combination of the cars.

The entire train, equipped with Type M Control, may thus be regarded as a unit; the motorman has the same control over a train that he would have over a single car with the ordinary cylinder controller.

Should the motorman remove his hand from the operating handle of the master controller, the current will be immediately cut off from the entire train, thus diminishing the danger of accident in case the motorman should suddenly become incapacitated.

The system will operate at any line potential between 300 volts and 600 volts, and the action of all contactors is absolutely reliable and instantaneous.

On heavy equipments the effort of the motorman in operating the master controller is so much less than that required to handle a large cylindrical controller that he can give more attention to the air brakes and other parts of the equipment, especially in cases of emergency.

The approximate total weight per motor car of control equipments, exclusive of supports, is 2,500 pounds for 300 H. P. of motors.

The approximate weight of the apparatus for each trail car, which comprises train cable, coupler sockets and connection boxes, is 100 lbs.

In many cases it will be found advantageous to anticipate the future growth of an interurban road by equipping each motor car with Type M Control. In these cases it will be easy to change from single car to train service whenever warranted by traffic conditions.

The position of the handle on that master controller which the motorman is operating always indicates the position of motor control apparatus on all cars.

Contactors.

The contactors are the means of cutting in and out the various resistances, of making and breaking the main circuit between trolley and motors, and of changing from series to parallel connection.

Each contactor consists of a movable arm carrying a renewable copper tip which makes contact with a similar fixed tip, and a coil for actuating this arm when supplied with current from the master controller. The contactor is so designed that the motor circuit is closed

Fig. 379. Contactors with Interlocks.

only when current is flowing through its operating coil; and gravity, assisted by the spring action of the finger, causes the arm to drop and open the circuit immediately, when the control circuit is interrupted. Each contactor has an effective and powerful magnetic blow-out, which will disrupt the motor circuit under conditions far exceeding normal operation. In closing, the copper tips come together with a wiping action, which cleans and smooths their surfaces.

All contactors in an equipment are practically identical, and the few parts which are subject to burning and wear are so constructed as to be readily replaceable.

In order to save space and eliminate interconnections as much as possible, several contactors are mounted on the same base (Fig. 379). The contactors should preferably be located under the car, and boxes are therefore supplied which facilitate installation, protect the contactors from brake-shoe dust and other foreign material, and provide the necessary insulation. These boxes are built with perforated openings for ventilation, but shields are supplied for closing these perforations whenever desirable.

Reverser.

The general design of the reverser (Fig. 380) is somewhat similar to the ordinary cylindrical motor reversing switch with the addition of electro-magnets for throwing it to either forward or reverse position. In general construction, the operating coils are similar to those used on the contactors, but in order to secure absolute reliability of action in throwing, the coil is given full line potential. The reverser is provided with small fingers for handling control circuit connections, and when it throws, the operating coil is disconnected from ground and is placed in series with a set of contactor coils, thus cutting the operating current down to a safe running value. These coils are protected by a fuse, which will immediately open the circuit if the reverser fails to throw. If the position of the reverser does not correspond to the direction of movement indicated by the reverse handle on the master controller, the motors on that car cannot take current. While the motors are taking current the operating coil is energized, and the electrical circuits are interlocked to prevent possibility of throwing.

Fig. 380. Reverser on Motor Cars.

Master Controller.

The master controller (Fig. 378) is considerably smaller than the ordinary street car controller, but is similar in appearance and method of operation. Separate power and reverse handles are provided, as experience has led to the adoption of this arrangement in preference to providing for the movement of a single handle in opposite directions.

An automatic, safety, open-circuiting device is provided whereby, in case the motorman removes his hand from the master controller handle, the control circuit will be automatically opened by means of auxiliary contacts in the controller, which are operated by a spring when the button in the handle is released. This device is entirely separate and distinct in its action from that of the main cylinder. Moving the reverse handle either forward or backward makes connections for throwing the reverser to either forward or backward position. The handle can be removed only in the intermediate or off position. As the power handle is mechanically locked against movement when the reverse handle is removed, it is necessary for the motorman to carry only this handle when leaving the car.

When the master controller is thrown off, both line and ground connections are severed from the operating coils of important contactors, and none of the wires in the train cables are alive.

The current carried by the master controller is about 2.5 amperes for each equipment of 400 H. P. or less. This small current carrying capacity permits a compact construction, and the controller weighs only 130 lbs

Master Controller Switch.

A small enclosed switch with magnetic blow-out is used to cut off current from each master controller, and is supplied with a small cartridge fuse enclosed in the same box. When this switch is open all current is cut off from that particular master controller which it protects.

Control Cable.

A special flexible cable, made up of different colored individually insulated conductors, is used for the train cable and, whenever possible, to make connections between the various pieces of control apparatus.

Connection Box.

Connection boxes are provided for connecting the control circuit cables at junction points without splicing, and small copper terminals are supplied for attaching to the ends of the individual conductors.

Control Couplers.

The master control cables of each car terminate in sockets and are interconnected by means of a short section of similar flexible cable fitted with plugs. Each socket contains a number of insulated, metallic contacts connected to the train wires, and the terminal plugs of the coupler contain corresponding contacts. The parts subject to wear are readily replaceable.

All coupler sockets are provided with spring catches which hold the plugs in contact under normal conditions, and permit them to automatically release in case two cars separate.

Control Cut-Out Switch.

This is a switch, usually nine-point, installed on each motor car and is used to disconnect the operating coils of the contactors and reverser from the train cable, and hence render them inoperative.

Control Fuses.

On each car several small enclosed fuses are placed in the control circuit at such points as to effectively protect the apparatus.

Fig. 381. Control Rheostat.

Control Rheostat.

While starting car, tubes of a high resistance rheostat are connected in series with the contactor coils to cut down the operating current to a value approximating that for the running positions of the controller. This rheostat is enclosed in a sheet iron case for protection. Fig. 381.

ELECTRIC RAILROADING 105

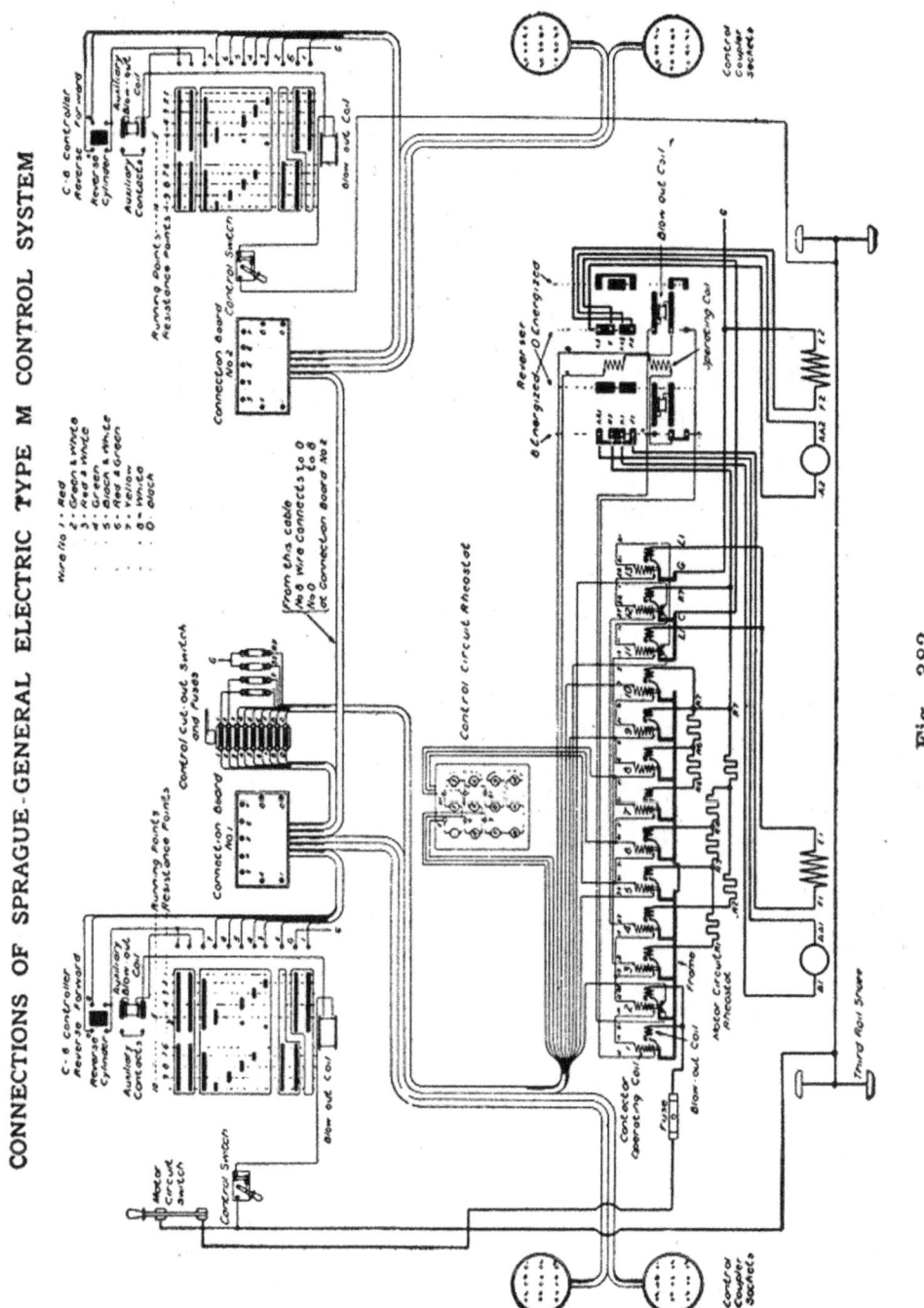

Fig. 382.

Circuits.

The motor circuit is local to each car, and on the first point the current on entering from the trolley or third rail shoe passes through the following pieces of apparatus in the order named: main switch and fuse, contactors, resistances, reverser, motors; thence to ground.

In the control circuit, the course of the current from trolley to ground is through the master controller switch and fuse, the master controller, connection box, to the cut-out switch. From the cut-out switch the current passes through the control cable to the operating coils of the reverser and contactors, and thence through fuses to ground.

Automatic Features.

The apparatus described is used with the standard equipment for hand control. If automatic features are desired they can be installed.

Wiring Diagram.

A diagram of the wiring of apparatus shown in Fig. 376 will be found in Fig. 382.

Rolling Stock.

The electric locomotive as a slow speed, heavy load tractor is quite old and there are many of them doing good service to-day that were built ten years ago.

Fig. 432 is in use by the American Bridge Co. Fig. 433 is used in the works of the Westinghouse Electric Co. Fig. 434 is in use in a lumber mill. Fig. 435 is used to haul scrap and pig iron. Fig. 436 is used by the Maryland Steel Co. to haul ingots and moulds. Fig. 437 is in use in Hawaiian Islands.

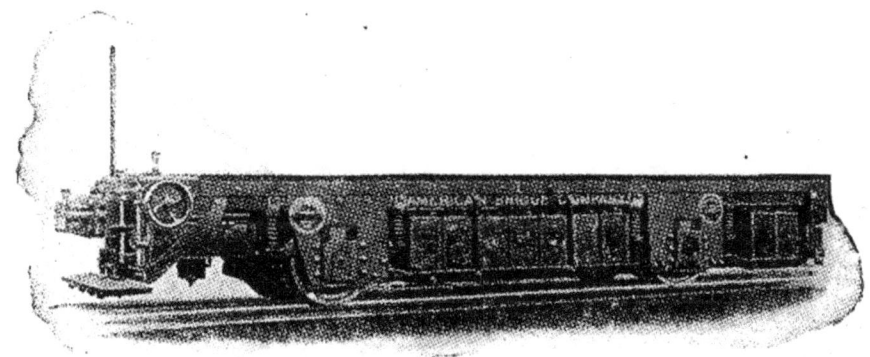

Fig. 432. 10,000-Pound Locomotive.

Fig. 438 shows how standard motors can be adopted to narrow gauge locomotive.

Figs. 439, 440 and 441 show conventional types of higher speed locomotives the latter showing the use of two trolleys allowing the collection of larger currents

108 ROLLING STOCK

Fig. 433. 95,000-Pound Locomotive.

Fig. 434. 2,600-Pound Locomotive.

without too great a resistance and sparking at trolley wheel.

Fig. 442 shows a 560 H. P. locomotive operating along the Hudson River steamship wharfs. Gear reduction is 3:1. It makes 8 miles an hour.

Fig. 435. 8,000-Pound Locomotive.

Fig. 443 shows an American locomotive operating in the Austerlitz Station of the Paris-Orlean R. R. The same locomtives also haul 160 ton trains under Paris in a tunnel to the Quai d'Orsay terminal.

Fig. 436. 10,000-Pound Locomotive

Fig. 437. 19,000-Pound Locomotive.

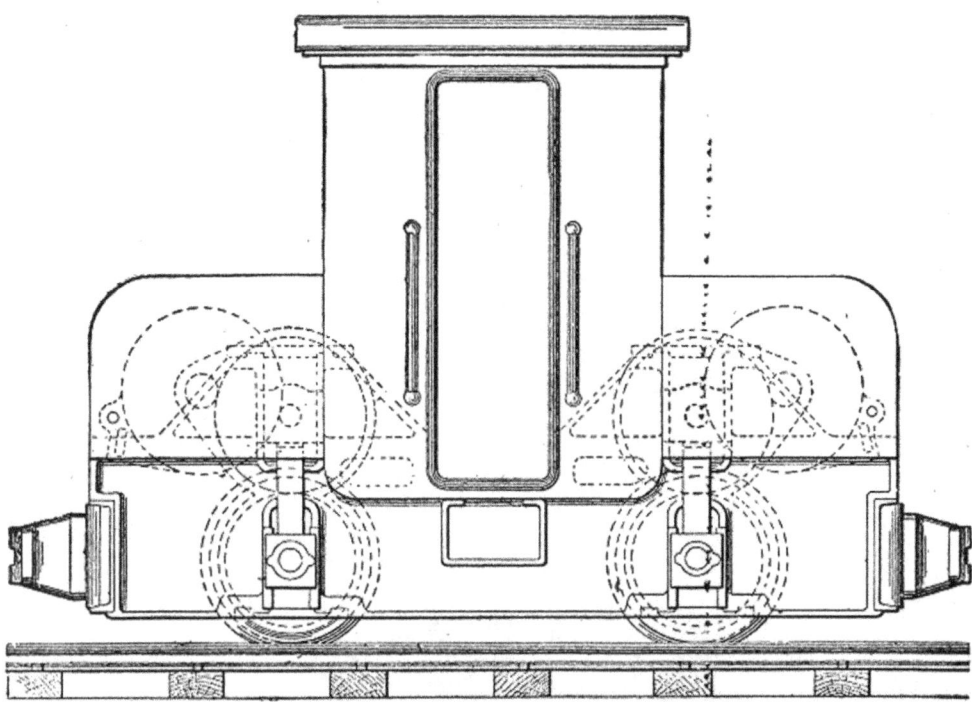

Fig. 438. Special Design for Using Very Large Motors on Narrow Gauge Track.

Fig. 439. 45,000-Pound Locomotive.

Fig. 444 shows the locomotive of the Buffalo & Lockport R. R., designed to handle freight and passenger service between these stations. They are equipped with motors capable of developing 600 H. P. Owing to slow speeds required (15 miles per hour) the motors are connected two in series permanently. They start with all

Fig. 440. 47,000-Pound Locomotive.

four in series and then place them in series parallel. They draw 500 amperes while accelerating a 450 ton train up to 14 miles an hour.

Fig. 445 shows a locomotive used in factory yard to drill freight cars.

The Baltimore & Ohio R. R. has been using 87 ton electric locomotives to haul its steam trains (locomotive and all) through the tunnel under the city of Baltimore.

Fig. 441. 55,000-Pound Locomotive.

Fig. 442. Steamship Connecting R. R. Draw-Bar Pull at 8 M. P. H. 10,000 Pounds.

Fig. 443. Electric Locomotive at Austerlitz Station. Paris and Orleans R. R.

Fig. 444. Buffalo and Lockport Locomotive.

ELECTRIC RAILROADING

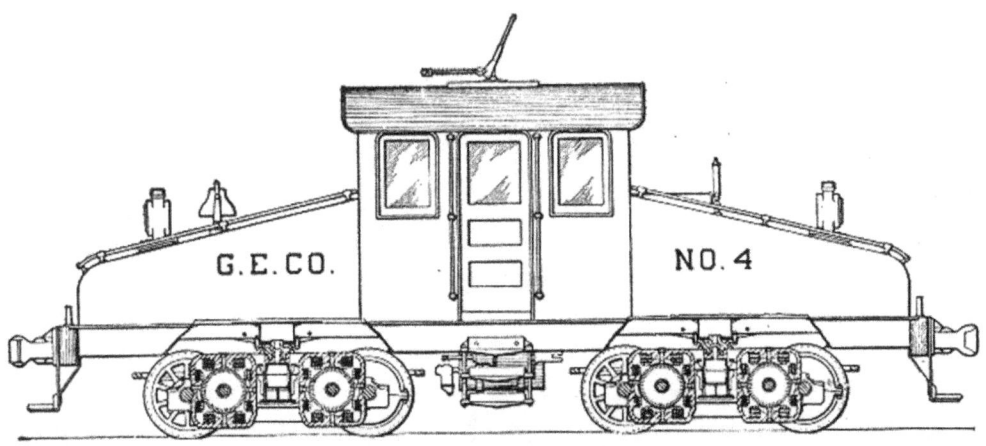

Fig. 445. Factory Yard Locomotive.

Fig. 446. B. & O. Gearless Locomotive.

One of these locomotives is shown in Fig. 446. Three we put in service in 1896 and for ten years have given good service: They will each haul a 2300 ton freight at 10 miles an hour, or a 500 ton passenger train at 35 miles an hour. They draw 2200 amperes at 625 volts during acceleration, dropping to 1800 at full speed.

Fig. 447a. B. & O. Locomotive Truck.

One of the two trucks is shown in Fig. 447. The motors are six pole and connected directly to axle. There are two motors in each truck making four in all.

In 1903 the B. & O. put in service two more locomotives. Each one is composed of two units. Each unit contains four motors, each geared to one of the axles by a 4:1 gear. The motors are 4 pole. Each unit weighs 73 tons. Thus the whole locomotive of 146 tons has 1600 horse power.

The geared type is perhaps best for such slow speed work.

Fig. 447b. B. & O. Locomotive Frame and Cab.

The freight locomotive of to-day will be a 16 wheel locomotive of the 0-16-0 type with a joint in the center of its frame like a Mallet Compound. This is called an articulated frame.

Each axle will have its motor. Its general dimensions are shown in Fig. 448.

A New York Central locomotive drawing a train is shown in Fig. 449.

118 ROLLING STOCK

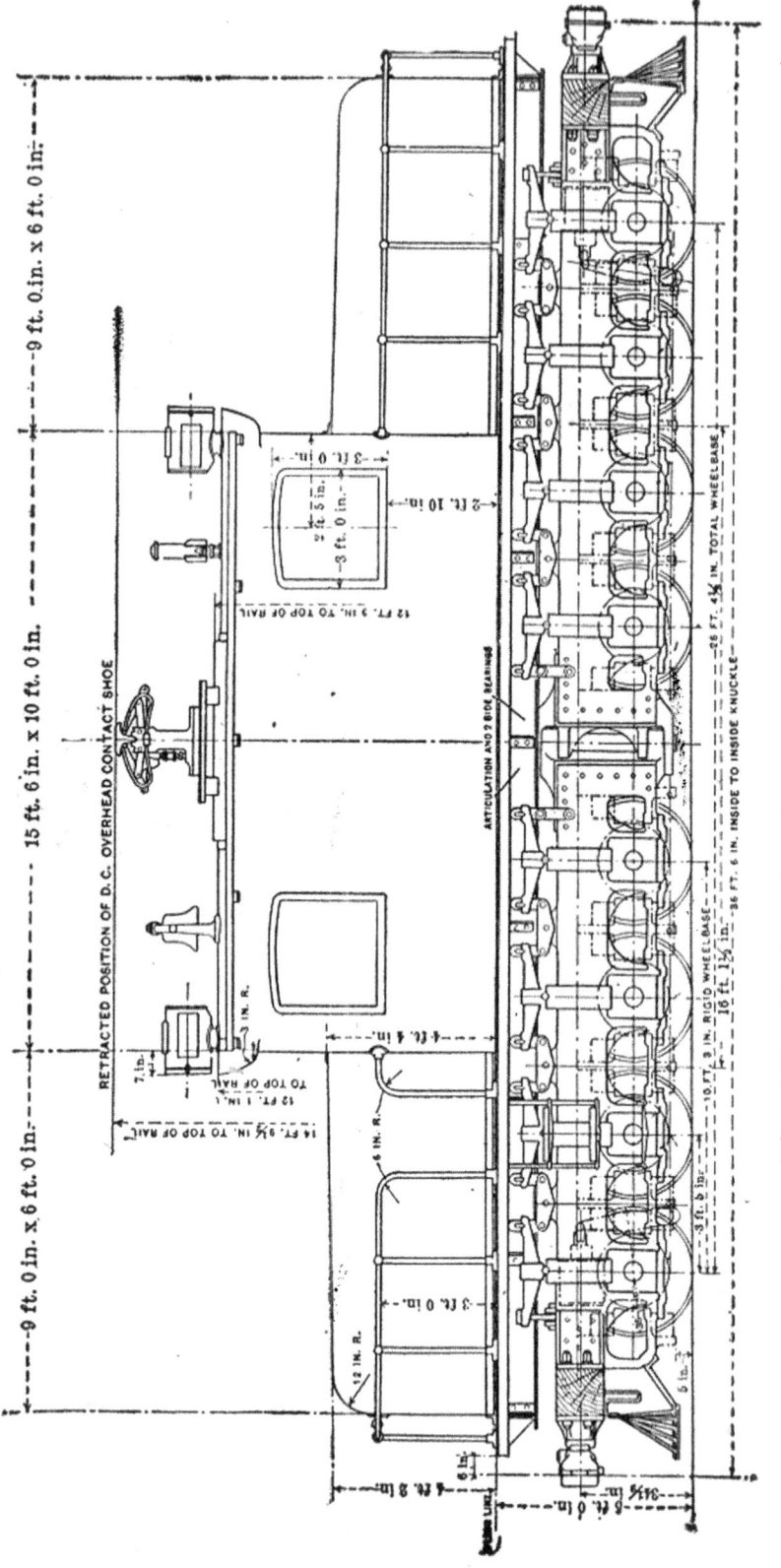

Fig. 448. Typical Freight Locomotive of 0-8-8-0 Type.

Fire proof cars are a very valuable asset to a road, as a means of gaining public favor and their actual calming influence in case of not only slight fires due to electrical troubles but also in slight collisions. Figs. 450 and 451 show a fire proof car designed by Mr. Gibbs. The Erie railroad is using similar ones for Postal Service. The Interborough Co. is using the Gibbs car for motor cars.

Fig. 449. New York Central Locomotive with Train.

These are finished inside with dark green enamel and aluminum paint which although a little hard looking makes a good appearance.

Fig. 452 shows a train on the West Shore R. R. operating between Utica and Syracuse.

Fig. 453 shows a locomotive and Fig. 454 a motor car of the Valtellina Rail Road of Italy. This is a 3 phase equipment.

Fig. 450. Gibbs' Fire-Proof Car. Long Island R. R. and New York Subway.

Fig. 452. West Shore Motor Car Train.

Fig. 453. Valtellina Three-Phase Locomotive.

Fig. 454. Valtellina Three-Phase Motor Car.

Trucks.

While the size of motors has been limited by the gauge of the rails, yet the demand for larger horse powers has influenced truck builders to put 36 inch wheels on the motor trucks. Such trucks will soon be standard for steam road work. The trailer truck at other end of car will have 33 inch wheels as standard.

Fig. 455 shows the general dimensions of a motor made for a 33 inch wheel truck. It will be noticed that the car axle goes through a set of bearings on the side of the motor frame. The large gear is fastened to the car. The motor shaft runs in bearings at either end of the frame. The pinion on motor shaft engages with gear on car axle.

Some of the weight of motor is given to car axle by the bearings in motor frame through which this axle passes. The rest is transferred through the truck frame.

Any motion of the motor must be in a circular arc around the car axle as a center, for the distance between center of car axle and motor shaft must always be same, else gear teeth will bind.

The Master Car Builders Association has given its sanction to certain constructions which are familiarly known by the initials, M. C. B.

A truck called the "M. C. B. equalizing truck" is shown in Fig. 456. The center pin is shown on center transom with bearing plates on either side. Outside of these are the side bearings to catch the weight when car rolls. Any up and down motion due to compressing the springs should not bring side bearing plates into contact. They generally come into contact when rounding curves, and to prevent interference with swiveling of trucks under

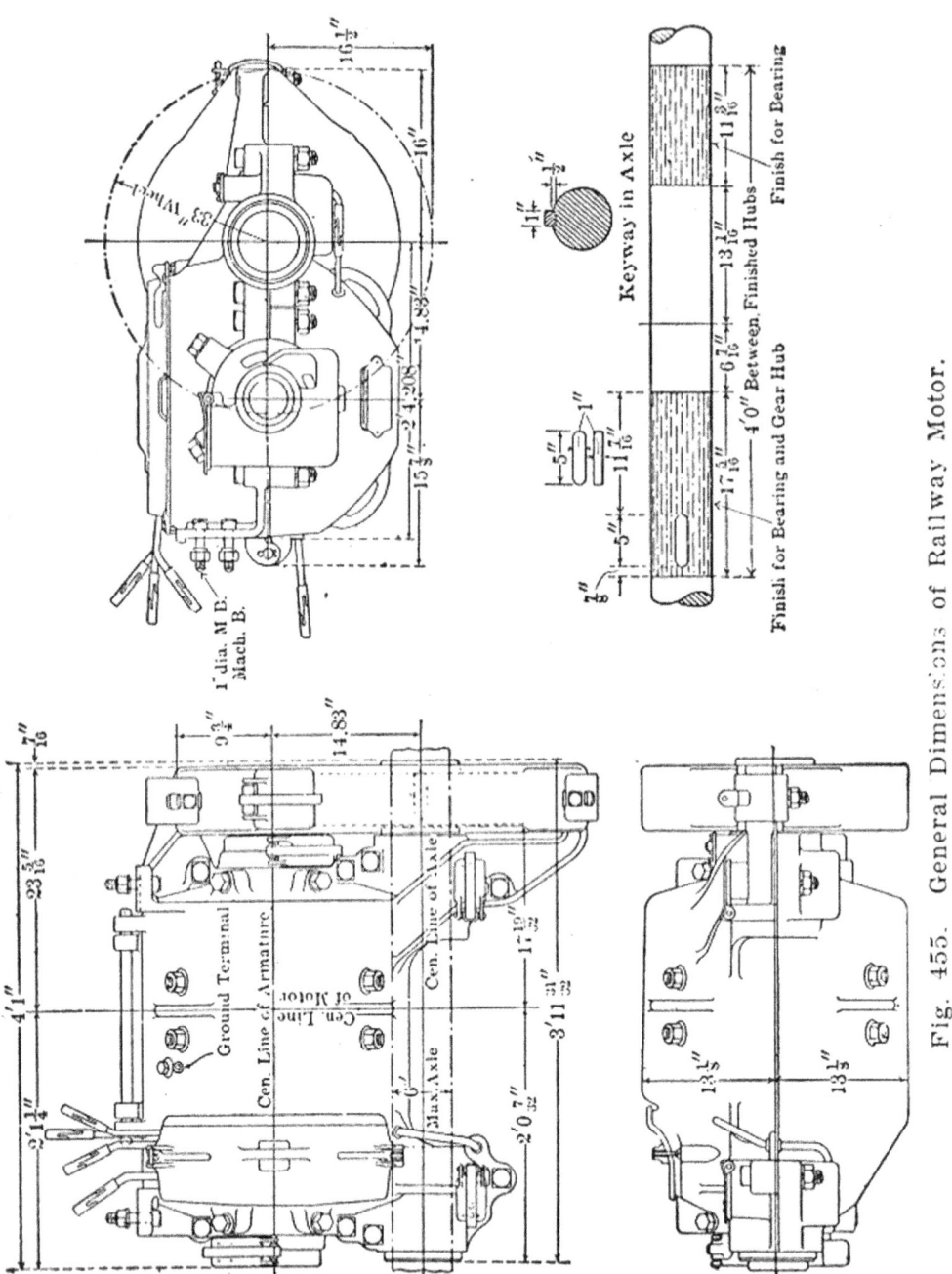

Fig. 455. General Dimensions of Railway Motor.

these circumstances, these bearings are frequently made with rollers.

In the plan view of Fig. 456 only one motor is shown to give a clearer view of the motor suspension. A rec-

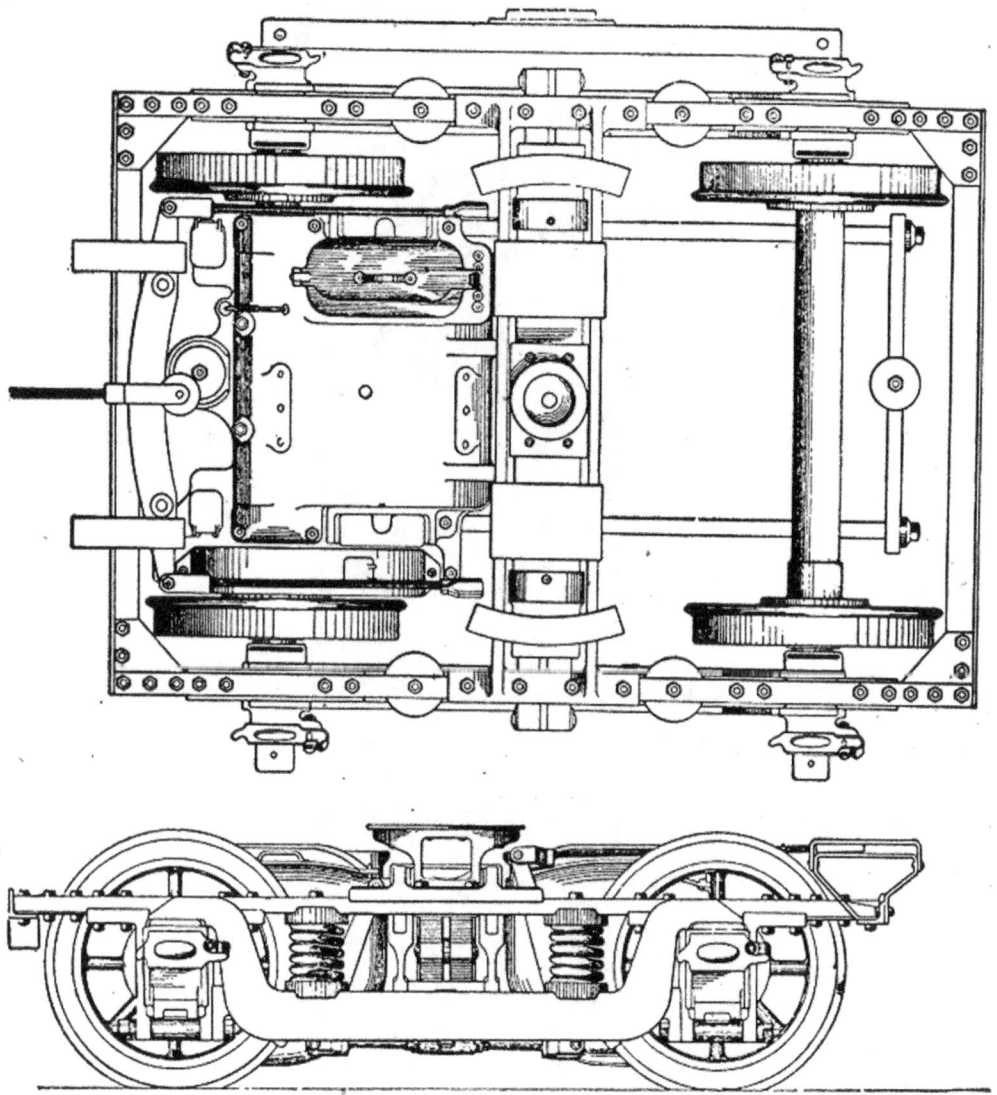

Fig. 456. M. C. B. Electric Truck. Cradle Suspension.

tangular frame of iron bars is hung by the centers of its shorter sides at each end of the truck. The connecting bolt at the same time compressing a spiral spring. On

Fig. 457. Cradle Suspension.

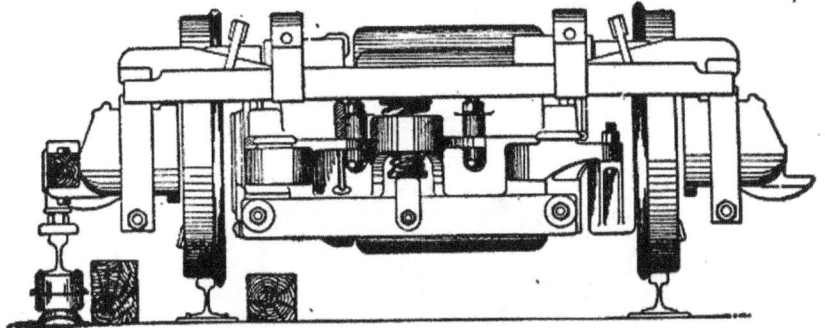

Fig. 458. Gibbs' Cradle Suspension, End View.

Fig. 459. Gibbs' Cradle Suspension with Truck Frame Lifted.

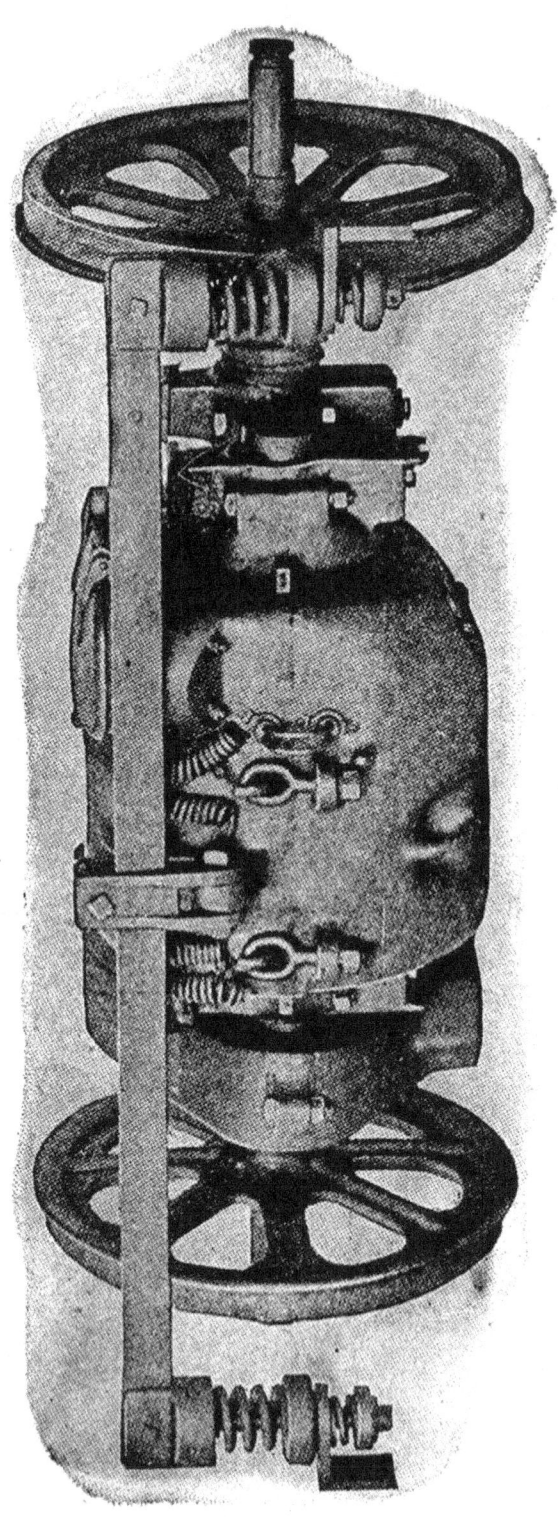

Fig. 460. Nose Suspension.

each side of the motor is a lug which is bolted to the long or side bars of this frame.

This suspension is the *cradle* suspension. It has many modifications. In Fig. 457 the center of end bar of cradle is slung without springs from a cross bar which is spring borne at the outside of the frame.

Fig. 461. Nose Suspension.

One of the best cradle suspensions is the Gibbs (Fig. 458) as shown in Fig. 459 the whole truck frame of a M C B truck may be hoisted clear of the wheels and motors.

The nose suspension is simpler than the cradle. The end of motor not resting on car axle is hung from a spring borne cross bar. See Fig. 460.

Another very simple nose suspension is shown in Fig. 461 where the truck transom has a frame bolted to it con-

Fig. 462. Parallel Bar Suspension.

taining a spring supported U or loop. A lug or nose on the motor sticks into this U. This illustration shows the king pin, bearing plate, and side bearings all mounted on transom.

Fig. 462 shows a suspension made of two bars running length-wise of truck which hold the motors. These bars are each spring borne at ends of truck, directly from frame. In the illustration two long bars are supporting the parallel bars because there is no truck there to do it. Such a suspension needs four spring supports and is no more flexible than the cradle suspension using only two. It is called the *parallel bar suspension*.

Car Equipment.

The electrical equipment of a car consists of the motor truck, the controller, resistances, iron pipe conduits containing the motor circuits, and the motor control circuits,

Fig. 463. Lightning Arresters.

a trolley or set of third rail shoes and a few auxiliary pieces of apparatus. Some arresters are shown in Fig. 463. An arrester installed with a kicking coil is shown in Fig. 464. A switch called a canopy switch is shown in Fig. 465. It is mostly used in interurban cars where the motorman's cab is built on front platform and this switch is installed over his head: It is a snap break switch and is used to cut off current from car at base of trolley.

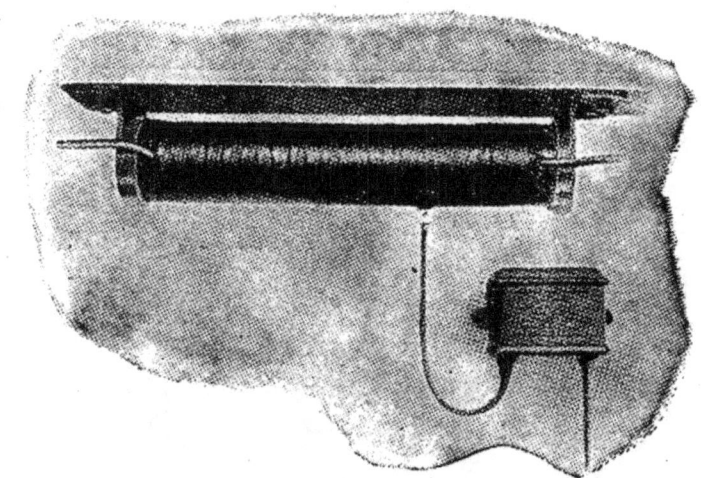

Fig. 464. Choke Coil and Lightning Arrester.

Fig. 465. Canopy Switch to Cut Off Current at Base of Trolley.

When a canopy switch has a magnet trip operated by current to motors it is called a current breaker. The one in Fig. 466 has a magnetic blow-out, which expels the arc through the chute shown on right side. The button on front is to trip the breaker. The handle on top is for closing it.

Main fuses (Fig. 467) should be protected by iron cases but wood boxes are still used.

Fig. 466. Automatic Circuit Breaker.

Fig. 467. Fuse Block.

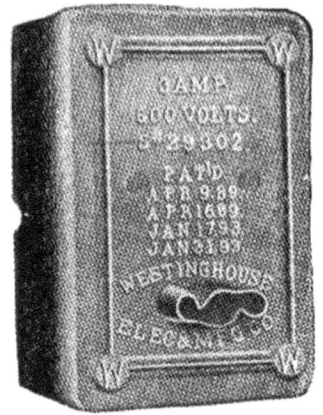

Fig. 468. Snap Switch for Lighting Circuits.

The car and vestibule lights are controlled by snap switches on porcelain bases, enclosed by porcelain or iron covers (Fig. 468). Head lights have same style switches of heavier construction.

Contact Devices.

The type of trolley with a wheel to collect current from wire is not satisfactory for high speeds. The wheel is apt

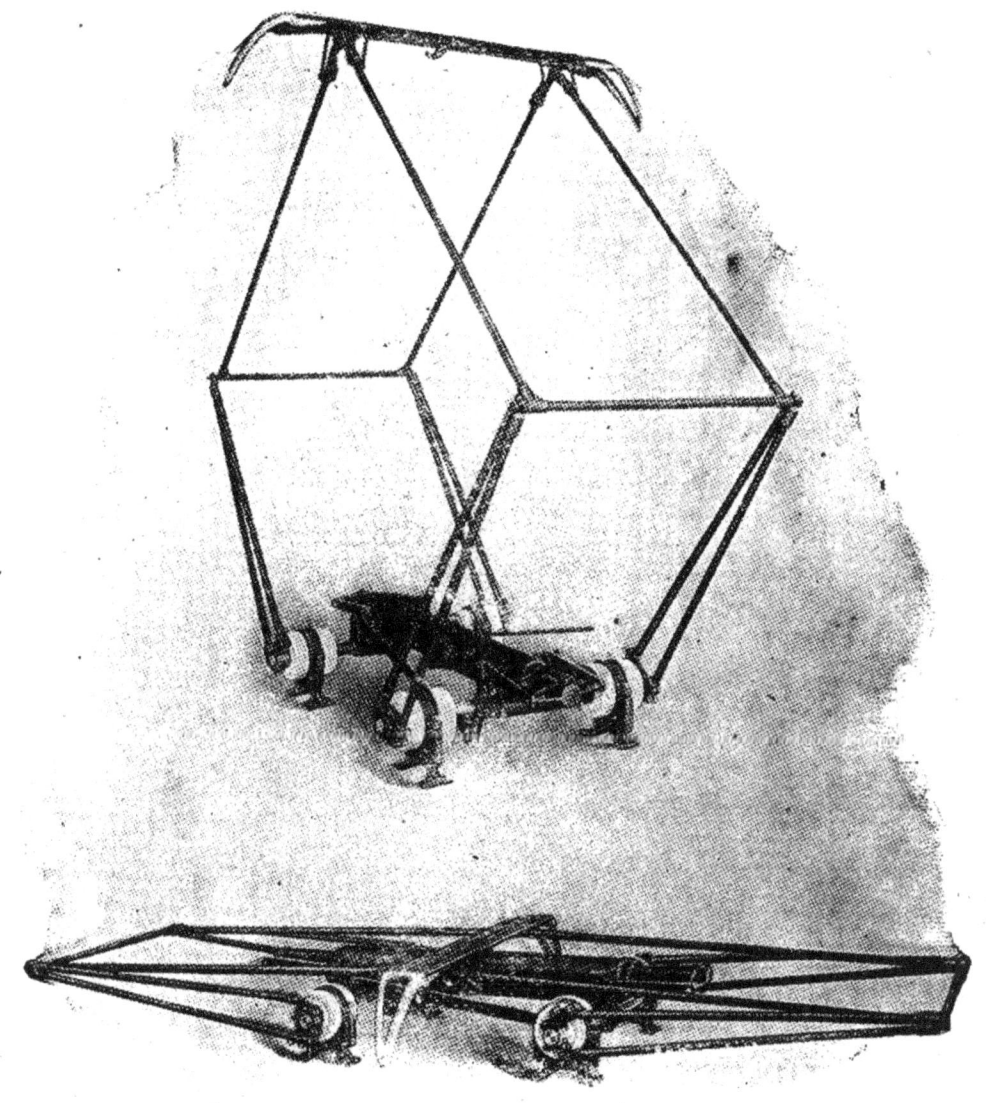

Fig. 469. Pantagraph Bow Trolley. Raised and Lowered.

to jump the trolley wire and smash the guy wires of ordinary, or the braces of catenary construction.

A bow trolley where the wheel is replaced by a broad plate of copper or iron some two or three feet wide and three inches across, must be used for high speeds. Then no matter how the train sways the trolley and wire always keep in contact.

The latest form of bow trolley is called The Pantagraph Trolley, as shown in Fig. 469. It is raised and lowered by an air cylinder shown in center.

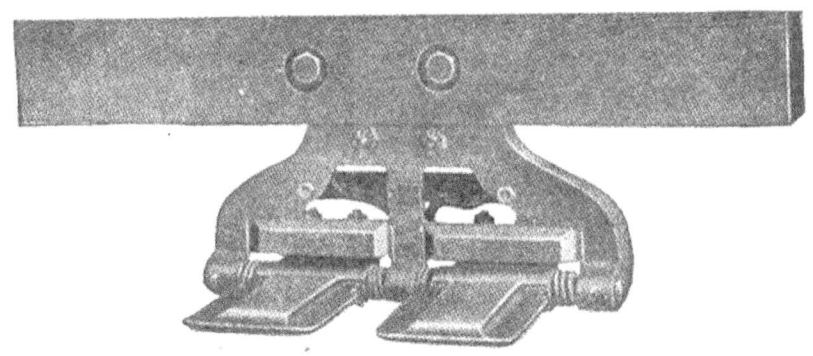

Fig. 470. Third Rail Shoes.

When a third rail is used shoes as in Fig. 470 are the current collectors. These are of cast iron pressed by springs against the top or bottom of the third rail.

Heaters.

In trains of motor cars the only way to heat cars is by resistances made hot by electric current. This is the most expensive way to heat and in interurban cars where motorman is always on front platform (the cars passing around a loop at each end of route) it is better to install a hot air or hot water heater and let motorman attend to it. This can be done at terminals and at turnouts or even at stops where eight or ten passengers are being let off or taken on.

When electric locomotives are drawing the standard railway coach, steam must be furnished. To do this steam heating plants with kerosene blue flame burners are placed in locomotives and attendance given by the second man in the cab.

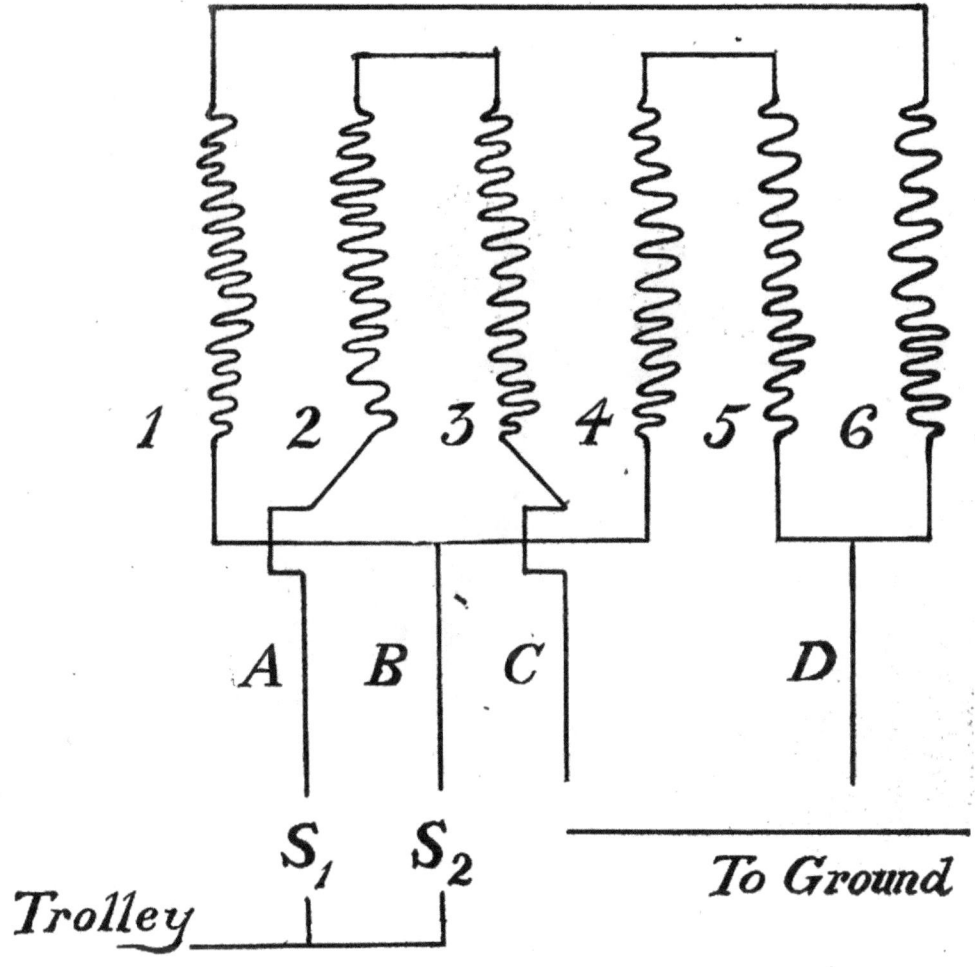

Fig. 471. Diagram of Car Heater Connections.

To furnish two degrees of temperature with electric heaters the heaters although all placed in series, are each individually connected as in Fig. 471.

Fig. 472. Car Equipment Straight Air Brake.

Terminals A, B, are connected to the same lettered terminal of heater behind; C and D are connected to C and D of heater ahead.

The first heater has A and B connected to switches S_1 and S_2 which are connected to trolley. The last heater has C and D connected to a ground wire which is connected to some part of frame of truck.

If with switch S_1 closed a certain amount of heat is generated, with S_2 closed twice the heat is obtained, while with both closed the maximum heat is obtained, being three times that given by the switch S_1 alone.

Air Brake.

For complete description of all air brake equipment read Vol. III.

Suburban lines feeding steam roads usually run single cars which are fitted with a straight air equipment like Fig. 472.

The electric locomotives of the New York Central R. R. have the Westinghouse E-T equipment.

Practically all the motor car of railway coach type running in trains have the regular automatic air brake with an air compressor on each motor car.

The parts of such a compressor are shown in Fig. 473, the complete compressor in Fig. 474, and a side view of compressor in its suspension is given in Fig. 475.

The New York Central motor cars have a governor of type shown in Fig. 472.

The New York Central locomotives and the Pennsylvania motor cars have a governor as in Figs. 476 and 477. Showing it closed and open.

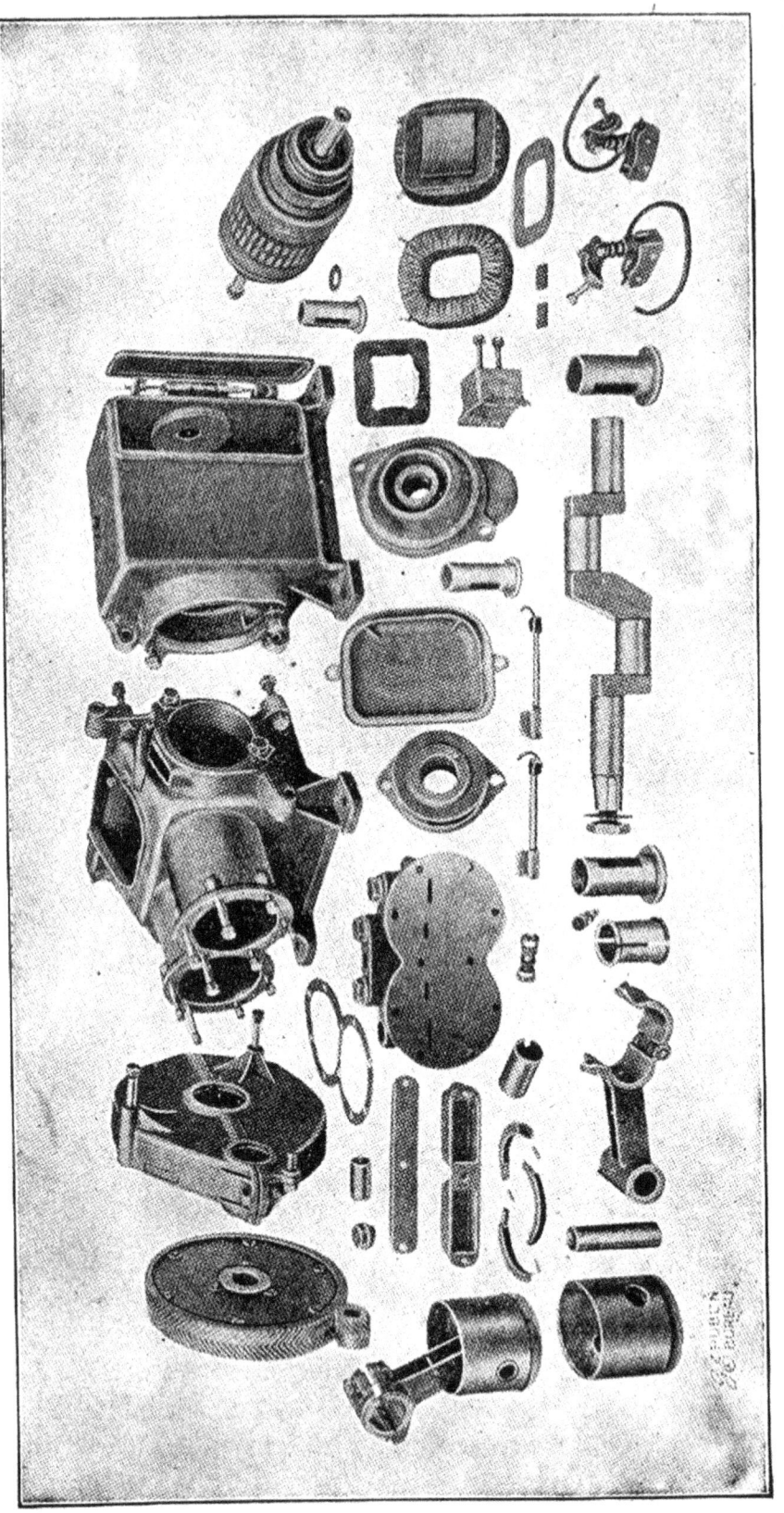

Fig. 473. Parts of Motor Driven (Geared) Air Compressor.

The construction is shown in Figs. 478 and 520. The cylinder head is provided with a tapped hole for the insulated pipe which makes connection between the governor and the compressor reservoir. The head is so con-

Fig. 474. Motor Driven (Geared) Air Compressor.

Fig. 475. Air Compressor (Fig. 474) in Suspension.

structed that this connection may be placed at the back or at either side of the governor, as desired. It is bolted to the frame and holds the rubber diaphragm A against the retaining ring. This ring serves as an abutment for the piston B against the upper surface of which the diaphragm A is pressed. The lower side of the piston is acted upon by the operating spring C, the pressure of which is adjusted by means of the screws R bearing against the washer S. Attached rigidly to the piston B is the rod D, the lower end of which is connected to one of the operating levers. The largest of these levers is

Fig. 476. Air Compressor Governor, Case Closed.

provided with a recess into which a mica insulated stud has been forced by hydraulic pressure. Attached to the stud are the cable terminal and the spring carrying the contact finger. The finger tip through which the circuit is completed and broken is so made as to be readily renewable when worn. This finger completes the circuit through the stationary contact, the tip of which is also renewable. Enclosing these contact members is the arc chute, which is composed of a special molded insulating compound and is provided with renewable plates of a highly refractory material. This material has the prop-

Fig. 477. Air Compressor Governor, Case Opened.

erty of resisting the action of the electric arc to a great degree. In series with this circuit is the blow-out coil O, for producing the magnetic field which extinguishes the arc when the circuit is broken. This coil is made of enameled copper ribbon wound edgewise, and connected with it is the line terminal, which is provided with two set screws for clamping the wire. The protecting cover is hinged at the back of the frame and is held in the

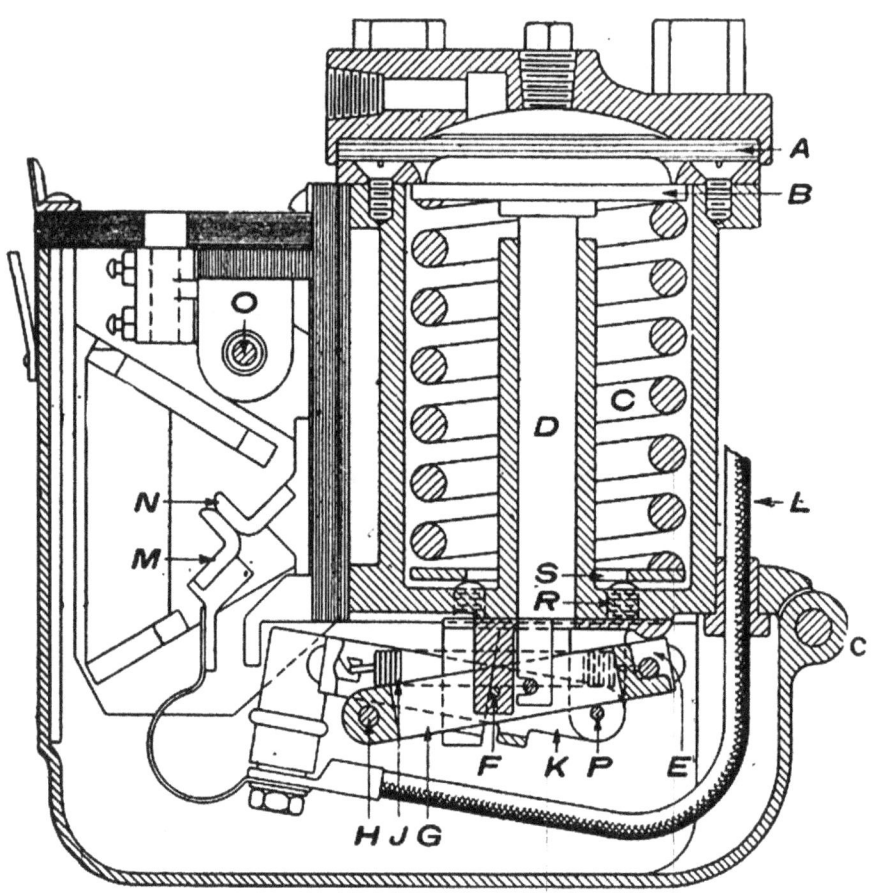

Fig. 478. Construction of Air Compressor Governor.

closed position by a spring catch. On the inside of this cover adjacent to the arc chute is a plate of insulating material which prevents the possibility of the arc striking the metal.

Operation.

The action of this governor in opening and closing the motor circuit of the compressor is as follows:

As the compressor continues to operate, thereby increasing the pressure of air in the reservoir, the pressure in the chamber above the diaphragm A rises and forces the piston rod downward against the action of the operating spring C, turning the lever E around its fulcrum F. This brings the pivot H above the centre line of the tension springs J, which connect the intermediate lever G with contact carrying lever K. The action of these springs then pulls the end of the intermediate lever downward; this movement quickly carries the centre line of the springs past the pivot P, thus reversing the action of these springs on the contact carrying K, and causing the free end of this lever to be drawn downward, separating the contacts M and N with a quick snap.

The object of this double system of levers is to maintain a constant pressure between the contacts until the tripping point is reached, thus preventing burning of the contacts.

As the pressure in the reservoir is reduced the piston rod O raises the rear end of the lever E, a projection of which engages with the intermediate lever G. This carries the center line of the tension springs J above the pivot of the contact carrying lever K and thereby pulls the contact finger upward, quickly closing the circuit.

The information given here is the same as that which the Pennsylvania R. R. demands that the motor-men should know before operating its trains.

The following pages contain a description of the electrical apparatus used on the motor cars of the West Jersey and Seashore R. R., one of the Pennsylvania lines running from Philadelphia to Atlantic City. This road is practically a straight line between the two cities with no grades worth mentioning. It is 60 miles long and can be done by express trains in very little over an hour.

These conditions while ideal for steam locomotives are even yet more suitable for electric traction. When it comes to local trains the electric cars are vastly superior and can make much better time with increased economy.

AIR-BRAKE EQUIPMENT ON MOTOR CARS.

A.—General.

The air brakes on the cars and locomotives in electric service are essentially the same as those on the other passenger equipment, except that the steam driven air pumps on the locomotives are replaced by electrically driven air compressors, one on each electric locomotive and each motor car, and the design of the air brakes is such that their release, as well as application, can be graduated.

The use of an air compressor and main reservoir on each motor car necessitates the use of an additional train pipe to connect all the main reservoirs together and to the motorman's brake valve. This extra train pipe is called the control pipe.

A safety valve is placed in the end of the main reservoir on each motor car to prevent overcharging the brake system in case the electric pump governor fails.

B.—Hints to Motormen.

In suburban service it is highly important not to block the road. Therefore, remember in case anything gets out of order that the first important thing is to get out of the way; learn carefully just what to do in order to make the proper move quickly; for example:

1. In case of a burst hose, if it be the control pipe hose, the cut-out cock on both sides of it should be closed; but if it should be the brake pipe hose, then it is neces-

sary to close the cut-out cock ahead of the brake and the double cut-out cocks on each of the cars back of it; then open, and leave open, the auxiliary reservoir bleed cocks on all of the cars that are cut out. In a case of this kind some one would be designated and prepared to operate the hand brakes on the cars that are cut out in case a car coupling should break and cause the train to separate.

2. In case of inability to release a brake, caused, for instance, by the emergency valve remaining unseated after an emergency application, close double cut-out cock and open and leave open, bleed cock of auxiliary reservoir on this car and proceed.

3. In case of brake sticking after service application, make about a ten-pound reduction and place the handle of the brake valve in release position. This will usually release the brake. If not, or further trouble is had with this brake, do as recommended in preceding case 2.

It will be seen by these examples that by a knowledge of the operation of the air-brake the motormen and trainmen can formulate rules for themselves that, in case of trouble, will enable them to get out of the way with little or no delay.

To gain time adapt the brake-pipe reduction, or application of brakes, to speed. For example, for high speed made a full application and graduate off when a short distance from the stop. To handle train smoothly make the application heavy and soon enough, so that if held on the train would stop a car length or so short of the mark. Then as the stop or mark is approached graduate the pressure out of the brake cylinder so that little remains when stop is made. If on a level, complete the release; if on a grade, hold until the signal to start is given, then release. As the pressure has been graduated down so that little remains in the cylinder, it will be seen that the start can be made promptly.

As the automatic brake is applied by the reduction of the brake-pipe pressure, no matter how produced, it is plain that leaks will produce results not intended or desired by the motorman, and sometimes interfere with the accuracy and smoothness of the stop. Therefore, they should be kept down and reported as surely and promptly as any other defect. Motormen should observe as carefully as possible the action of the governor, feed valve and gauges; that is, their adjustment, etc., as much better operation can be obtained if all are approximately uniform.

One of the things that the motorman should learn carefully regarding the automatic brake is, that after a certain reduction of pressure in the brake pipe, say eighteen to twenty pounds, the auxiliary reservoir and brake cylinder have equalized. Therefore, no greater braking power can be obtained, and to further reduce the brake pipe pressure wastes a great amount of air which must be restored to the brake pipe before a release can be made, and interfere with that release to such an extent that a rough stop is usually the result.

Properly handled this brake possesses all the flexibility of the straight-air brake, while the safety and reliability of the automatic brake has been greatly increased. Therefore the motorman should endeavor to understand its principles, so that he can handle the brake so as to obtain its maximum efficiency with credit to himself and comfort to the passengers.

AIR COMPRESSOR ON ELECTRIC LOCOMOTIVES.

A.—General.

The CP-19-B air compressor consists of a duplex, single-acting, vertical air pump, located between and directly connected to two 8-pole series, direct-current motors. It has a piston displacement of 75 cubic feet per minute, when operating on 600 volts, and against a tank pressure of 130 pounds per square inch. Fig. 523.

The compressor frame is so shaped as to form a large oil chamber for the cranks and connecting rods. It is provided with a pedestal-like base, arranged to support the machine, and bolted to the floor of the locomotive cab. To this frame the motor frames are bolted, one to each end. The vertical cylinders are bolted to the top, and large oil-tight doors are provided, one on each side, for admission to the cranks and bearings.

The pistons are provided with single rings of the three-section type. Each cylinder is provided with independent intake and exhaust valves. These valves are of the tubular type, operating in a vertical position on the tops of the cylinders.

The intake for the air is provided with a copper screen, located in a box, which can be easily removed and cleaned when necessary.

The crank chamber is provided with baffle plates, above and below, for the purpose of preventing too much splashing of oil into the cylinders.

The armatures are fastened directly to the **crank shaft**. Each end of the shaft is tapered and supplied with key and clamping nut, for the purpose of securing the armatures and providing means for their removal.

The pole pieces are made of soft iron sheets, securely riveted together and bolted to finished surfaces on the inside of the motor frame.

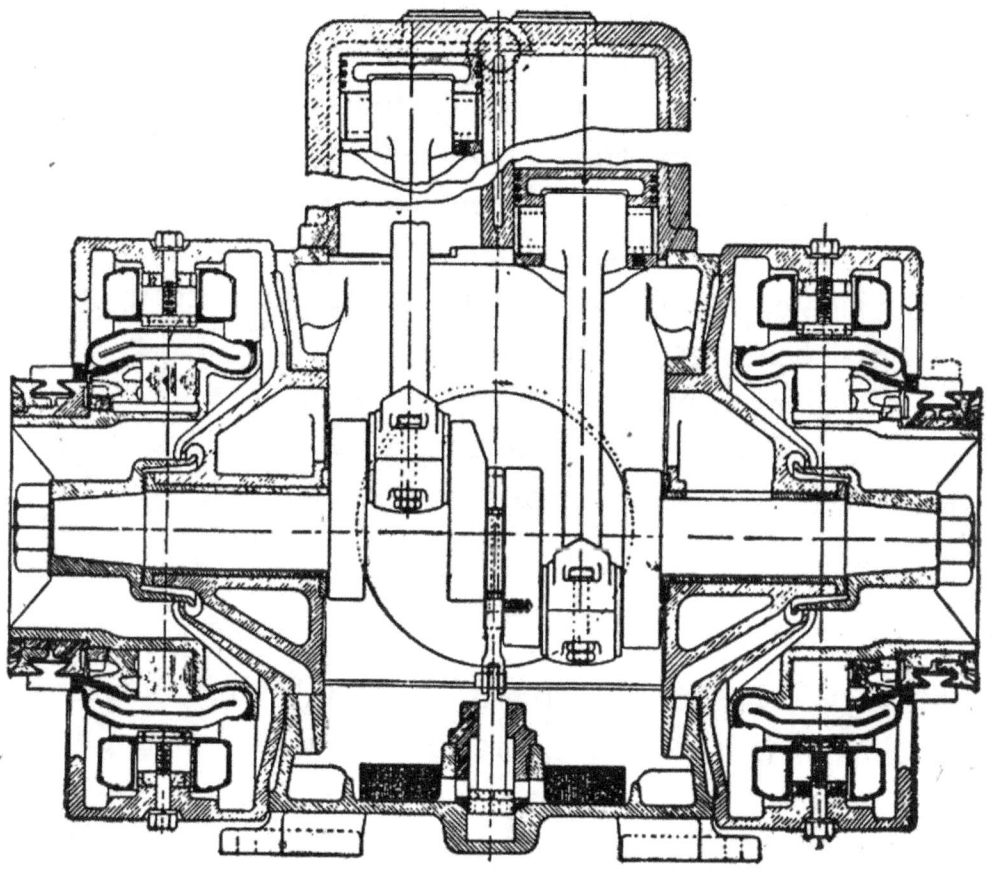

Fig. 523.

The brush holders are supported on insulated radial studs held by clamps bolted to the ends of the motor frames in such a manner as to permit adjustment to accommodate the wear of the commutator. The outside end of each motor is provided with a large ventilated shield, semi-closing the machine, and affording protection for the armatures and brush holders.

The machine has a total of six bearings, consisting of one crank bearing, and one wrist bearing for each of the two connecting rods, and two main bearings. The main bearings are located in the motor frames, one on each side of the crank portion of the driving shaft. All bearings are provided with removable bronze linings. The connecting rods are split on the diameter of the crank pin, and the crank bearings are held in place by caps bolted to the lower ends of the connecting rods. The main bearings are oiled from waste packed pockets formed in the motor frame castings. The crank bearings are lubricated by oil splashed by the connecting rods. The wrist bearings are lubricated by oil supplied to them through pipes connected to pumping devices located on the lower ends of the connecting rods so as to dip into oil in the bottom of the crank chamber.

B.—Operation.

The CP-19-B air compressor is intended to operate on 600 volts, and for such operation the motors should always be connected in series.

The direction of rotation of the armatures should be such that the top side of the commutator travels toward the observer, when standing on the side of the compressor where the air intake is located, and the intake openings in the oiling devices should recede while sweeping through the oil.

Should it be necessary to remove an armature, take off the end shield and remove brush holders; then take off the armature nut. Before removing the nut, it will be necessary to straighten out lock washer underneath the same. When the nut has been removed two bolts of proper length, with hooked ends, should be hooked behind two spokes of the armature spider diametrically opposite each other. The outside ends of these bolts should be threaded, and should pass through holes in a piece of iron, held against the armature shaft in such a manner that when tightened the armature will be loosened and pulled off.

When it becomes necessary to replace a lining for a main bearing it will be necessary to remove the armature and armature key. The lining can be then drawn out of the motor frame over the shaft by bolts screwed into tapped holes in the end of the lining.

As the commutator wears down it may become necessary to adjust the brush holders. The brush *holders* should be located about one-eighth of an inch from the commutator, and can be adjusted by loosening clamping bolt so the supporting stud can slide in the clamp.

In replacing brush holders which have been removed, care should be taken to move them over as far as possible in the direction opposite to the rotation of the commutator, so as to produce sparkless commutation.

If it should be observed that a compressor appreciably increases its speed, from causes other than increase in voltage, and seems not to be delivering the proper amount of air, attention should be given to the intake valves, as such a condition might be caused by valves sticking, or not properly seating due to accumulation of dirt. The valve in question should be taken out and thoroughly cleaned, care being taken not to leave particles of thread or lint sticking to it.

Should the intake valves fail to open with every stroke on the compressor, attention should be given to the exhaust valves. If the exhaust valves leak, or remain open for any reason, the cylinder will receive air from the reservoir, and will not give the intake valves an opportunity to open. When these valves are out care should be taken not to drop dirt into the cylinders, as the clearance between tops of cylinders and pistons is very small.

Valve trouble of any kind rarely happens with this type of valve, and can be caused only by accumulation of dirt. The operator will soon learn to know from the peculiar click of the valves whether or not they are working properly.

Should it become necessary to remove a piston or connecting rod, the cylinders must be taken off, then the crank caps removed from the connecting rods, upper baffle plate removed, and connecting rod and piston drawn upwards out of the compressor frame.

Oil should be maintained in the crank chamber to within about one-half inch of the centre portion of the lower baffle plate, and should never be allowed to become so low as not to permit the oiling device to properly dip into the same.

The frame of the machine is designed to catch oil splashed in the crank chamber and deliver it to the main bearings. However, the waste pockets around these main bearings should be examined from time to time to see that the waste is tight against the shaft, and is receiving the proper amount of oil. If splashing fails to supply oil to these bearings, the pockets should be filled by hand once a week.

Oil in the crank chamber should not be too thick, but should be of medium or light weight so that the oiling device can work to the best advantage. A light gas engine cylinder oil is recommended. When the oil in crank chamber becomes muddy it should be removed and replaced by a fresh supply.

Should pounding develop in the compressor, the crank bearings should be inspected, and if found in good condition, it is probable that the cylinder clearance has filled with dirt, or wrist bearings have become defective, and the cylinders should be removed and cleaned and bearings inspected.

In replacing pistons in cylinders care should be taken not to omit any of the little springs in the piston rings.

The machine should be thoroughly inspected from time to time, and bearings should not be allowed to become excessively worn before being replaced.

Brushes should be replaced when worn out, and commutators should be kept smooth, clean and round. Care should be taken not to allow oil to come in contact with the commutator or windings, as oil is injurious to insulating materials.

SUBURBAN MOTOR CAR CATECHISM—CAUSES FOR FAILURE OF TRAIN MOVEMENT.

Question 1. If train fails to move after instructions under train operation have been followed, what should be done?

Answer. Light circuit switches should be closed to ascertain if there is power in the contact rail, or motorman should note if trains in neighborhood are moved by power.

Question 2. If it is found that there is current in operating car, what should be done?

Answer. Master controller handle should be moved to first point, then master controller switch opened to ascertain whether the master control circuits are closed, which will be indicated by the sound of slight arcing at master controller switch.

Question 3. What would cause the failure of train cable circuits?

Answer. First, imperfect master controller fuse. Second, grounded train cable. Third, imperfect contact in master controller. Fourth, loose coupler jumper.

Question 4. What should be done to detect imperfect fuse?

Answer. Insert new fuse, and if this fails it is evident the trouble is elsewhere.

Question 5. What should be done when a grounded train cable occurs?

Answer. The master controller fuse should be replaced and the controller moved to the "on" position to determine if fault lies in construction of the fuse. If this fails, an attempt should be made to locate the ground in the train cable. The first thing to do is to throw the CONTROL CUT-OFF SWITCH on the operating car to the "off" position. If this proves ineffective, this operation should be repeated back through the train, cutting out, however, the train cable jumper between car tested and one to be tested.

Question 6. What should be done to detect imperfect contact in master controller?

Answer. Motorman should remove cover from controller and note the movement of contact fingers. The action of the train is dependent upon the contact of these fingers, and if it is found that the contact is imperfect he should endeavor to readjust the contacts, and if he fails in this it is then necessary to operate the train from the next car.

Question 7. What should be done to detect a loose jumper?

Answer. Motorman should lose no time in going back through his train to determine if the coupler plugs are properly inserted in the sockets, and, if not, he should insert them properly.

Question 8. What are the other causes that would prevent the operation of a train or reduce the speed?

Answer. First, the blowing of third-rail shoe fuses. Second, the blowing of main motor circuit fuses. Third, the blowing of circuit breakers or main fuses. Fourth, an imperfectly acting triple valve causing brakes to remain set on one or more cars in train.

Question 9. How can enclosed fuse that is blown be detected?

Answer. If an enclosed fuse has blown there is a deposit or collection of greyish powder at the ends of the box.

Question 10. What should be done in the event of a third-rail shoe fuse blowing?

Answer. This fuse will blow only when there is a short circuit on the car equipment, and fuse should not be replaced but train continued in the regular manner, and report promptly made to the train despatcher or person in charge of nearest terminal.

Question 11. If a circuit breaker acts or blows, what should be done?

Answer. The circuit breaker setting switch should be moved to the "on" position.

Question 12. What should be done when a triple valve acts imperfectly?

Answer. Air-brake instructions should be followed, i. e., valves should be cut out and auxiliary reservoir cock opened to release brakes.

Question 13. If a train is standing on crossover and current cannot be obtained on the operating car, although the other cars of the train and trains in the neighborhood have current, what does this indicate?

Answer. This indicates that the bus line fuses between the operating and adjacent cars have blown, or that bus jumper is loose or disconnected.

Question 14. What should be done to continue operation of train?

Answer. Motorman should go back to the first motor car where current can be obtained and move train through crossover, then go back to the first car again and proceed in the usual manner until a point of inspection can be reached and inspector notified.

Question 15. If a fire occurs in any car in the train, what should the motorman do?

Answer. Open all circuit breakers by moving the circuit breaker switch to the "off" position, and if this fails he should then open the main or motor circuit switch and the main cut-out switch on the car on which the trouble occurs.

Question 16. If smoke or fire is observed by the trainmen in any of the light or heater circuits within the car, what should be done?

Answer. The trainman should immediately cut out the light or heater switches, whichever the case may be, and the trouble be reported to the despatcher in charge of the nearest terminal.

Question 17. If an unusual noise is observed in the movement of train, what should be done?

Answer. To prevent delay the motorman should have the conductor stand beside the train to locate the noise while he moves the train, after which, if the trouble is with the brake rigging, same should be tied up.

Question 18. If the noise is located within the motors, what should be done?

Answer. Motorman should open the cut-out switch on the car affected, and proceed after reporting trouble to despatcher in charge of terminal.

Question 19. If a third-rail shoe support is broken, what should be done?

Answer. Motorman should first pull the bus line jumpers, at both ends of the car, insert wooden insulating slippers between the contact shoe and rail and then proceed to detach or tie up remnants of device, exercising extreme care that the contact device is kept clear of the truck frame, contact rail, structure, or any grounded parts to prevent injury to himself.

Question 20. If either pilot or emergency air-brake valve leaks badly, what should be done?

Answer. First try applying brakes by releasing the knob in the controller handle several times, and if this does not remedy the defect or difficulty cut the valves out by means of a cut-out cock located in the pipe leading to them from the train line.

INSTRUCTIONS FOR THE OPERATION OF MULTIPLE UNIT CONTROL.

GENERAL DESCRIPTION OF APPARATUS.

1. THE MOTOR CARS ON THE WEST JERSEY AND SEASHORE RAILROAD are equipped with two General Electric (No. 69-C) 200 horse power railway motors, both of which are mounted on one truck, known as the MOTOR TRUCK. The Sprague-General Electric (type M) multiple unit system of control is used.

2. BY MULTIPLE UNIT CONTROL is meant the operation of a train of two or more motor cars from a single master controller on any car in the train; that is, a train of several cars, each propelled independently by its own motors, is controlled as one car.

3. THERE ARE TWO CONTROL CIRCUITS on each car: First, the MASTER CONTROL, which is operated by the motorman; second, the MOTOR CONTROL, which depends for its operation on the master control. Both master control and motor control cables are enclosed in iron pipe conduit.

4. EACH MOTOR CAR is provided with two master controllers, one at each end of the car in the motorman's compartment. All master controllers are connected to a seven-wire TRAIN CABLE running the entire length of each car and connected together between cars by the TRAIN CABLE JUMPER. Current received through the master controller and train cable

operates electrically controlled switches known as CONTACTORS on each car, and establishes the motor control on their respective cars. The motor control is local with each car and can be governed by any master controller on the train.

5. EACH MOTOR CAR TAKES CURRENT from the third rail, through the third rail shoes, or from the trolley wire, through the trolley. All third rail shoes and trolleys are connected through switches to a BUS LINE, which runs the entire length of each car and is connected together between the cars by the BUS LINE JUMPER; therefore, if any third rail shoe or trolley is in contact with the third rail or trolley wire, all motors of the train can be supplied with current through the bus line.

MOTOR CONTROL.

6. THE MOTOR CONTROL CIRCUIT (Fig. 479) is the circuit forming the path of the current from the third rail shoes or trolley through the motor control apparatus and motors to the track rails, and is THE MAIN CIRCUIT.

7. THE ESSENTIAL PARTS of the motor control of each car comprise the following apparatus:

> One set of fifteen CONTACTORS, which close and open the circuit to the motors.
> One REVERSER, which determines the direction of train movement.
> One set of eight RESISTANCES, which limit the flow of current to the motors when starting.

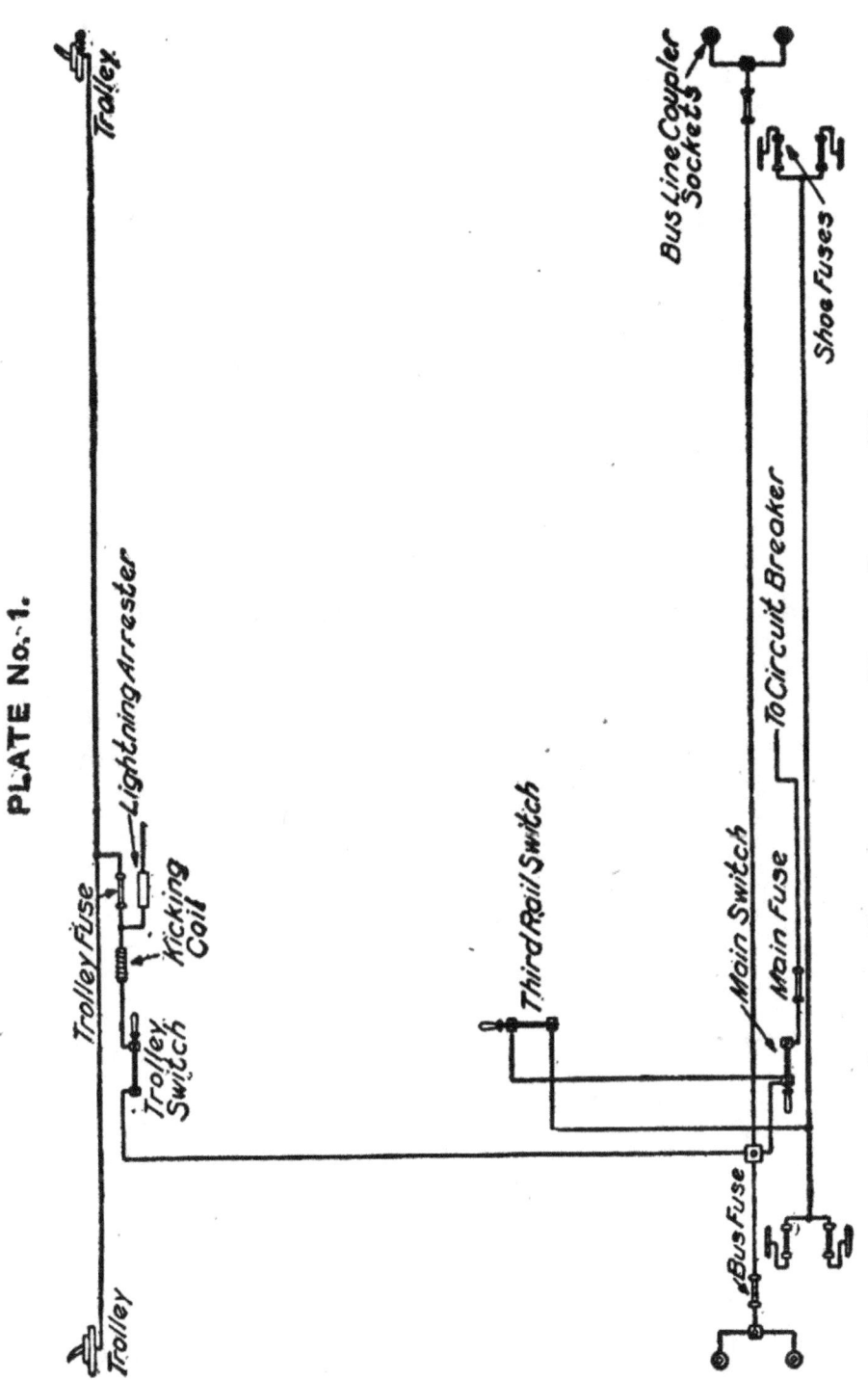

General Arrangement of Motor Control Wiring.
Fig. 479.

ONE CIRCUIT BREAKER, which protects the motors and motor control apparatus against excessive current.

ONE MAIN FUSE, which—like the circuit breaker, and in addition to it—protects the motors and motor control apparatus against overload in case circuit breaker fails to operate.

ONE MAIN SWITCH, by which the current can be cut off from motor control circuit for inspection or in case of defective apparatus.

ONE THIRD RAIL SWITCH, by which current can be cut off from third rail shoes when operating from trolley.

ONE TROLLEY SWITCH, by which the trolley can be cut off from the bus line.

FOUR THIRD RAIL SHOES, which collect current from the third rail.

FOUR SHOE FUSES, which protect the apparatus and car wiring against excessive current.

TWO TROLLEYS, either of which take current from the trolley wire.

One TROLLEY FUSE, which protects the apparatus and car wiring from excessive current.

One BUS LINE, which, together with the bus line jumper, connects all shoes and trolleys of a train together.

TWO BUS LINE FUSES, which protect the bus line against excessive current.

ONE KICKING COIL and one LIGHTNING ARRESTER, which protect the circuits and apparatus against lightning discharges.

8. THE FOUR THIRD RAIL SHOES are connected together through the shoe fuses by a cable, from which a connection is made through the third rail switch on switchboard, through the main switch, main fuse, circuit breaker, contactors, resistances, reverser and motors to the track rails.

9. THE TWO TROLLEYS are connected together by a cable, from which a connection is made through the trolley fuse, then through the kicking coil and trolley switch, located in a box on the roof of the car, to the bus line, from which a connection is made between switch. From the main switch the circuit is the same as from the third rail shoes. A connection is made between the trolley fuse and kicking coil through a lightning arrester, located in the box with the kicking coil on the roof of the car, to ground.

10. THE CONTACTORS, fifteen in number, are enclosed in an iron box, known as the contactor box, located under the car.

The Contactor (Fig. 480) is a switch, the movable portion of which is operated by an electro-magnet receiving line current through the master controller and the train cable. The main contact is made between two heavy copper tips, which are enclosed in an arc chute. A magnetic blowout is provided, having poles extended along two sides of the arc chute, for extinguishing the arc formed in breaking the circuit.

By means of the contactors the motor control is established on individual cars.

11. THE CONTACTOR BOX (Fig. 481) is located beneath the car, about midway between the trucks.

Fig. 480. Contactor.

This box is of iron, lined with asbestos and other insulating materials to prevent short circuits, and is provided with two hinged sheet iron covers. When it is desired to inspect the contactors the sheet iron covers

ELECTRIC RAILROADING

Fig. 481. Contactor Box. Contain 15 Contactors and Potential Relay. Train Cable Connection Box is Mounted on Left End.

can be dropped by releasing the catches which hold them in place.

12. THE REVERSER (Fig. 482) is enclosed in a metal box, and located near the end of the contactor box toward the trailer truck.

The movable part of the reverser is a rocker arm, controlled by two electro-magnets, one for each direction. These magnets are operated by current from the master controller through the main cable, the connections being made so that only one magnet can receive current at a time. Cables from the motor armatures and fields are connected to the fingers of the reverser, and by means of contact pieces mounted on, but insulated from, the rocker arm, proper connections of armatures and fields are established for producing forward and backward movement of the car.

The control connections for the reverser are so arranged that, unless the reverser is at the proper position, current is cut off from the contactors, and consequently the motors on that car receive no current. When the reverser is in the correct position it is electrically locked and cannot be operated while the motors are taking current.

The reverser is always closed, either in the forward or backward position, depending on whether the master controller handle has been moved to the left or to the right.

13. THE RESISTANCE (Fig. 483) is located beneath the car, near the contactors, and is made up of cast iron grids mounted in, and insulated from, an iron frame.

These resistances are used to regulate the flow of current to the motors while the car is accelerating. Cables

Fig. 482. Reverser.

connect the various resistances to different contactors, so that sections of the resistance may be cut out to increase the speed. Resistances are used only in starting, switching, or moving at low speeds, and are entirely cut out either in the one-half or full speed positions of the master controller handle.

Fig. 483. Motor Control Rheostat.

14. **THE CIRCUIT BREAKER** (Fig. 484) is enclosed in an iron box, located beneath the car at the end of the contactor box toward the trailer truck.

The circuit breaker is similar in construction to the contactor, but designed to carry and break the full current taken by the car. It is closed and opened by means

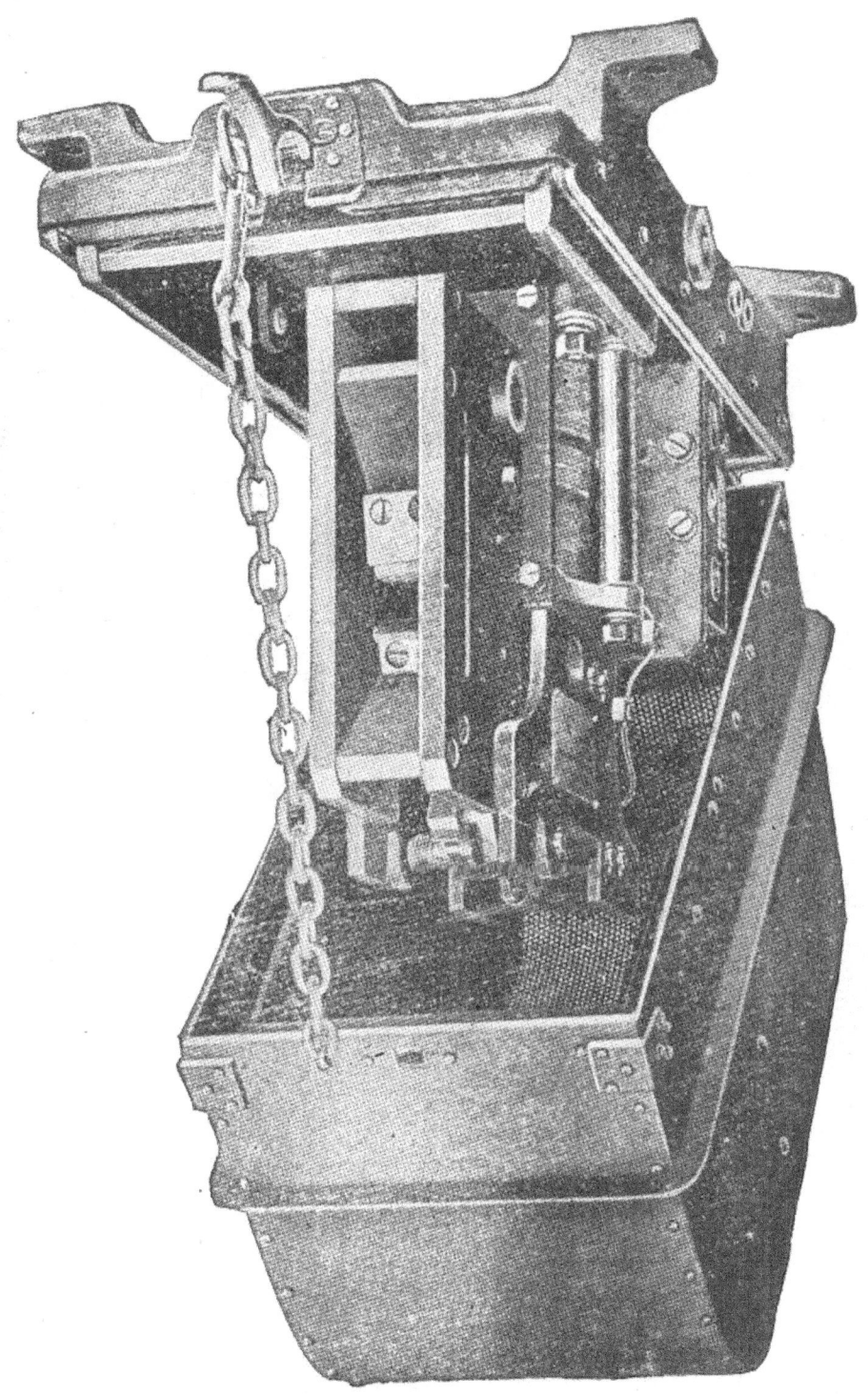

Fig. 484. Circuit Breaker.

of two electro-magnets, acting independently, and operated by current through the train cable and the circuit breaker switch (Fig. 485) which is located in the motorman's cab, above the master controller. The circuit breaker on any car is opened automatically when exces-

Fig. 485. Circuit Breaker Setting and Tripping Switch.

sive current flows through the motor circuits on that car. As the setting and tripping circuits of all circuit breakers of a train are connected through the train cable, all circuit breakers are closed and opened simultaneously by operating the circuit breaker switch.

The circuit breakers are normally closed when the train is ready for operation.

15. **THE MAIN FUSE** (Fig. 486) is located beneath the car, at the trailer end, near the main switch.

It is made from a thin copper ribbon and is contained in a box composed of insulating material. Sheet iron poles partially surround the insulation and provide a magnetic blowout for extinguishing the arc formed when the fuse blows.

Fig. 486. Main Fuse.

The fuse is held in place by copper clamps, fastened with thumb screws having insulated handles. It may be replaced after opening the main switch, loosening the clamps and removing the ends of the old fuse. Ordinarily the current breaker will open automatically from excess current before the fuse has time to blow.

16. THE MAIN SWITCH (Fig. 487) is located in a box beneath the car. It is a quick-break, knife-blade switch, and is used to cut off the supply of current to

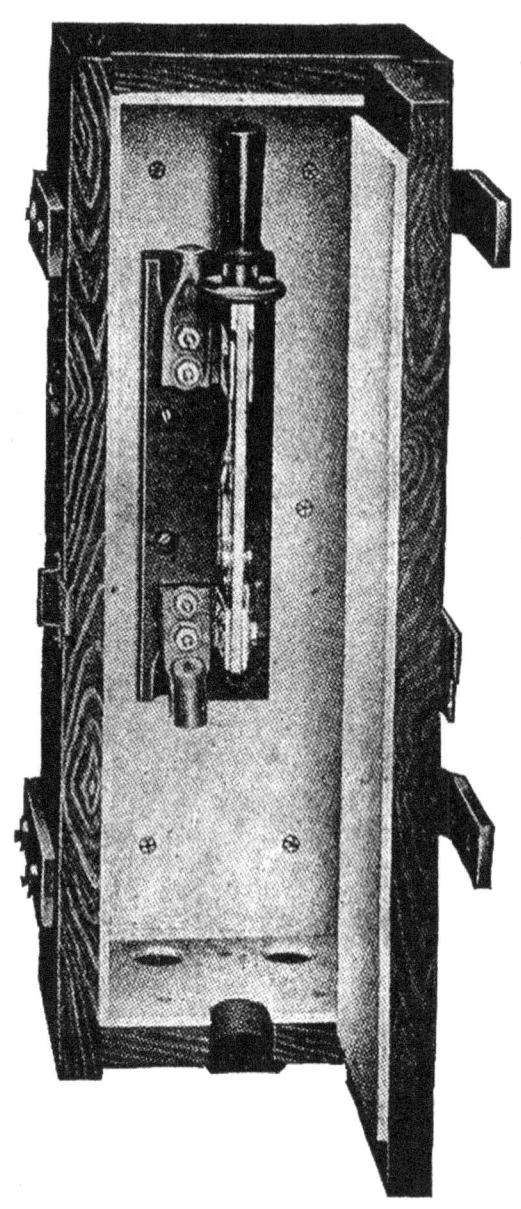

Fig. 487. Main Switch.

the motor circuit from both trolley wire and third rail. This switch is normally closed, BUT SHOULD ALWAYS BE OPEN when examining or working on the motor control apparatus.

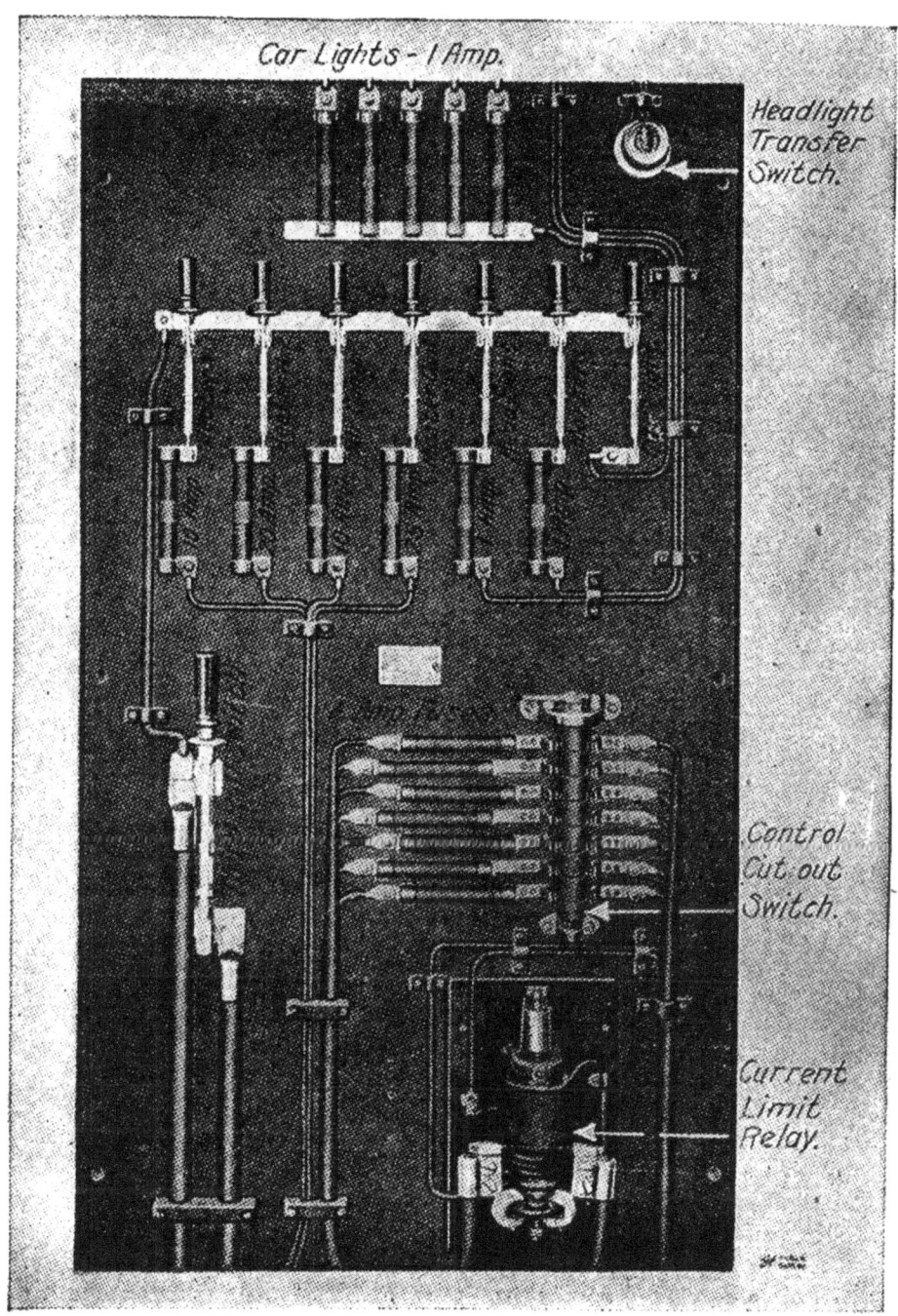

Fig. 489. Switchboard on West Jersey & Seashore Cars.

17. THE THIRD RAIL SWITCH is located on the switchboard (Fig. 489). It is a quick-break, knife-blade switch, and is used to cut off current from the third rail to the motor control circuit and to cut out the third rail shoes when operating from the trolley wire.

This switch is normally closed when the car is taking current from the third rail and open when taking current from the trolley wire. THE SWITCH SHOULD NOT BE OPENED WHILE THE MOTORS ARE TAKING CURRENT, EXCEPT IN AN EMERGENCY.

18. THE TROLLEY SWITCH is located in a box on the car roof. It is a quick-break, knife-blade switch, and is used to cut off the trolley and its fuse from the bus line circuit. This switch is normally closed, BUT SHOULD ALWAYS BE OPEN WHEN WORKING ON THE TROLLEY OR RENEWING A TROLLEY FUSE.

19. THE BUS LINE COUPLER SOCKETS, four in number, are located under the platforms, two at each end of the car.

The coupler socket (Fig. 490) is composed of a body of moulded insulating material, containing a large split plug contact. Supporting feet of malleable iron are secured to this insulating body for attaching to the under side of the car platform. The socket is provided with a hinged lid, having a projection on the inside to hold the jumper plug in place. The cover also excludes dirt and water when the jumper is not inserted. Only one of the two bus line coupler sockets at each platform is in use at a time.

20. **THE BUS LINE JUMPER** (Fig. 491) is used to connect the bus line coupler sockets on adjacent cars. It consists of a short section of flexible cable, with a plug attached to each end, and completes the bus line between the cars. Only one bus line jumper is required

Fig. 490. Bus Line Coupler Socket.

for connecting between adjacent cars, the additional sockets being provided so that cars may be turned end for end or coupled in any desired relation.

21. **THE BUS LINE FUSES**, two in number, are located beneath the car, one at each end. They are similar to the main fuse. These fuses are placed in the bus line circuit to protect it against excessive currents.

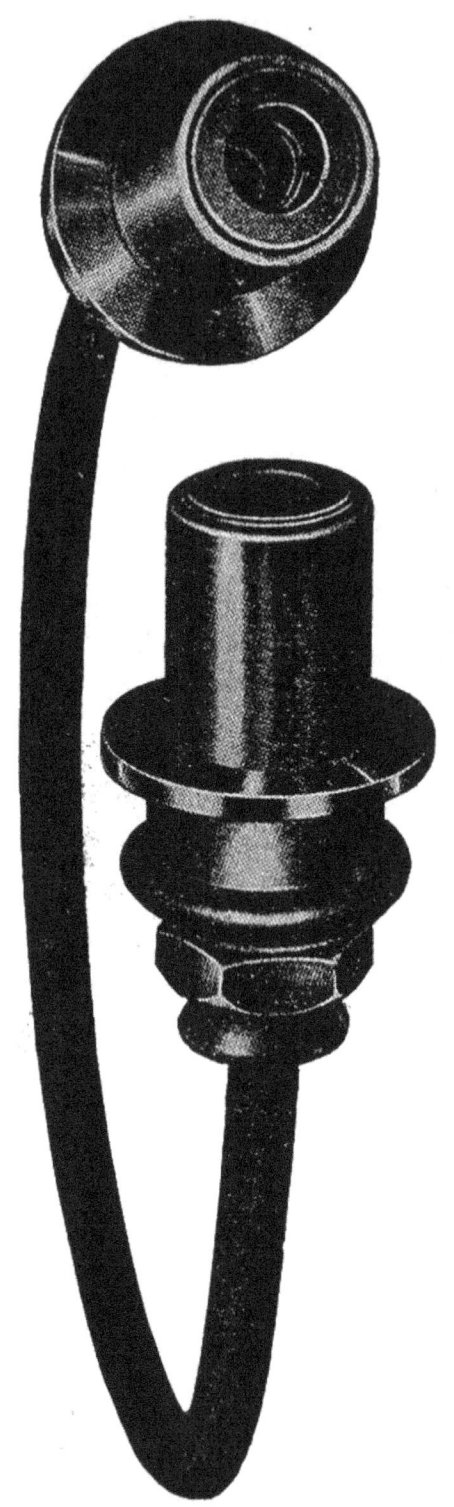

Fig. 491. Bus Line Jumper.

22. **THE BUS LINE JUNCTION BOXES**, two in number, are located beneath the car, one at each end.

The box is made of cast iron and contains an insulated board, to which is secured a single stud bolt for holding the cable terminals. This box is provided for connecting the bus line coupler sockets to the bus line cable.

23. **THE BUS LINE CONNECTION BOX** is located beneath the car, midway between the trucks.

This box is similar to the bus line junction box, and is provided for connecting the third rail and trolley circuits to the bus line cable.

24. **THE SHOE FUSE BOXES**, four in number, are located on the wooden shoe beams, one on each side of each truck. The box is similar to the main and bus line fuse boxes and contains the shoe fuse.

25. **THE TROLLEY FUSE BOX** is located on the roof of the car. It is similar to the main and bus line fuse boxes and contains the trolley fuse.

MASTER CONTROL.

26. THE MASTER CONTROL CIRCUIT (Fig. 492) is the circuit forming the path for the current from the bus line, through the master controller and the train cable, to the operating coils of the motor control apparatus.

27. THE ESSENTIAL PARTS of the master control of each car comprise the following apparatus:

TWO MASTER CONTROLLERS, which operate the motor control.

TWO MASTER CONTROLLER SWITCHES, used to cut off current from their respective master controllers when not in use.

ONE MASTER CONTROL SWITCH, to cut off current to master controller and circuit breaker switches.

ONE TRAIN CABLE, which connects the master controllers to the motor control apparatus.

FOUR TRAIN CABLE COUPLER SOCKETS, to which the train cable jumpers are connected.

ONE TRAIN CABLE JUMPER, which connects the train cable between cars.

TWO TRAIN CABLE CONNECTION BOXES, where connection is made to master controllers, coupler sockets and seven-point cut-out switch.

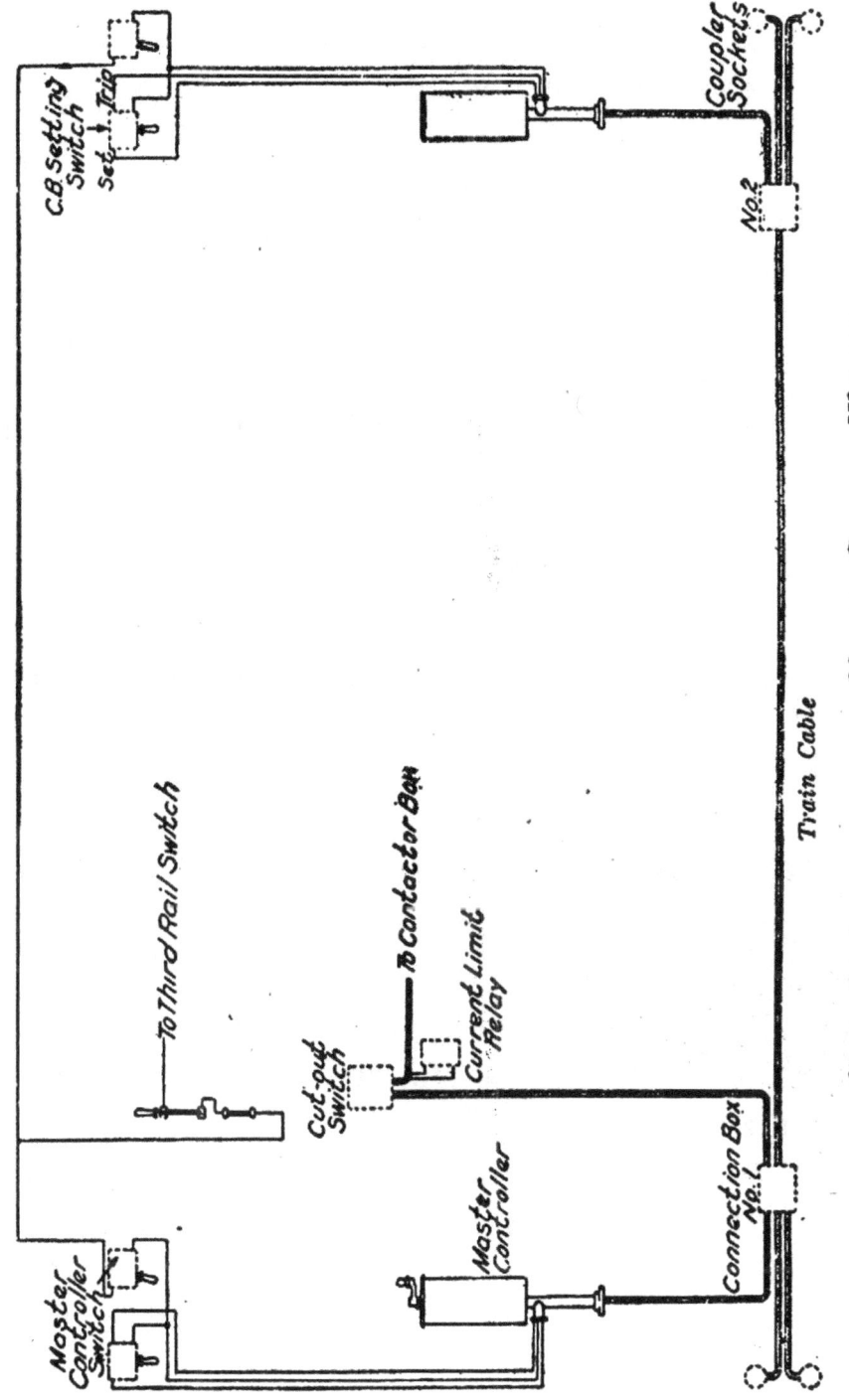

General Arrangement of Master Control Wiring.
Fig. 492.

ONE SET OF RESISTANCE TUBES, which limit the current in the master control circuits.

ONE CURRENT LIMIT RELAY, which limits the rate of acceleration.

ONE POTENTIAL RELAY, which opens the master control circuit when power is cut off from the train.

ONE SEVEN-POINT CUT-OUT SWITCH, to disconnect motor control apparatus from train cable.

TWO CIRCUIT BREAKER SWITCHES, for setting and tripping circuit breakers.

CONTROL FUSES, which protect master control wiring against excessive current.

DESCRIPTION OF MASTER CONTROL APPARATUS.

28. THE MASTER CONTROLLERS, two in number, are located in the motorman's compartments, one at each end of the car.

The master controller (Fig. 493) contains a single movable contact cylinder and stationary fingers, mounted on an insulated support. The controller has a single handle for both forward and reverse direction of train movement. Four points are indicated on the cap plate for forward direction and two for reverse. The first point in either direction is called the "Switching" or "Lap" position; the second, "Full Series." The third point is called the "Parallel Lap" position, and the fourth, "Full Parallel."

The master controller governs the admission of current to the train cable for operating the reverser and contactors.

Fig. 493. Master Controller.

29. THE MASTER CONTROLLER SWITCHES,

two in number, are located above each master controller, one at each end of the car.

Fig. 494. Master Controller Switch Without Fuse. Also Negative Control Switch on Locomotive.

The master controller switch (Fig. 494) is a pivoted switch mounted in an iron box and having a projecting handle. It is provided with a magnetic blowout. This switch is used to cut off current from its master controller when the latter is not in use. It also serves as an emergency switch in case of any failure of the master controller.

ELECTRIC RAILROADING

30. **THE MASTER CONTROL SWITCH** is located on the switchboard and is of the quick-break, knife-blade type.

The switch is used to cut off current from the master controller and the circuit breaker switches.

The normal position of the switch is open except when the train is being operated from a master controller on that car.

31. **THE TRAIN CABLE** is located in an iron pipe placed beneath the car.

The train cable is composed of seven conductors, each being covered with a different colored outer braid for identification. These conductors are attached to numbered plugs in the coupler sockets at the ends of the car. Branch cables run from connection boxes in the train cable to the master controllers, seven-point cut-out switch and coupler sockets.

The train cable is used to connect the operating master controller of the motor control apparatus of the car or train. The seven wires are used as follows:

    No. 1. (Red) for accelerating or notching up.

    No. 2. (White) for series connection of motors.

    No. 3. (Green) for parallel connection of motors.

    No. 4. (Green and White) for operating reverser one direction.

    No. 5. (Yellow) for operating reverser other direction.

    No. 6 (Red and Black) for tripping circuit breakers.

    No. 7 (Black) for setting circuit breakers.

32. THE TRAIN CABLE COUPLER SOCKETS

(Fig. 495), four per car, are attached to the under side of the car platform. These sockets are of malleable iron and contain a body of moulded insulation, into which are set seven bronze split plugs, one being attached to each conductor of the train cable.

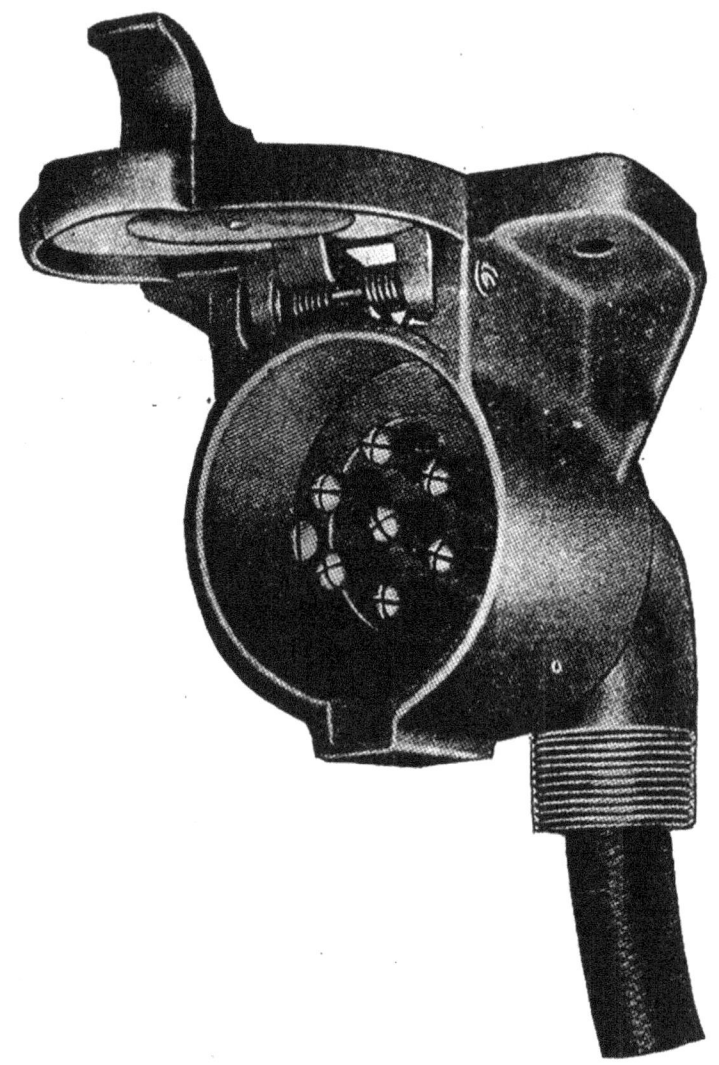

Fig. 495. Train Cable Coupler Socket.

Each socket is provided with a hinged cover adapted to hold the jumper plug in place and to prevent the entrance of dirt and moisture when no jumper is inserted.

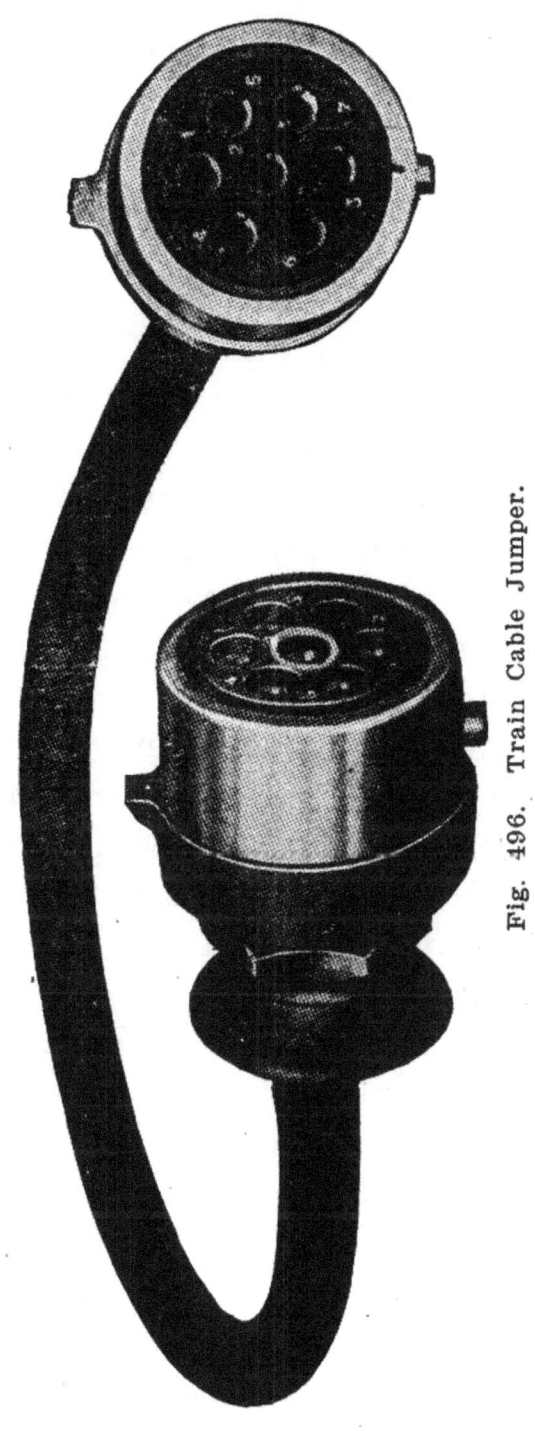

Fig. 496. Train Cable Jumper.

33. THE TRAIN CABLE JUMPER (Fig. 496) is used for connecting the train cables on adjacent cars. It consists of a short length of seven-conductor cable, with iron heads or plugs attached to the ends, each containing seven insulated contacts, one being secured to each conductor. The jumper heads fit into the coupler sockets on adjoining cars, and connect together their train cables.

34. THE TRAIN CABLE CONNECTION BOXES, two in number, are located beneath the car.

The train cable connection box (Fig. 497) is of iron and is used for making the connections from the master controller, circuit breaker, coupler sockets and cut-out switch to the train cable. Seven screw studs, which are held in an insulating board, are used for securing the terminals attached to the ends of the entering cables.

Conductors provided with the same colored covering are connected together, except at one connection box on each car, where Nos. 4 and 5, which operate the reverser, are crossed in order to obtain a direction of car movement to agree with the position of controller handle in either controller.

35. THE RESISTANCE TUBES are located in the contactor box, and consist of twelve tubes wound with resistance wire. They are used to regulate the current in the operating coils of the contactors.

36. THE CURRENT LIMIT RELAY (Fig. 498) is located on the switchboard. It consists of an electromagnet provided with two coils. The master control circuit passes through the upper coil and the main circuit for motor No. 1 through the lower coil. The master control circuit coil lifts the plunger for each step during acceleration and interrupts the contactor pick-up circuit.

Fig. 497. Train Cable Connection Box.

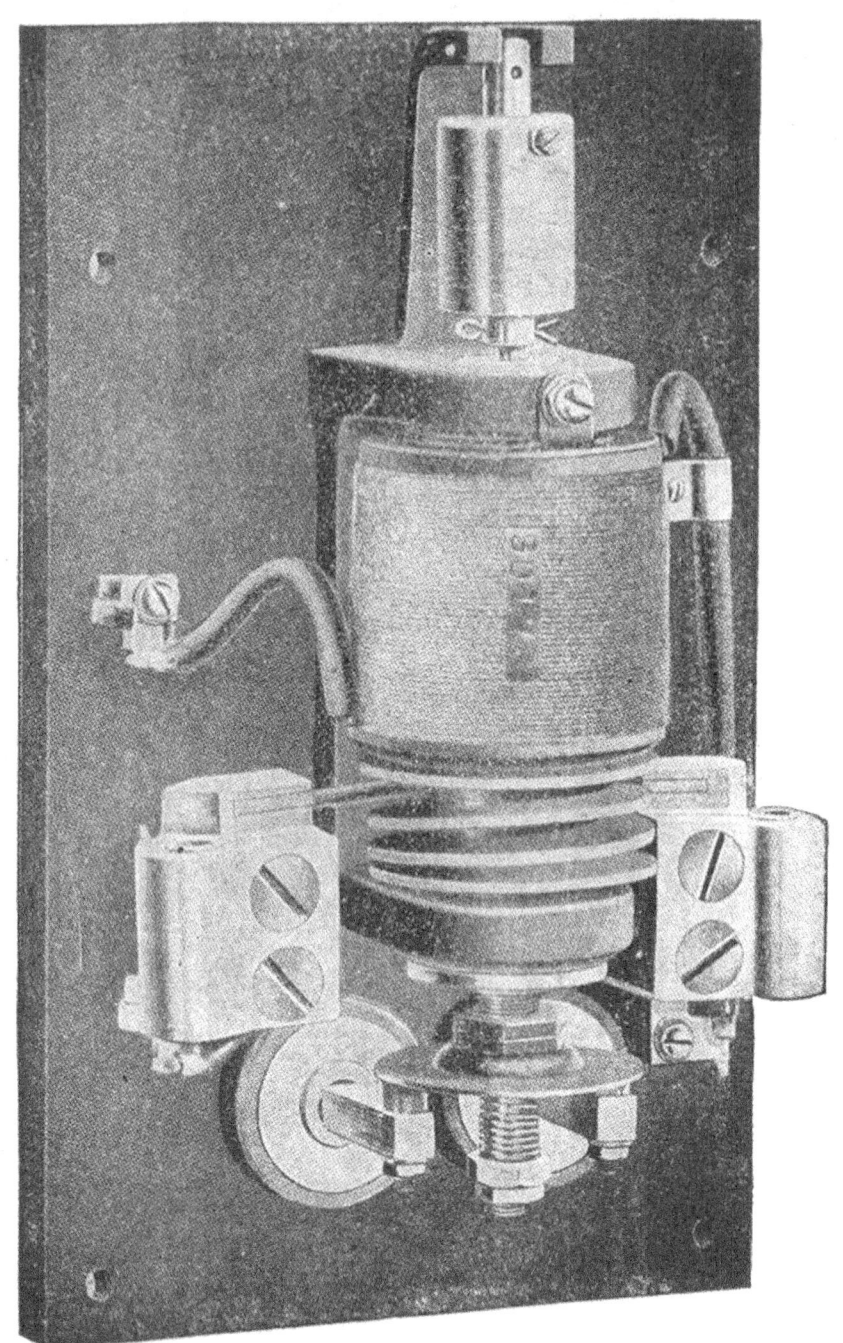

Fig. 498. Current Limit Relay.

If the current flowing through the main circuit coil is more than a certain amount the plunger is held in its upper position and cannot drop until the motor current as fallen to the desired amount.

The relay is provided for the purpose of producing an automatic control during acceleration.

37. THE POTENTIAL RELAY (Fig. 499) is mounted in the contactor box. It is similar to the current relay in construction, but is used for a different purpose. The relay has a coil which is connected between a point in the motor circuit, ahead of the first motor, and ground. If for any reason the motor current is interrupted on a car, this relay will open the master control circuit to the contactors on that car, causing them, in turn, to open. When current is restored to the car, the relay will again pick up and complete the master control circuit. The contactors will then pick up in regular succession, the same as if the motorman had shut off power and immediately turned the master controller handle on again.

38. THE CONTROL CUT-OUT SWITCH is mounted upon the switchboard. It consists of copper contacts, mounted on an insulated drum, and two sets of fingers fastened to the switchboard. It is provided for the purpose of disconnecting the master control circuit, to the contactors reverser and circuit breaker on the car, from the train cable.

39. THE CIRCUIT BREAKER SWITCHES, two in number, are located one above each master controller.

The circuit breaker switch (Fig. 485) is mounted in a cast iron box and consists of a pivoted blade, with a handle extending below the box.

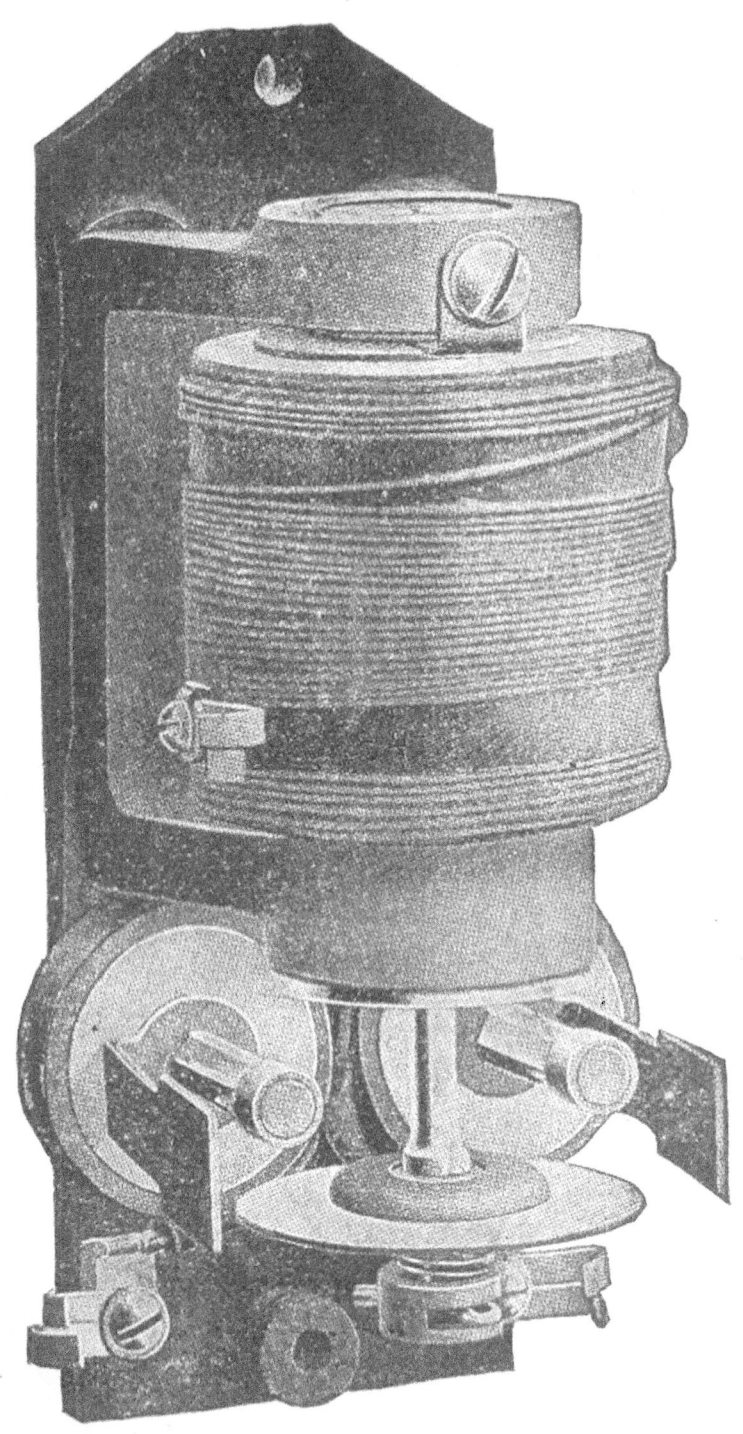

Fig. 499. Potential Relay.

The handle, when turned to the right, makes connection through a contact with the setting coils of the circuit breakers; when turned to the left, with the tripping coils of the circuit breakers. These positions are indicated by the words "On" and "Off" on the face of the box.

The normal position of the handle is vertical, and is held in this position by two springs.

40. CONTROL FUSES are mounted on the switchboard beside the control cut-out switch. A fuse is placed in each of the seven control circuits between the train cable and the cut-out switch.

41. THE SWITCHBOARD (Fig. 489) is located in the vestibule at the trailer end of the car, and has mounted upon it the following apparatus:

> The THIRD RAIL SWITCH. (Paragraph No. 17.)
>
> The SEVEN-POINT CUT-OUT SWITCH and FUSES. (Paragraph Nos. 38 and 40.)
>
> The CURRENT LIMIT RELAY. (Paragraph No. 36.)
>
> The MASTER CONTROL SWITCH AND FUSE. (Paragraph No. 30.)
>
> SWITCHES AND FUSES FOR AIR COMPRESSOR, LIGHTS AND HEATERS.

EMERGENCY AIR BRAKE ATTACHMENT.

42. **THE EMERGENCY AIR BRAKE ATTACHMENT** for master controller (Fig. 493) consists of a main valve outside of the controller (Fig. 500), and a small pilot valve (Fig. 501) within it. The main valve

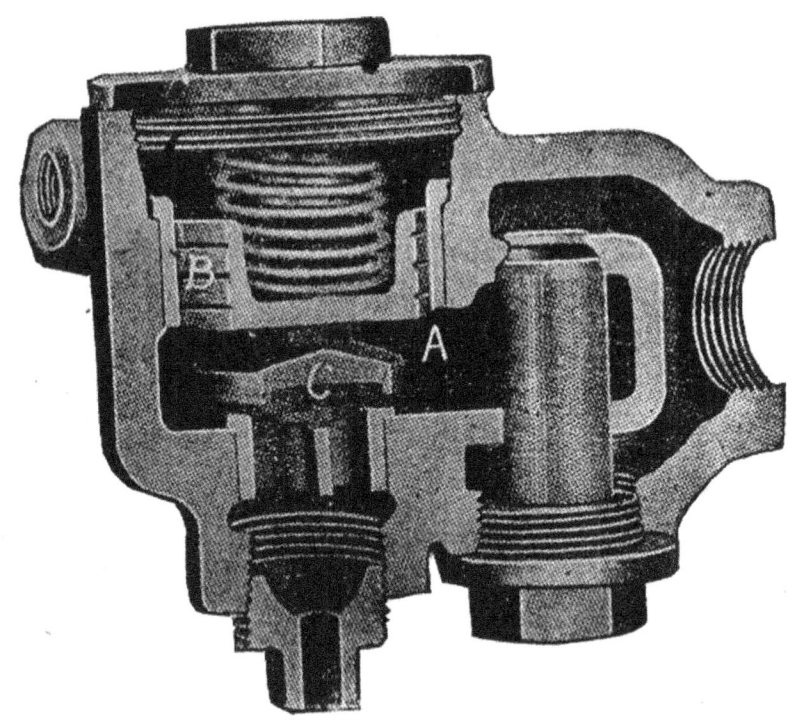

Fig. 500. Main Valve. Emergency Air Brake Attachment.

contains a chamber "A," divided into two parts by a piston "B" connected to a valve "C," exhausting to atmosphere. The lower part of the chamber "A" connects directly to the brake pipe. The upper part of "A" connects to the pilot valve through "F" and pressure in both parts is equalized by a small hole in the piston "B." When the pilot valve is opened, pressure in the upper part of the main valve is reduced, and the piston lifts, allowing the brake pipe to exhaust through a hole in the bottom of the main valve to atmosphere. The pilot valve is opened by a loose collar on the cylinder shaft in the controller, which presses against the stem of the valve when the controller handle is at the "Off" position and the button released.

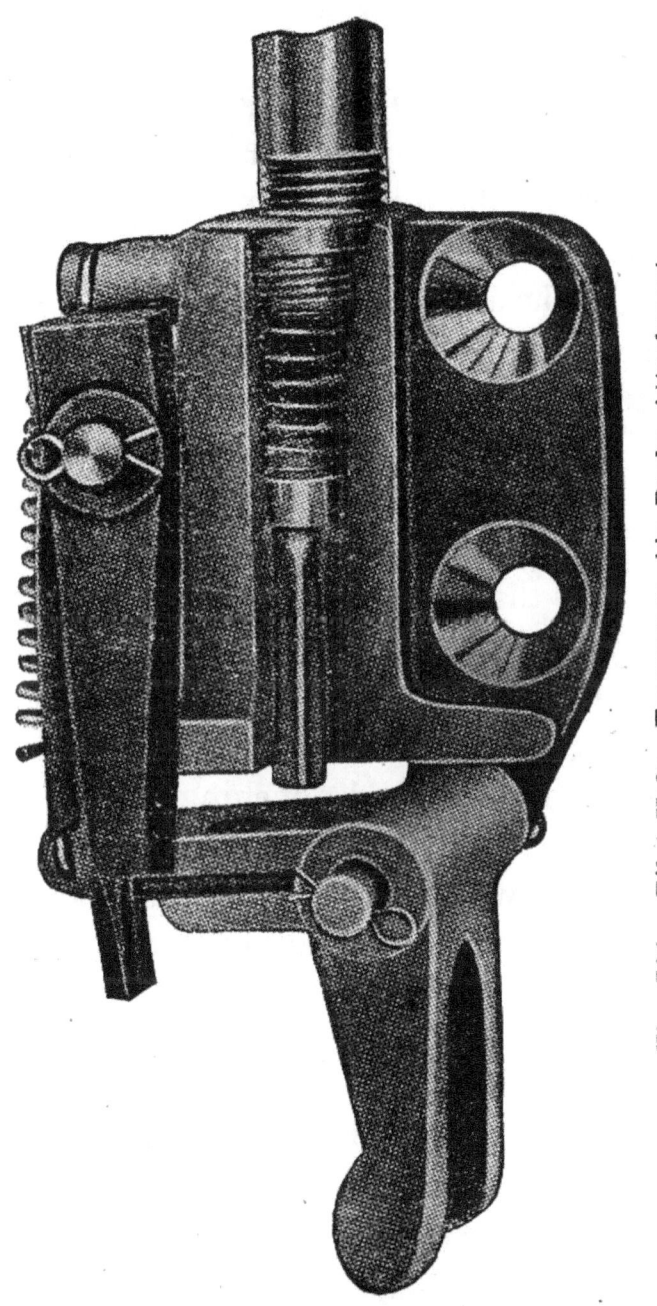

Fig. 501. Pilot Valve Emergency Air Brake Attachment.

TRAIN OPERATION.

43. GENERAL—The apparatus will be inspected and the train put in condition for operation by the inspectors; but the motorman will be held responsible for the operation of the apparatus while in his charge, and he should, therefore, familiarize himself with the location, use and operation of all apparatus on the cars, and should carefully follow the instructions below:

44. PREPARATIONS FOR STARTING—When the train is turned over to motorman, he should:

>FIRST—Pass along the outside of train, carefully examining bus line and train cable jumpers between cars, to assure himself that all connections are properly made and that main switches are closed.
>
>SECOND—Pass through the train, closing air compressor and third rail switches in each car, and opening master control switches in all cars except head car or car from which train is to be operated.
>
>THIRD—Pass along outside of train again and satisfy himself that the air compressors are working properly.
>
>FOURTH—Take position in the motorman's compartment at forward end of train and note the brake pipe pressure, which should be seventy pounds, close master controller switch. The circuit breakers should then

be set by moving the circuit breaker switch, over the master controller, to the "On" position—holding it there about one second to allow time for all circuit breakers to set.

FIFTH—Test the brakes as required by "Air Brake Instructions," making, upon request of the trainmen or inspectors, a full service application (twenty-pound reduction of pressure), holding them on until the trainmen or inspectors have examined the brakes on each car.

If the brakes are found in proper condition, trainmen or inspectors shall signal the motorman, from the rear of the train, who will then release the brakes.

The test is not complete until the trainmen or inspectors have re-examined the brakes, which should be done as quickly as possible, to see that they have released properly, after which the inspectors must report their condition to the motorman.

The train is now ready to be started.

45. TO START—Press down the button in the controller handle, insert the handle key and give it a quarter turn. The button must now be held down to prevent the pilot valve in the controller from operating and applying the brakes. Move the controller handle to the left as far as it will go, holding it there against the spring, which tends to return it to the "Off" position. The motor control will then notch up to full speed position by the automatic progression of the contactors, in successive steps, under the control of the current limit relay. In this

position it is not necessary to hold the button down to prevent application of the brakes.

46. COASTING—Hold the button down and move controller handle to "Off" position. In this position power will be shut off and the train may coast free.

47. SERVICE STOP—The service stop will be made by the air brake valve in accordance with the "Air Brake Instructions."

48. EMERGENCY STOP—The emergency stop may be made by releasing the controller handle, which will then return to the "Off" position, shutting off the power and applying the brakes.

49. TO START SLOWLY—Move the controller handle to the left to first point. In this position both motors on each car are connected in series with all resistance in circuit and the motor control will not "notch up" to higher speed.

50. TO INCREASE SPEED SLIGHTLY—Move the controller handle to the second point and quickly return it to first point. This operation results in the cutting out of one step of resistance, and may be repeated until all the resistance is cut out, thus slowly notching up under the control of the motorman and not automatically.

If the controller handle is left on the second point for a sufficient length of time, all resistance will be automatically cut out in successive steps, under the control of the current limit relay, until full series or half speed is reached.

51. RUNNING POSITIONS—The second and fourth notches are running positions, and the train should not be operated for more than a few minutes at a time with the controller handle on intermediate notches.

52. TO REVERSE—Move the controller handle to the right to the first point. The reverser will change the direction of train movement, and the motors will be connected in series with all resistance in circuit.

It is not possible to run above half speed in the reverse direction, and if higher speed is required, it can only be obtained by operating the master controller at the other end of the car or train.

TRAIN FAILURE.

53. A TRAIN FAILURE, that is, a failure of a train of one or more cars to move or to attain full speed, when the directions for train operation have been followed, may be due to one or more of the following causes:

FIRST—FAILURE OF POWER.

SECOND—DEFECT IN MASTER CONTROL CIRCUIT.

    (a) Master control fuse blown or imperfect.
    (b) Grounded train cable.
    (c) Poor contact in master controller.
    (d) Loose train cable jumper.

THIRD—DEFECT IN MOTOR CONTROL CIRCUIT.

    (a) Circuit breakers open.
    (b) Bus fuses blown.
    (c) Loose or disconnected bus jumper.
    (d) Main fuse blown.
    (e) Shoe or trolley fuses blown.

FOURTH—FAILURE OF AIR BRAKES TO RELEASE.

FAILURE OF POWER.

54. A FAILURE OF POWER can be detected by closing the lighting switches; if lights burn, power is on.

DEFECT IN MASTER CONTROL CIRCUIT.

55. TO DETERMINE IF MASTER CONTROL CIRCUIT IS OPEN turn master controller handle to the first notch and open the master controller switch. The noise of slight arcing indicates that the master control circuit is closed and that the trouble is elsewhere. No arcing shows that the master control circuit is open and indicates that fuse is blown or imperfect. A black or charred spot in the center of the label, called a "Tell-tale," indicates that the fuse is blown and should be replaced. A fuse which shows no indication of being blown should be tested to detect faulty construction by removing a fuse from a lighting circuit and inserting the fuse to be tested. The lights burning indicate that the fuse is good, and it can then be replaced.

56. TO DETERMINE IF TRAIN CABLE IS GROUNDED, operate the master controller. If the master controller fuse blows, it indicates that one or more wires of the train cable are in contact with the ground, and the cable is said to be "grounded."

To locate a ground in the train cable, disconnect train cable on operating car from rest of train by removing train cable jumper from its socket on second car. If the fuse now blows, when the controller handle is operated, it indicates that the ground is either in the operating car or its train cable jumper.

To determine whether ground is in train cable or jumper, remove the jumper. If the fuse blows when the controller is operated, the ground is in the car. If it does not blow, the ground is in the jumper, and a new one should be inserted. If the fuse does not blow when the jumper is disconnected from the second car, the jumper should be replaced, and the one between the second and third cars disconnected from its socket on the third car, and so on until the fault is located.

If the fault is found to be caused by a defective jumper, and if the train is not provided with an extra jumper, the jumper between the two last cars of the train should be taken to replace the defective one.

If the fault is found to be on the car and not in the jumpers, the seven-point control cut-out switch on that car should be turned to the "Off" position, and the test repeated. If the fuse still blows when the handle is operated, the fault is in the train cable. If the fuse does not blow, the ground is between the cut-out switch and the contactors, reverser and circuit breaker. If this is the case, the cut-out switch on the defective car should remain in the "Off" position, thus cutting out the fault as well as rendering the car inoperative, but in no way interfering with the train cable, and permitting the operation of other cars in the train, through the train cable in the usual manner.

If opening the cut-out switch does not remove the fault, that is, if the fault is in the train cable and the defective car is near the rear end, the train should be operated from the front car as usual, the defective car and those following being cut out by removing both train cable jumpers on that car; if at or near the head of the train, the train should be run from the following car, all cars ahead being cut out.

57. **TO DETECT POOR CONTACT IN MASTER CONTROLLER**, open the master controller switch, remove the cover from the controller and turn the handle slowly, noting if each finger makes good contact with the drum. If any contact is poor and cannot readily be readjusted by the motorman, he should run the train from the next car.

58. **TO DETECT LOOSE TRAIN CABLE JUMPER**, the trainmen should note if the contactors on each car are working while the train is accelerating. If there is a loose train cable jumper, all cars ahead of the jumper will operate; others will not. The motorman should be immediately informed if any car is not operating.

DEFECT IN MOTOR CONTROL CIRCUIT.

59. **IF ONE OR MORE CIRCUIT BREAKERS OF A TRAIN BLOW** when starting or running, return the controller handle to the "off" position and move the handle of the circuit breaker switch to the "on" position. If the circuit breakers again blow when the controller handle is operated, the brakes should be examined to see if they have released.

If the circuit breaker on any car repeatedly blows, the motorman should make an examination to see that it is properly adjusted. If the trouble is not with the circuit breaker, the car should be cut out by opening the seven-point cut-out switch on the switchboard and the main switch beneath the car.

Blowing of the circuit breaker is accompanied by a loud report.

60. AN OPEN CIRCUIT IN BUS LINE may be detected when the train is at a crossover and current cannot be obtained on operating car, although other cars of the train have current. This indicates that the bus line fuse or fuses are blown, or that a bus line jumper is loose or disconnected between the operating and adjacent cars.

The motorman should inspect the bus line jumpers, and if the trouble cannot be quickly remedied, he should go back to the first car having current and move the train through the crossover. The motorman should then return to the first car and proceed in the usual manner.

61. WHEN THE MAIN FUSE IS BLOWN, the motors will not operate, although the contactors may be in working order and the circuit breaker closed. This should occur very seldom, as it can only be caused by short circuit or grounding in the motors or motor circuits, which are usually protected by the quicker acting circuit breaker. This fuse should not be replaced on the road except to avoid serious delay to the service, as in the case of single cars. BEFORE RENEWING MAIN FUSE, OPEN THE MAIN SWITCH.

62. A SHOE FUSE MAY BLOW from short circuit, grounding of the car wiring on some part of the car or truck, or may be caused by a contact shoe on the car or train grounding, due either to being broken or from fouling or picking up something along the line. If it is necessary to replace a shoe fuse on the road so as to prevent delay to service, the motorman should open the third rail switch on the switchboard and insert the wooden paddles, provided for that purpose, between all shoes on that car that are in contact with the third rail.

63. A TROLLEY FUSE MAY BLOW from short circuit or grounding of the car wiring on the car or

truck, or because it has been overloaded by running in a train with other trolleys down and taking current for the whole train through the one fuse. If this latter has been the cause, the fuse should be replaced on the road if it is required to prevent delay to service. Before replacing the fuse, pull down both trolleys and open the trolley switch.

GENERAL DIRECTIONS.

64. IN CASE OF FIRE beneath any car in the train, the motorman should open all circuit breakers by moving the circuit breaker switch to "OFF" position. If this fails, he should open the main switch beneath the car and the seven-point cut-out switch on the switchboard.

65. IF SMOKE OR FIRE IS OBSERVED by the trainmen in any of the lighting or heater circuits within the car, they should IMMEDIATELY open the switch controlling the circuit, and extinguish the fire with SAND. NEVER USE WATER to extinguish a fire when power is "ON," as water is liable to increase the danger by causing further short circuits.

66. UNUSUAL NOISES in train movement should at once be located. To avoid delay the conductor or brakeman should stand beside the train while it is moved slowly. If noise is caused by brake rigging, the same should be tied up; if the noise is located within the motors, and the schedule permits it, the motors should be cut out by opening the seven-point cut-out switch on that car.

67. A BROKEN THIRD RAIL SHOE or shoe support should be broken completely off or tied up, whichever, in the judgment of the motorman, will cause the least delay. In either case, open the third rail switch on switchboard and insert wooden paddles between third rail and all contact shoes on the car. To break off remainder of shoe, use some tool with a wooden handle, as a hammer or ax. NEVER USE A CROWBAR OR COUPLER PIN FOR THIS PURPOSE.

68. TO STOP TRAIN WHEN AIR BRAKES FAIL, turn controller to first notch in reverse position. THIS SHOULD ONLY BE DONE IN CASE OF EMERGENCY AND TO AVOID ACCIDENTS.

69. CAUTION—Employes should exercise extreme care while working about or on car wiring. The switch controlling the circuit on which work is being done should always be open.

70. MOTORMEN MUST REPORT at the end of each trip, on the regular form provided for the purpose, all detentions and reasons for such detentions and any defects in electrical, air and signal apparatus.

AUTOMATIC AIR-BRAKE CATECHISM.

MOTOR CARS.

A.—General.

Question 1. What is the power used to operate an air-brake?

Answer. Compressed air.

Question 2. How is the air compressed for use in the brake system?

Answer. By air compressors on the motor cars.

Question 3. How does it apply the brake?

Answer. By being admitted to a brake cylinder and forcing a piston out, which, by means of connecting rods and levers, pulls the brake shoes against the wheels.

Question 4. How is the brake released?

Answer. By allowing the air in the brake cylinders to escape to the atmosphere. A spring in the brake cylinder then shoves the piston back and the brake shoes are forced away from the wheels by the brake release springs on the trucks.

Question 5. What is the form of air-brake now generally used?

Answer. The quick-action automatic brake.

Question 6. Why is it called an automatic brake?

Answer. Because if anything, no matter what, causes a reduction of pressure in the brake pipe, the brake will apply automatically.

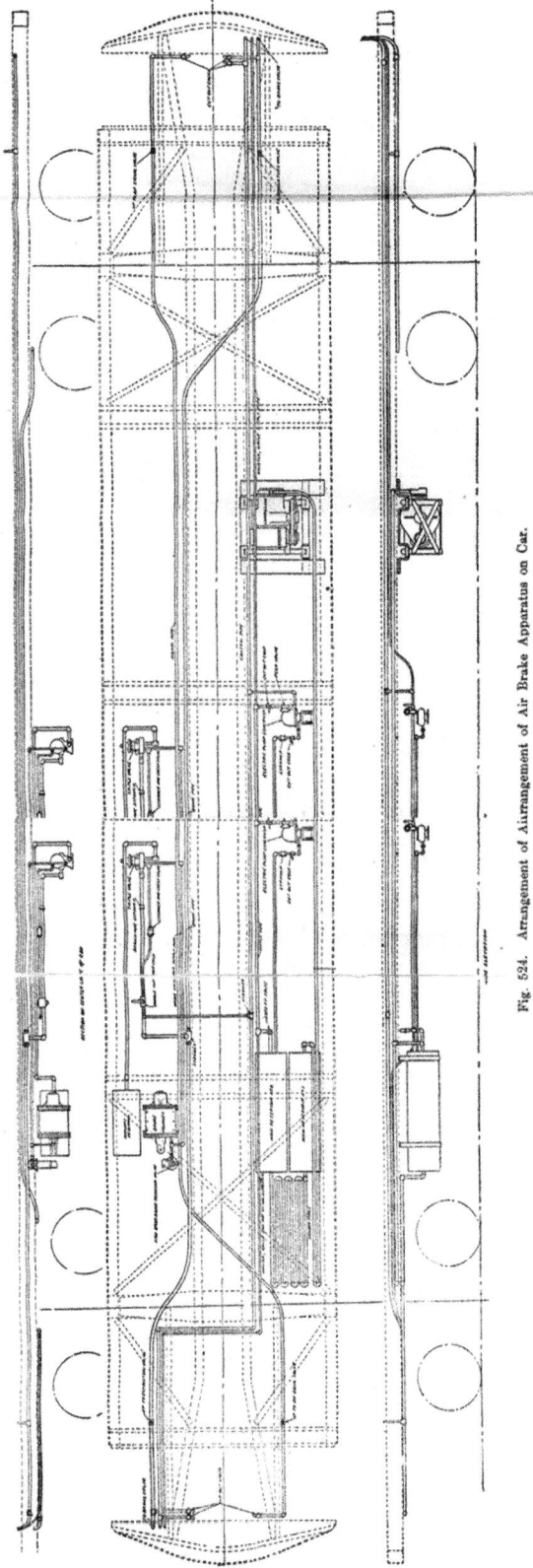

Fig. 524. Arrangement of Airrangement of Air Brake Apparatus on Car.

Question 7. What parts has the quick-action automatic brake on a motor car?

Answer. An air compressor, pump governor, two main reservoirs, safety valve, slide-valve feed valve, control pipe, two brake valves, two air gauges, brake pipe, triple valve, auxiliary reservoir, brake cylinder, conductor's valve, two air strainers, one bleed cock, two pair of hose and couplings, six cut-out cocks, one double cut-out cock, one air strainer with check valve, and one branch pipe air strainer (Fig. 524).

Question 8. Where are the brake valves and air gauges located?

Answer. In the motorman's cab at each end of the car.

Question 9. What parts has the quick-action brake on a trailer car?

Answer. Auxiliary reservoir, brake cylinder, triple valve, brake pipe, control pipe, conductor's valve, two air strainers, one bleed cock, four cut-out cocks, two pair of hose and couplings, one double cut-out cock, one air strainer with check valve, and one branch pipe air strainer.

Question 10. Is there any difference between the reservoirs, triple valves, and brake cylinders used on motor cars and trailer cars?

Answer. No.

Question 11. Where is the pressure that supplies the brake cylinder stored or carried with the automatic system?

Answer. In the auxiliary reservoir under each cab.

Question 12. What has to be done to apply the automatic brake?

Answer. Reduce the brake-pipe pressure, which reduction causes the triple valve to admit the pressure from the auxiliary reservoir to the brake cylinder.

B.—*The Air Compressor.*

Question 13. Where is the compressor installed, and how?

Answer. It is placed under the car, suspended from the sills by a cradle. (See Fig. 525).

Question 14. Does it make any difference in which direction the compressor rotates?

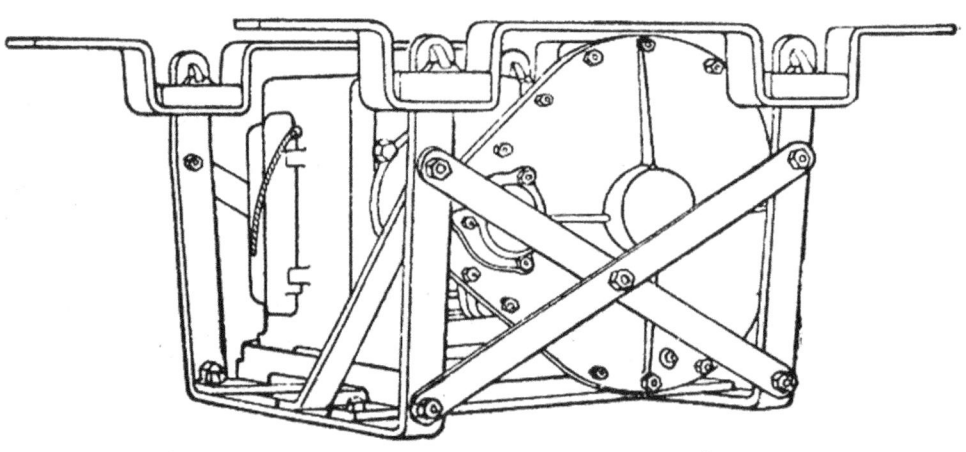

Fig. 525. Suspension Cradle of Air Compressor.

Answer. The shaft must always turn so that the compression part of the stroke is on the upper half revolution. This will be assured if the rotation is the same as the hands of a clock when looking at the compressor at the gear side.

Question 15. How are the pump parts lubricated?

Answer. The crank case is filled with oil (preferably Arctic Ammonia Oil) up to a point determined by the oil fitting 18, Fig. 526, on the side of crank case. When the level of the oil is visible in this fitting, the cap being removed, the oil level in the crank case is correct. As

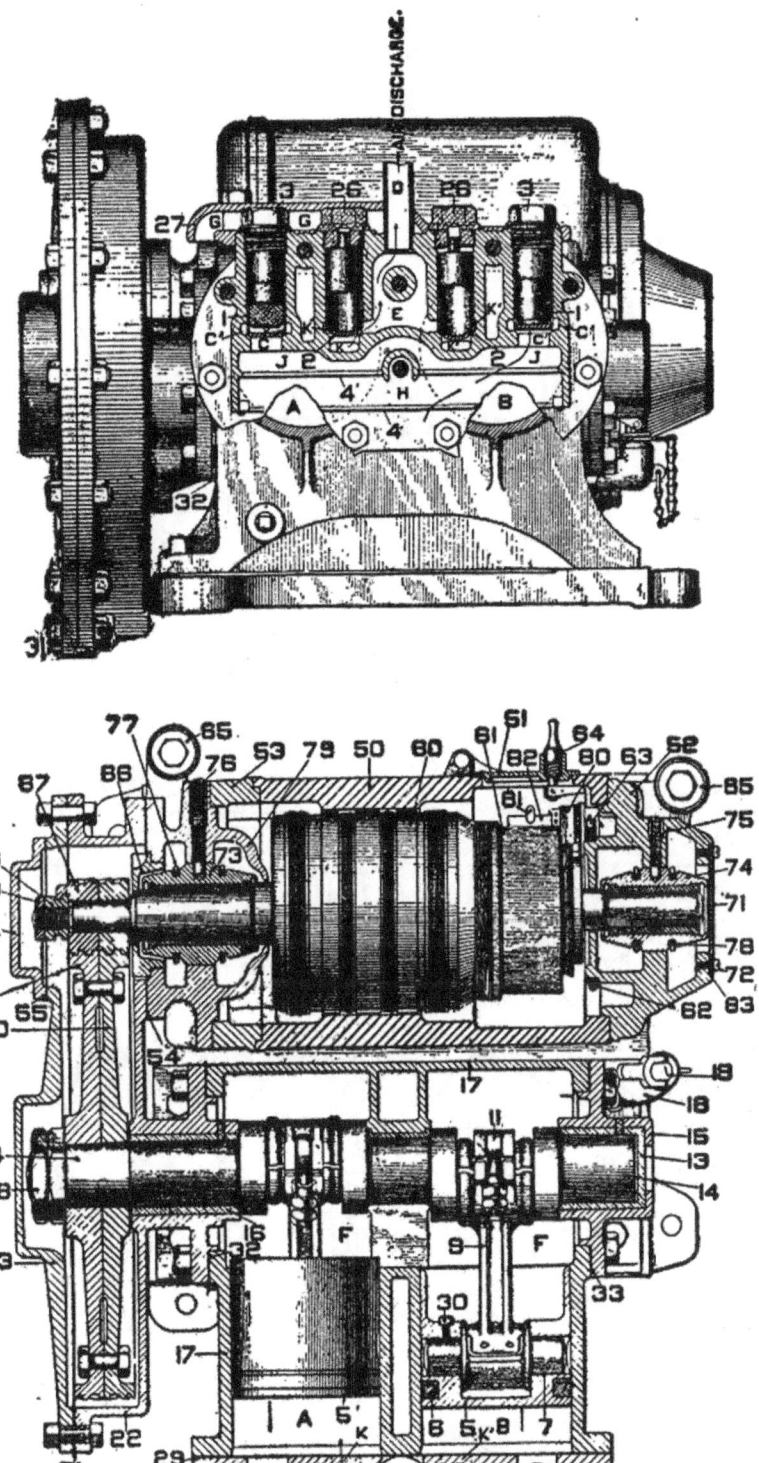

Fig. 526. Air Compressor on Motor Cars.

the shaft turns and the connecting rod heads are forced downward, they drive the oil over the inside of the crank case and such parts of the cylinders as are exposed. In this manner all the crank-shaft bearings as well as the cylinders themselves and wrist pins are thoroughly lubricated.

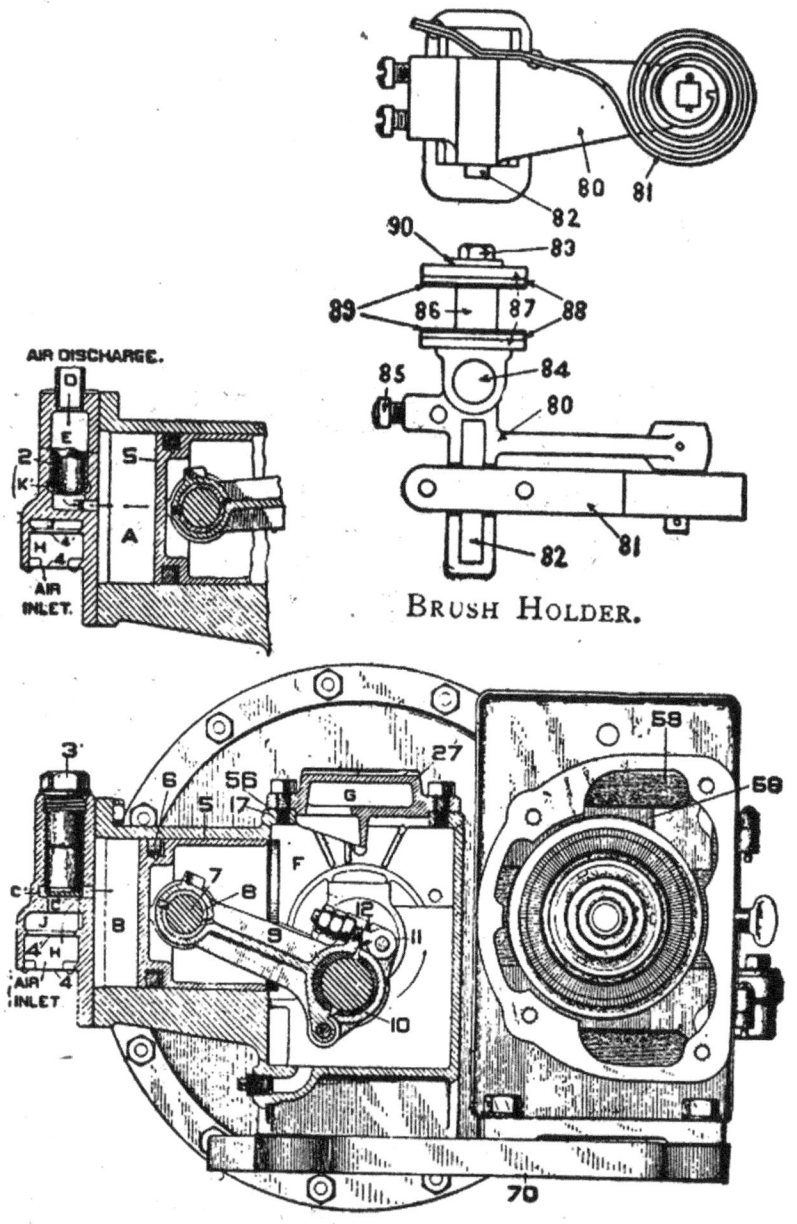

Fig. 527. Air Compressor on Motor Cars.

Question 16. How often should the oil in the crank case be replenished?

Answer. Once a week.

Question 17. How often should the suction box be cleaned?

Answer. This depends largely upon the locality in which the car operates. Generally it is not required more than once or twice a month. In very dusty localities it may be required oftener.

Question 18. How is the suction box cleaned?

Answer. The outer perforated plate 4 (Fig. 527) covering the air inlet on the lower side of chamber H should be removed and the pulled curled hair taken out and thoroughly cleaned by beating in a bag, by the use of compressed air or some other efficient means. It may then be replaced and the outer perforated plate put back in place.

Question 19. How is the motor lubricated?

Answer. By removing plug 65 (Fig. 526) in both end bearing housings and filling with oil until the level can be plainly seen. These bearings should be replenished at the same time as the crank case.

Question 20. Should a compressor which frequently blows fuses be sent out temporarily with a heavier fuse than that prescribed?

Answer. Not under any circumstances. Such a practice is almost sure to result in burning out the motor.

C.—*Electric Pump Governor.*

Question 21. What is the purpose of the electric pump governor? (Fig. 528).

Answer. It starts and stops the compressor automatically when certain predetermined minimum and maximum air pressures occur in the main reservoir by alternately making and breaking the circuit to the air-compressor motor.

Question 22. Where is this governor located?

Answer. It is placed in a sheet-iron box under the

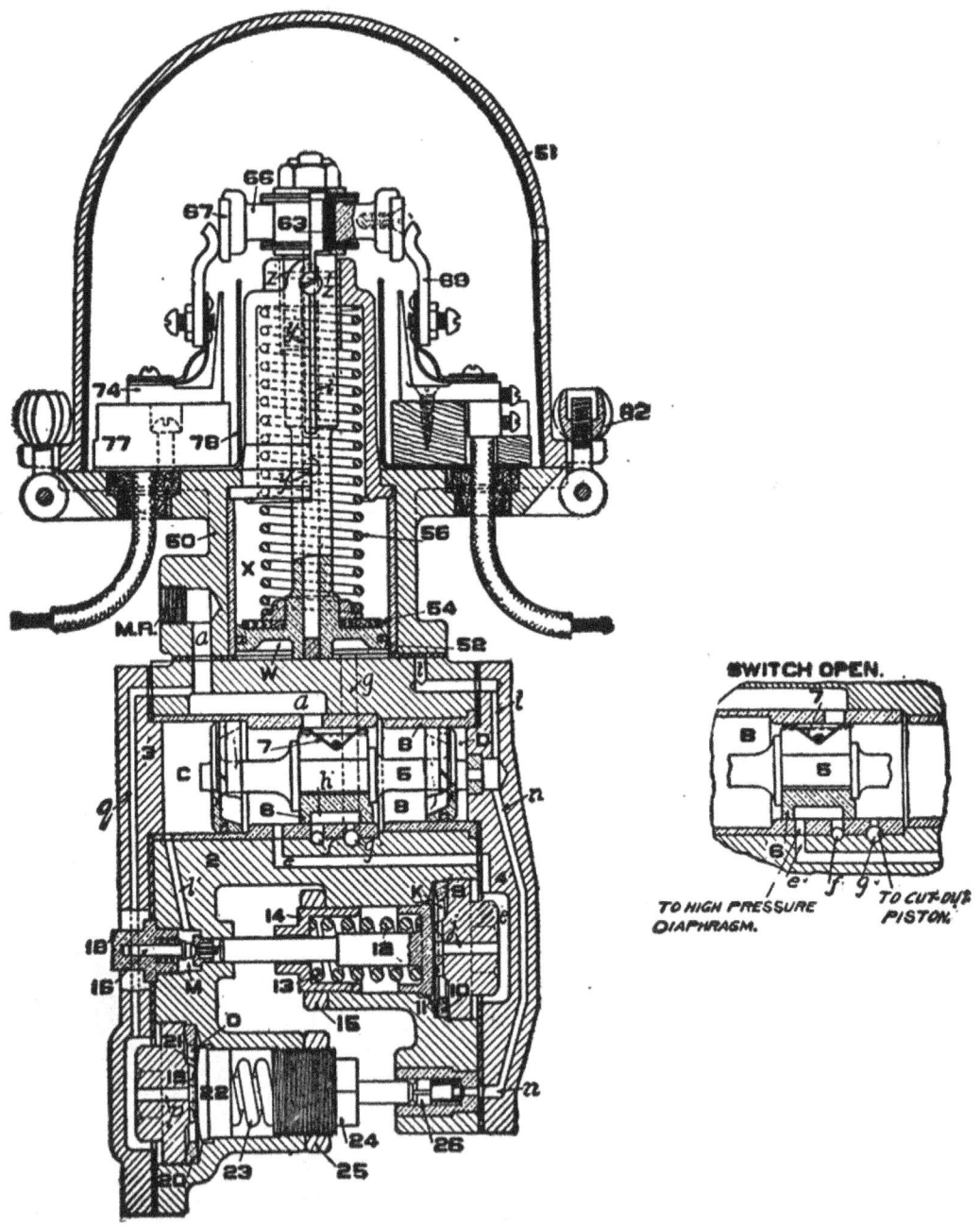

Fig. 528. Air Compressor Governor on Motor Cars.

car on the motor compressor side. This box is located between the grid resistances.

Question 23. At what pressure is the governor set to start the compressor?

Answer. One hundred and five pounds.

Question 24. At what pressure is the governor set to stop the compressor?

Answer. One hundred and twenty pounds.

Question 25. Why is there such a difference between the maximum and minimum pressures?

Answer. By having this difference a number of applications of the brake can be made before reducing the main reservoir pressure to the cutting-in point. This gives the compressor a longer rest between periods of operation, thereby allowing it more time to cool.

D.—*The Main Reservoirs.*

Question 26. From the compressors where does the air pressure go?

Answer. To the main reservoirs.

Question 27. Where are the main reservoirs located?

Answer. Under each motor car.

Question 28. How much main-reservoir pressure should be carried?

Answer. One hundred and twenty pounds maximum and 105 pounds minimum.

Question 29. How often should the reservoir be drained?

Answer. Daily.

Question 30. From the main reservoir where does the air go?

Answer. Through the feed valves to the control pipe and thence to the motorman's brake valve.

E.—Safety Valve.

Question 31. What is the purpose of the safety valve? (Fig. 529).

Answer. It prevents overcharging of the brake system in case the electric pump governor fails.

Question 32. Where is it placed?

Answer. In the end of the main reservoir.

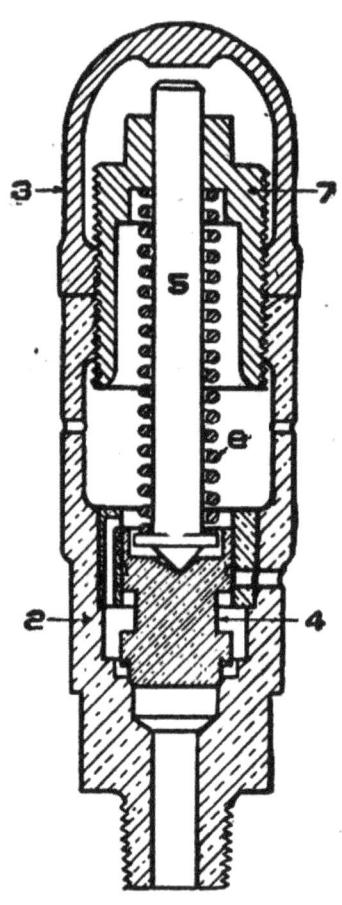

Fig. 529. Safety Valve.

F.—Slide-Valve Feed Valve.

Question 33. From the main reservoir, where does the air go?

Answer. To the slide-valve feed valve (Figs. 530 and 531).

Question 34. Where is it located?

Answer. In the box under the car between the resistances on the motor compressor side, in which the electric pump governor is also located.

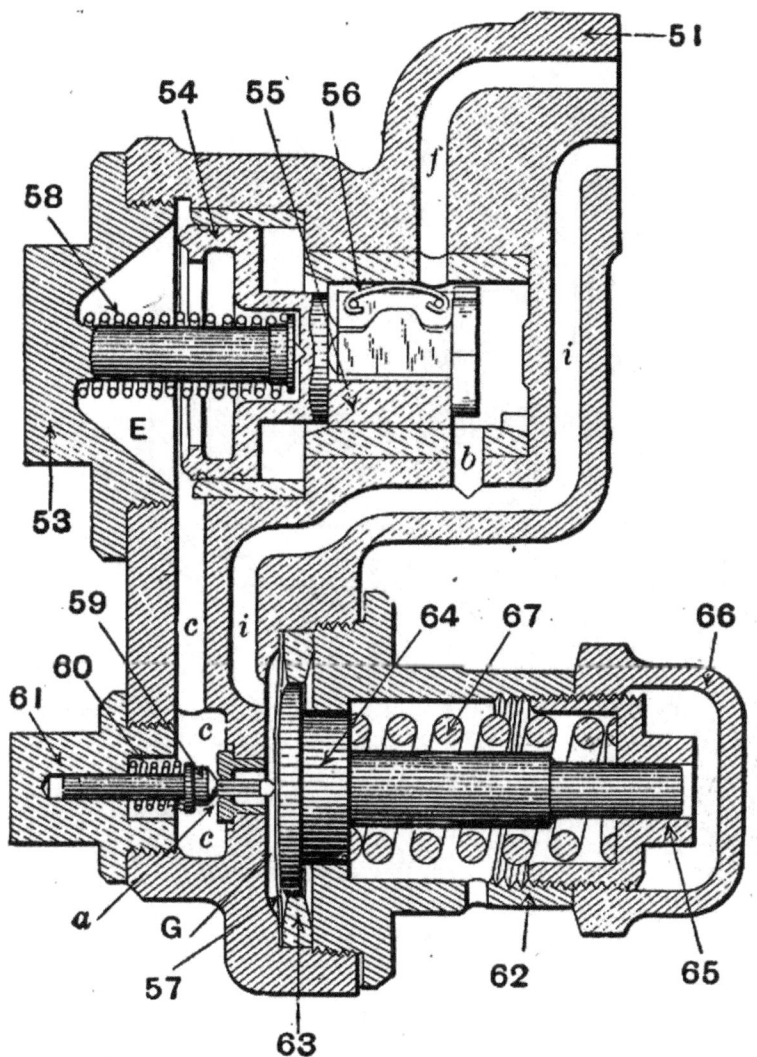

Fig. 530. Slide Valve—Feed Valve Open.

Question 35. What is meant by the slide-valve feed valve?

Answer. It is a device in the pipe from the main reservoir to the control pipe which automatically reduces main-reservoir pressure to a constant control-pipe pressure.

Question 36. What tends to lower the control pipe pressure, thereby causing the slide-valve feed valve to act?

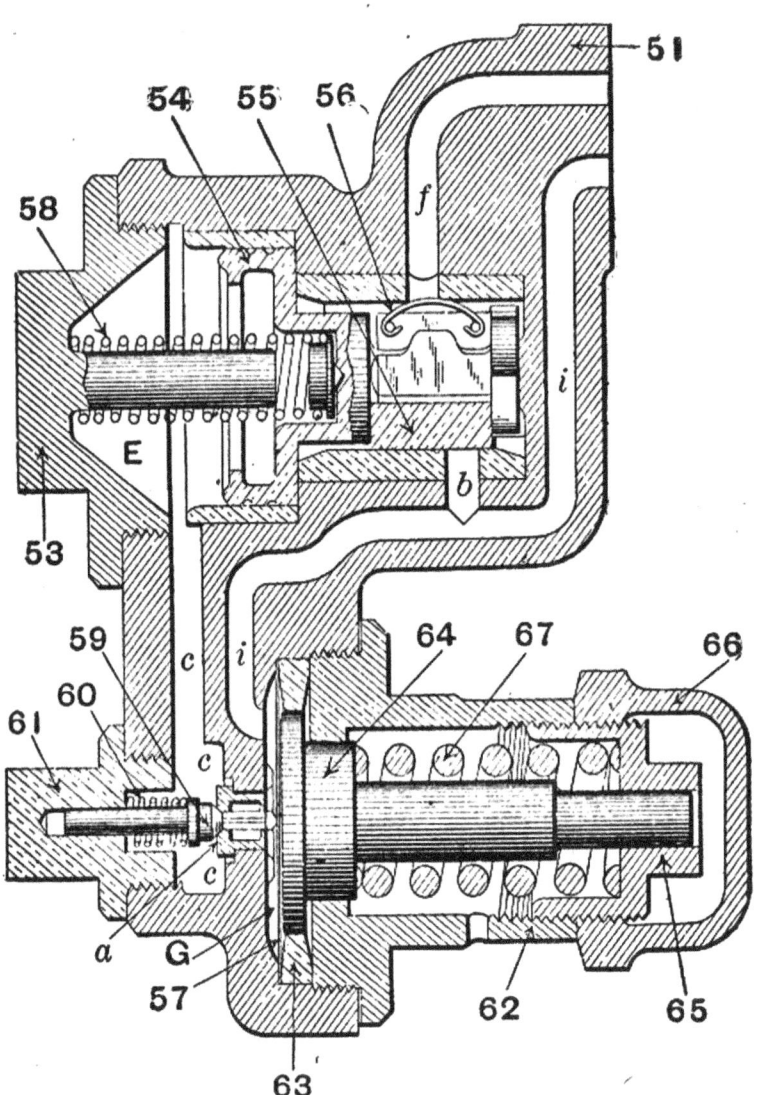

Fig. 531. Slide Valve—Feed Valve Shut.

Answer. Reinstating the brake-pipe pressure at release; recharging the auxiliary reservoirs; maintaining an air pressure of 90 pounds in the system against leakage, when the brakes are not applied.

Question 37. What care should be given this feed valve?

Answer. The piston and its slide valve should occasionally be taken out, all dirt and gum removed from them and the chambers where they work, being careful to leave no lint and to avoid bruising the parts removed. A very small amount of some light lubrication oil (engine oil will do in the absence of a better) should be applied to the piston, the face of the slide valve and the spring on the latter. In replacing the parts move them back and forth a few times to insure that they work freely. Next, remove the regulating valve, carefully clean it, its valve seat and the bushing through which the valves extend, using no metal to do this, so as to avoid scratching, and replace the valve dry.

Question 38. Must the main reservoir be drained to do this?

Answer. No. Close the cut-out cock between the feed valve and the main reservoir.

Question 39. When properly regulated, what can cause pressure to feed too high in the control pipe?

Answer. A leaky slide valve.

Question 40. What will tend to prevent the feed valve properly maintaining the pressure in the control and brake pipes?

Answer. A leaky regulating valve, leakage past cap nuts. If this leakage is great enough the effect will be the same as opening the regulating valve.

Question 41. What will tend to prevent the feed valve from opening promptly?

Answer. The piston becoming heavily coated with a greasy deposit, which prevents rapid equalization of the pressure on both sides of the piston, thus reducing its sensitiveness.

Question 42. Should the feed valve be carefully regulated?

Answer. As there are a number of these valves in a train they should all be regulated alike as nearly as possible, since that valve which is regulated the highest will stay open the longest and furnish the most air, thus making the work imposed on the compressor of that car more than that done by the others.

G.—*Control Pipe.*

Question 43. After leaving the feed valve, where does the air go?

Answer. Through the control pipe to the brake valve that is being operated by the motorman.

Question 44. What is the purpose of the control pipe?

Answer. It is the means of conveying to the brake valve that is being operated by the motorman the supply of air furnished by all the main reservoirs of the train.

Question 45. What are the connections to the control pipe?

Answer. From the feed valve; to the brake valve, and to the triple valve.

Question 46. What pressure is maintained in the control pipe?

Answer. Ninety pounds.

Question 47. Does this pressure vary during the application of the brakes?

Answer. No.

H.—The Motorman's Brake Valve.

Question 48. From the feed valves, where does the air go?

Answer. Through the control pipe to the brake valve being operated by the motorman.

Question 49. From the feed valves to the control pipe to the brake valve is all what pressure?

Answer. Ninety pounds.

Question 50. It passes through the brake-valve into what?

Answer. The brake pipe, and thence through the triple valve to the auxiliary reservoir.

Question 51. What is the purpose of the brake valve?

Answer. To connect the control pipe to the brake pipe; to release the brakes, charge the system and maintain the pressure; to connect the brake pipe through suitable passages to the atmosphere to apply the brakes, and to break all connection between the brake pipe and control pipe or atmosphere; to hold the brakes applied.

Question 52. In what position of the brake valve is there a direct opening from the control pipe to the brake pipe?

Answer. In release or running position.

Question 53. In this position how would the control pipe and brake-pipe pressure stand, comparatively speaking?

Answer. Equal.

Question 54. What is the release or running position to be used for?

Answer. For recharging the brake pipe quickly, so as to insure a prompt and simultaneous release of the brakes; for recharging the auxiliary reservoir, and prevent brake-pipe leakage from setting the brakes.

Question 55. What is the next position of the brake valve and what does it signify?

Answer. Lap position; all ports closed.

Question 56. When is it used?

Answer. When holding the brakes on after an application; or when graduating the release; or when they have been applied by opening a conductor's valve. This position should also be promptly used when train breaks in two; hose becomes uncoupled or bursts; when coupling to air-brake cars or at any time a sudden reduction of brake-pipe pressure takes place when not made by the motorman himself.

Question 57. How should the brake-valve handle be turned to lap?

Answer. Slowly after making a brake-pipe reduction so as to cut off the exhaust gradually, that the head brakes will not be "kicked off" by the air surging forward; quickly when going to the release position, to graduate the release.

Question 58. Why should it be returned quickly when graduating the release?

Answer. Because the longer the brake-valve handle is in the release position the lower the brake-cylinder pressure will reduce. In other words, the reduction of brake-cylinder pressure is governed by the same principle as the increase of brake-cylinder pressure during an application, but oppositely. For example, the increase of brake-cylinder pressure up to the point of equalization is proportional to the decrease of brake-pipe pressure; on the other hand, the decrease of brake-cylinder pressure is proportional to the increase of brake-pipe pressure.

Question 59. What is the next position and its use?

Answer. Service application; should be used for all ordinary stops.

Question 60. How is the air discharged from the brake-pipe in making a service application?

Answer. Through ports in the rotary valve of the brake-valve, and the "quick service" ports of the triple valve. The further the brake-valve handle is moved in the service-application direction the more rapid the discharge of air.

Question 61. Would the blow, or escape, of air from the brake-pipe be longer with a six-car train than with a three-car train, the same reduction in pounds being made in each case?

Answer. Yes; if the brake-valve handle is moved to the same notch in both cases. The capacity of the long brake-pipe being so much greater it would require a larger volume of air to escape to make the same reduction in pounds.

Question 62. How many service-application notches has the brake-valve?

Answer. Two: service and intermediate service.

Question 63. When should they be used?

Answer. With a six-car train the brake-valve handle can be moved to the second service-application opening; but with not more than three or four cars the first or intermediate notch should be used.

Question 64. Why not use the service notch with a three or four-car train?

Answer. Because owing to the comparatively short brake-pipe the reduction of brake-pipe pressure would be sufficiently rapid to cause quick action, resulting in a full emergency application of all the brakes when only partial service application was intended.

Question 65. What is the next position?

Answer. The emergency or quick-action; in this position a large direct opening is made from the brake-pipe to the atmosphere.

Question 66. When is this position to be used, and how?

Answer. Only in case of emergency; and then the handle should be moved directly to that position and allowed to remain there until the train stops or the danger is passed.

I.—Brake-Pipe.

Question 67. What is the purpose of the brake-pipe?

Answer. It is the connection between the brake-valve and the triple valves, auxiliary reservoirs and brake cylinders.

Question 68. What is the difference in pressure between the brake-pipe and the control pipe?

Answer. When the brake-valve handle is in full release there is no difference; during an application of the brakes the brake-pipe pressure is lower than the control pipe, an amount depending on what brake-pipe reduction is made by the motorman.

Question 69. What special devices are placed in the connection from the brake-pipe to the triple valve?

Answer. The double cut-out cock and the branch-pipe air strainer.

Question 70. What is the double cut-out cock?

Answer. It is a cock having two entirely separate passages through it, one tapped at each end for one-inch pipe and the other for three-eighth-inch pipe. The larger one is for the branch pipe from the brake-pipe to the triple valve, and the smaller one for the branch pipe from the control pipe to the triple valve. The turning of the cock handle shuts off communication from both the brake-pipe and the control pipe to the triple valve. (Fig. 532).

Question 71. Why should it be arranged to shut off communication from both the brake-pipe and the control pipe to the triple valve at the same time?

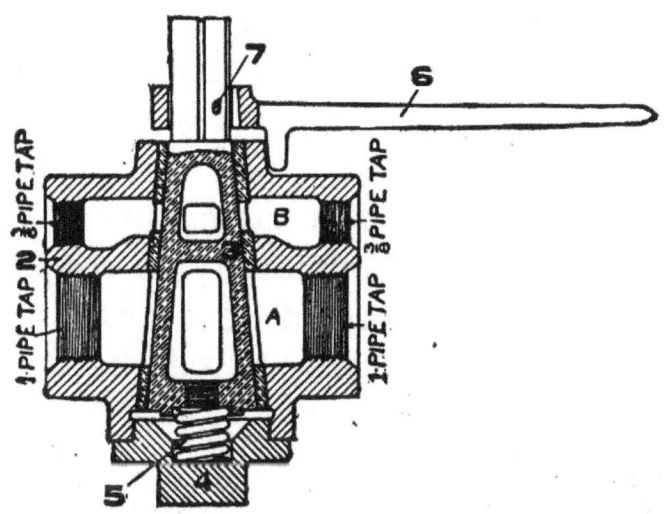

Fig. 532. Double Cut-out Cock.

Answer. It makes it impossible in case anything should happen to the brake cylinder, reservoir or triple valve to cut them out from one of these pipes and not from the other, which might easily occur if a single cock were placed in each of the branch pipes separately.

Question 72. When is the double cut-out cock to be closed?

Answer. Only when the brake apparatus on that car becomes out of order sufficiently to make it inadvisable to use it.

Question 73. What is the purpose of the branch-pipe air strainer?

Answer. It prevents dirt and scale from entering the triple valve, where it might result in cutting the slide valve and piston; or during an emergency application lodge on the emergency valve and hold it open.

Question 74. How are connections made between the cars?

Answer. By hose and couplings.

Question 75. What is it necessary to do when coupling or uncoupling hose connections between cars?

Answer. To uncouple it is necessary first to close the cocks at the end of each car, both for the brake-pipe and the control pipe, before attempting to uncouple the hose. In coupling it is necessary to see that the hose couplings for both the pipe lines are securely made before opening the cocks in each pipe on the cars; open the cocks of the control pipe FIRST, and AFTERWARDS those in the brake-pipe.

Question 76. In making up trains what should be done with the hose couplings at each end of the train?

Answer. They should be fastened up to the dummy couplings which are supported on the end of the car in order to keep any dirt or foreign matter from getting into the couplings and pipes, and to prevent anything lying in the track from striking them. Also, to reduce the wear due to the swinging of the hose when free.

J.—*The Triple Valve.*

Question 77. To what is the brake-pipe connected under the car?

Answer. The triple valve.

Question 78. Where is it located?

Answer. On a bracket in a special box underneath the car, between the grid resistances, on the side opposite to the box containing the electric pump governor and feed valve.

Question 79. Why is it called the triple valve?

Answer. Because of the three distinct operations it performs in response to variations of brake-pipe and auxiliary reservoir pressures. It (1) charges the auxiliary reservoir; (2) applies, and (3) releases the brakes.

K.—*Auxiliary Reservoir.*

Question 80. What is the auxiliary reservoir?

Answer. It is a wrought steel reservoir in which is stored the air for applying the brakes on the car to which it is attached.

Question 81. To what is it connected?

Answer. Its only connection is to the triple valve.

L.—*Brake Cylinder.*

Question 82. What is a brake cylinder?

Answer. It is the cylindrical casting secured to the car framing at the side of the auxiliary reservoir. It is provided with a piston having an air-tight leather packing and a hollow piston rod. This piston, together with the cylinder and the head on the packing leather side, form a chamber into which the compressed air is admitted from the triple valve, and by forcing the piston outwardly applies the brakes to the wheels by means of foundation brake gear and brake shoes to which it is attached by a loose push rod; a head on the other end of the cylindrical casting forms the guide for the piston and a seat for a coiled spring by which the piston is forced back to the inner end of its stroke when the air pressure is exhausted from the brake cylinder by the operation of the triple valve.

M.—Levers.

Question 83. How is the piston rod connected to the brake shoes?

Answer. By a system of levers generally called "foundation brake gear." When the piston is pushed out the levers are so arranged as to draw the shoes up against the wheels. (Fig. 533).

Question 84. What is especially necessary in arranging these levers?

Answer. That the retarding effect on each wheel should be in proportion to the weight of the car bearing upon it and that it should be equal for both wheels on the same axle. When a car weighs equally on all the axles the brake-shoe pressure should be equal on all the wheels.

Question 85. How is the necessary brake-shoe pressure against the wheels determined?

Answer. By the light weight of the car.

Question 86. What proportion of light weight is taken as a basis for the brake-shoe pressures?

Answer. The total pressure of the brake-shoes against the wheels should be 100 per cent of the weight of the motor cars and 90 per cent of the light weight of the trailer cars.

Question 87. What is the general arrangement of foundation brake gear?

Answer. Fig. 533 shows the general arrangement of brake rods and levers and their relation to the brake

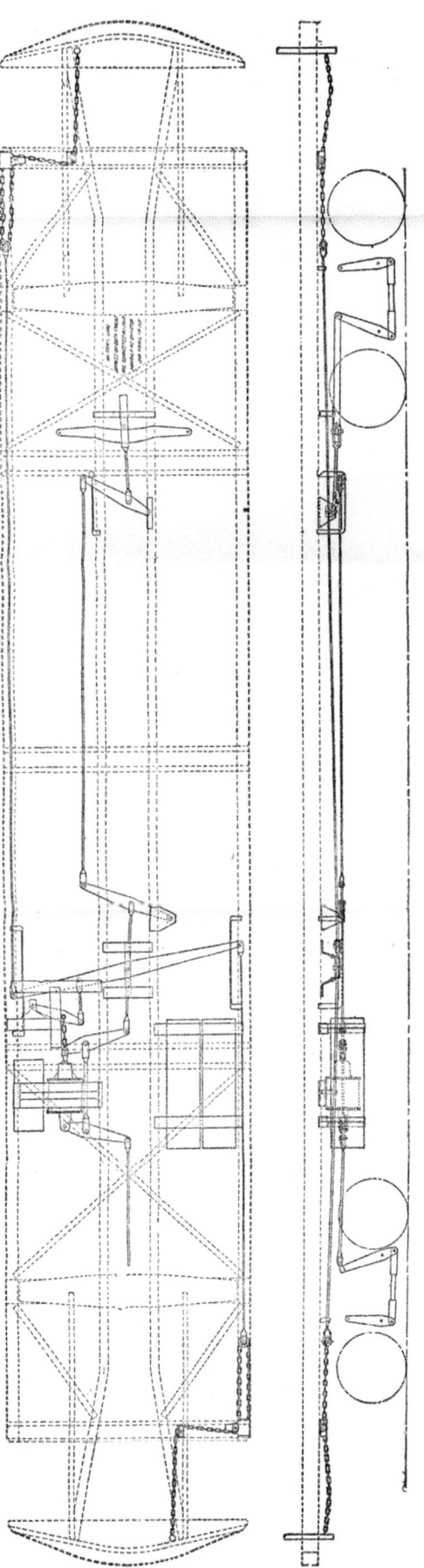

Fig. 533. Arrangement of Brake Levers.

cylinder. To the push rod is connected the PUSH-ROD LEVER. A similar lever, called the CYLINDER LEVER, is attached to the slack adjuster and connected with the push-rod lever by the CYLINDER ROD. Through these two levers the pressure developed in the brake cylinder is carried to each of the trucks. As the piston is pushed out by the air pressure the upper end of the push-rod lever is forced to the left. This transmits the force through the cylinder rod to the cylinder lever, and as a result the lower ends of both levers are drawn together, transmitting a pulling force through both of the TRUCK PULL RODS. The push-rod and cylinder levers are so proportioned that the amount of force transmitted to each truck is in the same proportion as that of the weight of the car resting on each truck. The amount of pull transmitted to each of the truck pull rods is equal.

The truck pull rod engages with the upper end of the LIVE TRUCK LEVER. The lower end of the live truck lever is connected with the lower end of the DEAD TRUCK LEVER by a TIE ROD. These truck levers are proportioned, so that each brake beam gets an amount of pressure in proportion to the weight on that axle.

Question 88. What is the total leverage?

Answer. It is the ratio* of the sum of the pressures on all the wheels of the car to the pressure on the push-rod.

Question 89. How is the hand-brake connected to the lever system?

Answer. Through the HAND-BRAKE ROD, HAND-BRAKE LEVER, HAND-BRAKE CONNEC-

---

*Ratio: The quotient obtained by dividing one into the other is obtained. Suppose it is 7. Then we say the ratio is 7 to 1.

TION, MULTIPLYING LEVER, and the chain which connects the multiplying lever to the push-rod.

Question 90. What is the use of the chain?

Answer. It provides a flexible connection between the hand-brake and power-brake rigging, so that when the power brake is in operation the hand-brake levers do not move, thus reducing the amount of friction to be overcome by the air pressure and also reducing the wear on the hand-brake rods and levers.

Question 91. What is the object of the multiplying lever?

Answer. To increase the power of the hand-brake to that ordinarily obtained by the air pressure.

Question 92. When applying the brakes by hand does the piston in the brake cylinder move out?

Answer. No. The push-rod is loose in the push-rod holder and can be forced out by the piston, but cannot pull the piston out when it is pulled out.

N.—*General Operation.*

Question 93. How should brakes be tested in preparing trains for service?

Answer. First, see that hose coupling cut-out cocks on the head and rear end of train are closed and those between the cars are opened. Next, that all the brake valves are lapped with the exception of the one that is to be used, and this must be placed in release position. Then start the compressors, charge the brake-pipe and auxiliary reservoirs, allowing the compressor to operate until the governor cuts it out. Motorman will then apply brakes by moving handle of brake valve to service-application notch until a reduction of ten pounds has been made in the brake-pipe. Then after placing handle on lap, remove handle, and carrying same, motorman will proceed throughout length of train and see that each cylinder piston of every car has moved out such a distance as to indicate that brakes are properly applied on all cars of the train. The brakes are then to be released from the last cab at end of train. Then again remove handle, and return to other end of train, examining all cylinder pistons. Be careful to see that they have moved back to full release, thus indicating that all brake shoes hang free.

Question 94. In making an application of the brakes for any purpose, except testing brakes or emergency applications, what is the least pressure that should be drawn from the brake-pipe at the first reduction?

Answer. Five pounds.

Question 95. Why not less than this amount?

Answer. Because the reduction might not be sufficient to force the brake piston against the release spring and friction of brake rigging.

Question 96. What reduction of train-line pressure is necessary to fully apply the brakes on service application?

Answer. From eighteen to twenty pounds.

Question 97. Why should the reduction, as stated in the last question, fully apply the brakes?

Answer. Because eighteen to twenty pounds reduction in brake-pipe pressure causes an equalization of auxiliary reservoir and brake-cylinder pressure, thus fully applying the brakes. A further reduction in the brake-pipe is simply a waste of air.

Question 98. What is the possible result of this waste of air?

Answer. The brakes are slower in releasing, fail to

release simultaneously, cause a shock to the train upon stopping, and seriously overtax the compressor.

Question 99. How many applications should be made in making the ordinary service stop?

Answer. As a general rule, one.

Question 100. What is meant by one application?

Answer. From the time the brakes are applied until they are fully released, no matter how many brake-pipe reductions or graduated releases, is one application; after the brakes have been fully released, and are reapplied, is a second application.

Question 101. How is the application to be made for an ordinary service stop?

Answer. A fifteen to eighteen-pound brake-pipe reduction should be made obtaining a full cylinder pressure at once, if at fair speed and gradually reducing same as the speed of the train decreases.

Question 102. Should this plan of operation invariably be followed?

Answer. No. If the train is drifting or running at very low speed it is not necessary to have such a high cylinder pressure.

Question 103. Why is it that the cylinder pressure should be gradually released as the speed of the train decreases?

Answer. Because the friction between the brake-shoes and the wheels is less for high speed than for low, having the same pressure in both cases. Consequently, if maximum cylinder pressure is used at a high speed it is necessary to decrease it as the speed decreases; also to make stop in less time and to avoid rough stops; also stops can be made much more accurately; otherwise, skidding of the wheels would be likely to follow at low speeds.

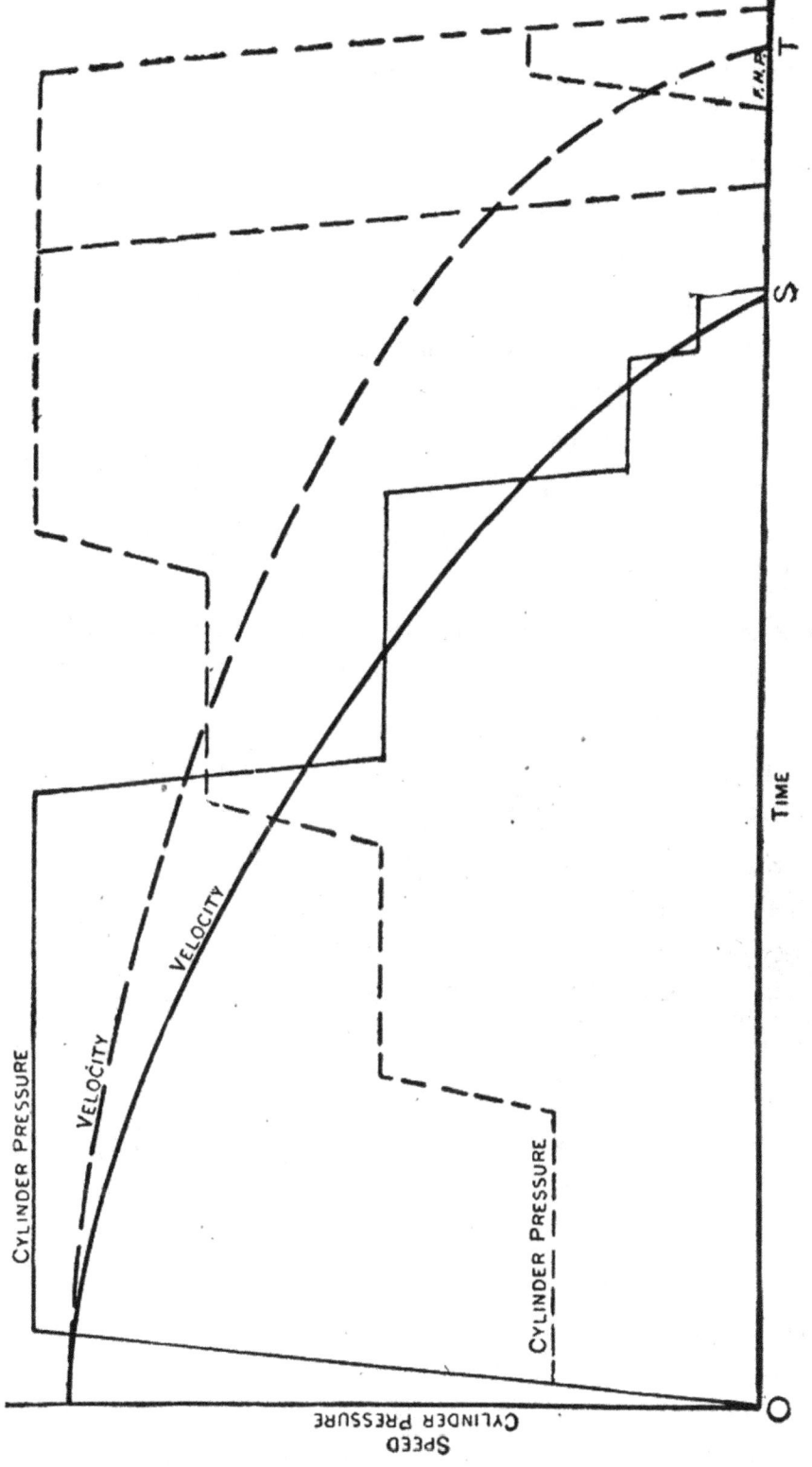

Fig. 534. Diagram of Stops.

Question 104. What would be the result if the cylinder pressure should be gradually increased during the application?

Answer. Pressure would be least when the speed was greatest, and, therefore, have a much smaller retarding effect than it ought to; and would be greatest when the speed was considerably reduced, thereby making the skidding of the wheels very probable and bring the train to a stop with a sudden jerk.

Fig. 534 illustrates the proper and improper method of handling the brakes in a service application. The brakes are applied at O and the train comes to a stop at S or T. The curve shows the decreasing velocity after the brakes are applied. The diagram shows the variations of cylinder pressure during the stop. The full lines show the proper method of handling, and the dotted lines the improper. It will be seen by the dotted diagram and curve that the retardation of the train during the first part of the stop is comparatively small. The motorman is afraid to put on his brakes, and as a result applies them little by little, till at the end of a stop he has full cylinder pressure, and the retardation of the train is very sudden and dangerous. Often motormen will find, when using such a method, that he has to make full release of the brakes and then reapply, as shown on the diagram, in order to keep the train from stopping short of the station. This causes jerks and uneven motion throughout the train and a great waste of air, resulting in overworking the compressor and causing unnecessary wear on the train apparatus.

On the other hand, if the motorman throws full pressure at once into the cylinder the retardation during the first part of the stop is much greater, and as the speed gradually decreases, the motorman gradually releases the cylinder pressure in such a way as to keep the retardation of the train at a maximum. The amount gained in retardation during the first part of the stop by the proper method of braking makes the time required for the entire stop much less than in the other case, the time saved being represented by the distances S T.

Question 105. What other reason is there besides making quicker stops for using the proper method of braking outlined above?

Answer. By gradually releasing the brakes the auxiliary reservoirs are partially recharged at each partial release, till when the train comes to a stop the auxiliary reservoirs are almost completely recharged. In the other case, when the train comes to a standstill the brake-pipe pressure is the least of any time during the stop, so that the entire system has to be completely recharged after the train comes to a standstill. This means, in the latter case, more time is required for the brake system to be fully prepared for subsequent applications. Also with proper method start can be made quickly if desired, as there is little, if any, cylinder pressure remaining. This is also true if grade necessitates holding brake on during stop, as it can be graduated almost off.

Question 106. In making partial release during a brake application, how should the brake valve be handled?

Answer. It should be moved to the release position for a moment and immediately returned to lap.

Question 107. To make a complete release of brakes, how should the brake-valve be handled?

Answer. It should be moved to the full release position and allowed to remain there.

Question 108. If brakes release after a service-application, where should cause be looked for?

Answer. Examine brake valves in train until trouble is located. Either a brake-valve has not been fully lapped or has a leaking rotary valve.

Question 109. In case of emergency, when it is essential to stop the train in the shortest possible distance, how should the brake-valve be handled?

Answer. The handle should be thrown to the full emergency position and left there until the train has come to a stop, or the danger is passed.

Question 110. Would it not be better to return the handle to lap position after a quick reduction has been made? The object to save brake-pipe pressure to assist in releasing?

Answer. No. The first consideration in a case of emergency is to stop and to do that as quickly and surely as possible. The handle should be left in emergency position.

Question 111. If the motorman has the brake partially applied with service application and should be suddenly flagged, what should he do?

Answer. Put the valve handle in the emergency position and leave it there until stopped, the same as before.

Question 112. Would he get quick action under those circumstances?

Answer. That depends on the amount of reduction made in service and the length of the piston travel. With only a slight reduction he would get partial quick action, but would not get full quick-action brake-cylinder pressure.

Question 113. Could anything be gained by placing

the handle in release position for a moment before going to emergency position?

Answer. No; it would be dangerous to do so. Such an action would release the brakes when they were most needed and would make them slower to apply.

Question 114. If the motorman had the brakes applied with a thirteen to fifteen-pound service application, and was flagged, would it be policy for him to put the brake-valve in the emergency position?

Answer. Yes; if it were a case of emergency. Possibly some of the brakes have partially leaked off; the emergency application would set them fully.

Question 115. In the case of emergency should a motorman reverse his motors?

Answer. Yes. As a last resort to prevent collision or to save life he may reverse his motors. Handle on master controller should be thrown into opposite direction to the first, or switching notch, which notch is usually found to have the greatest retarding effect. Motors may also be reversed in the event of brakes being inoperative, but in ordinary service conditions motormen must never reverse motors.

Question 116. In case the brakes are applied suddenly from the train, what should the motorman do?

Answer. Place the brake-valve handle on lap position until a signal is given to release the brakes.

Question 117. Why is this done?

Answer. To maintain the main reservoir pressure and to prevent its escape, thereby providing for a prompt release of the brakes.

Question 118. How should the conductor's valve be operated when necessary?

Answer. It should be pulled wide open and allowed to

remain or be held in that position until the train stops, and then before leaving it the valve should be closed.

All cars have a conductor's valve which, when opened, remains in that position until closed by hand.

Question 119. Why is it necessary to leave the conductor's valve open until the train has stopped, if it is used?

Answer. Because if it is closed and the motorman fails to place the brake-valve on lap position the brakes will release.

Question 120. What does this valve do when it is open?

Answer. It makes a direct opening from the brake-pipe to the atmosphere, the same as when the brake-valve is placed in the emergency position.

Question 121. Can the brakes be released with the conductor's valve?

Answer. No. It must be remembered that to release brakes it is necessary to either put air into the brake-pipe or take it out of the auxiliary reservoirs. The conductor's valve will not do either of these.

Question 122. Should the brake apply suddenly, without the aid of the motorman or train crew, what should be done?

Answer. Place the brake-valve handle on the lap position as before.

Question 123. What would be the probable cause of this?

Answer. Either a burst hose, burst brake-pipe, or train breaking in two.

Question 124. In the event of a burst brake-pipe hose, what should be done?

Answer. Close the flat handled cut-out cock imme-

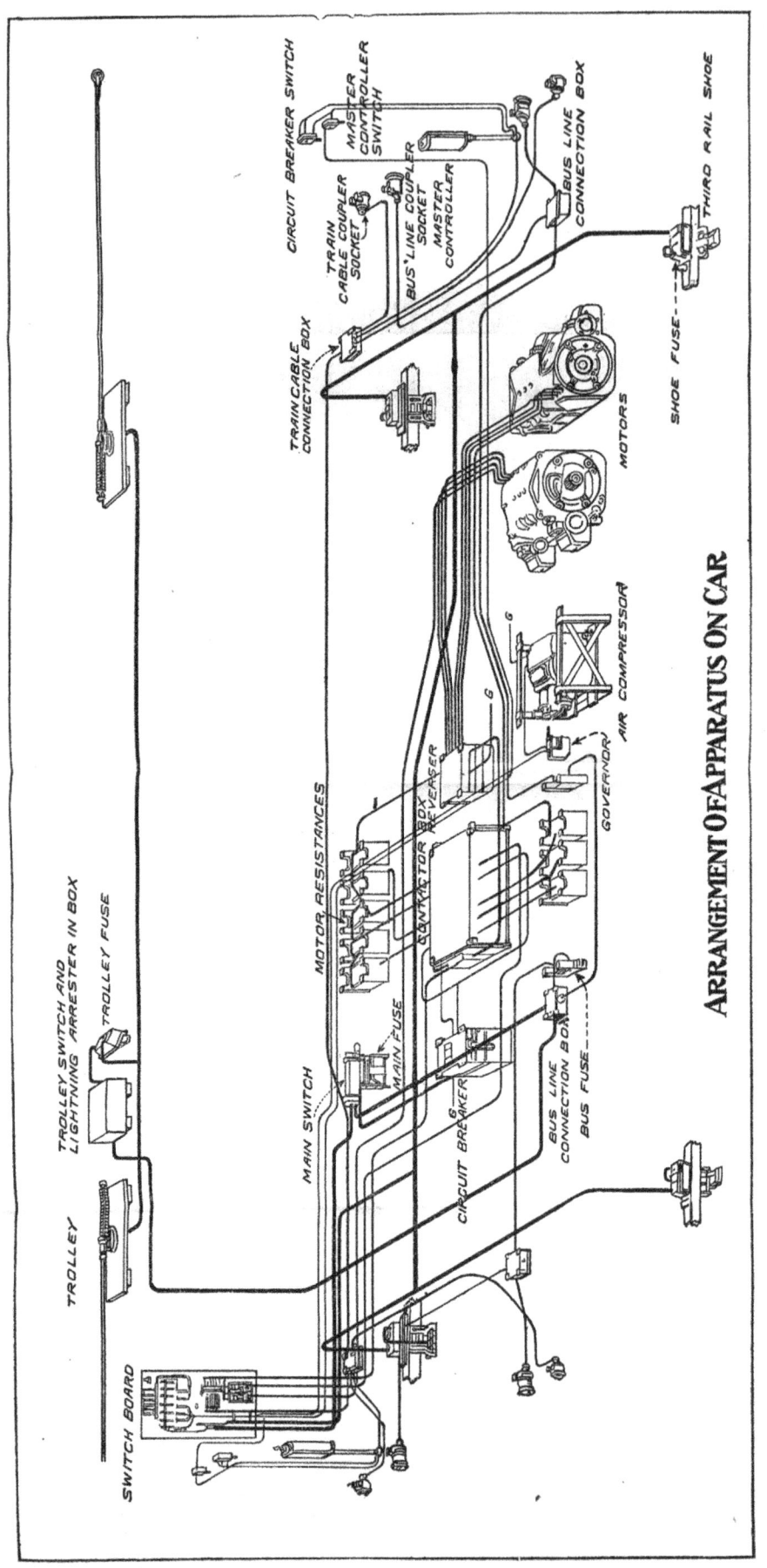

Fig. 535. Pennsylvania Equipment.

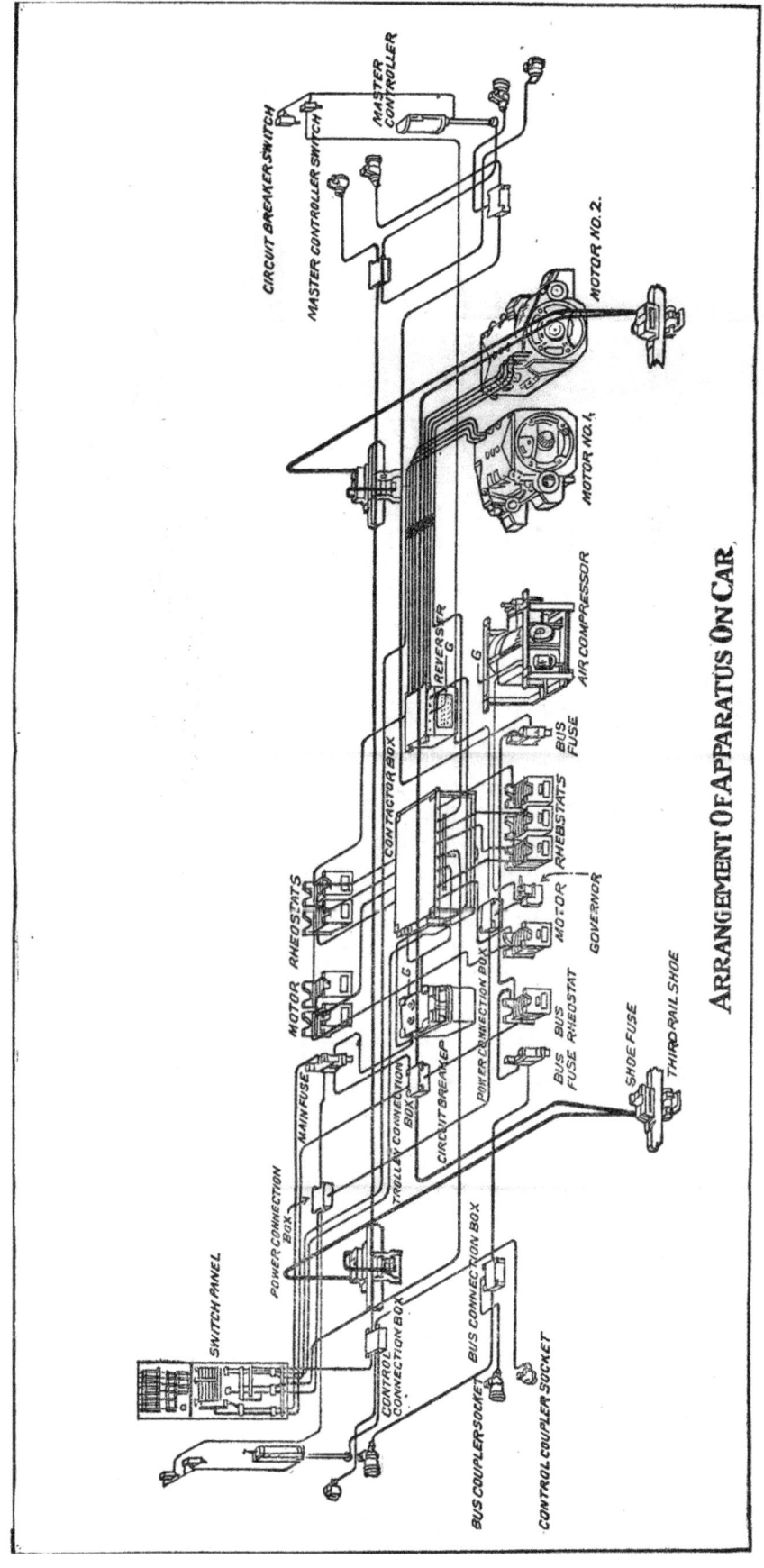

Fig. 536. New York Central Equipment.

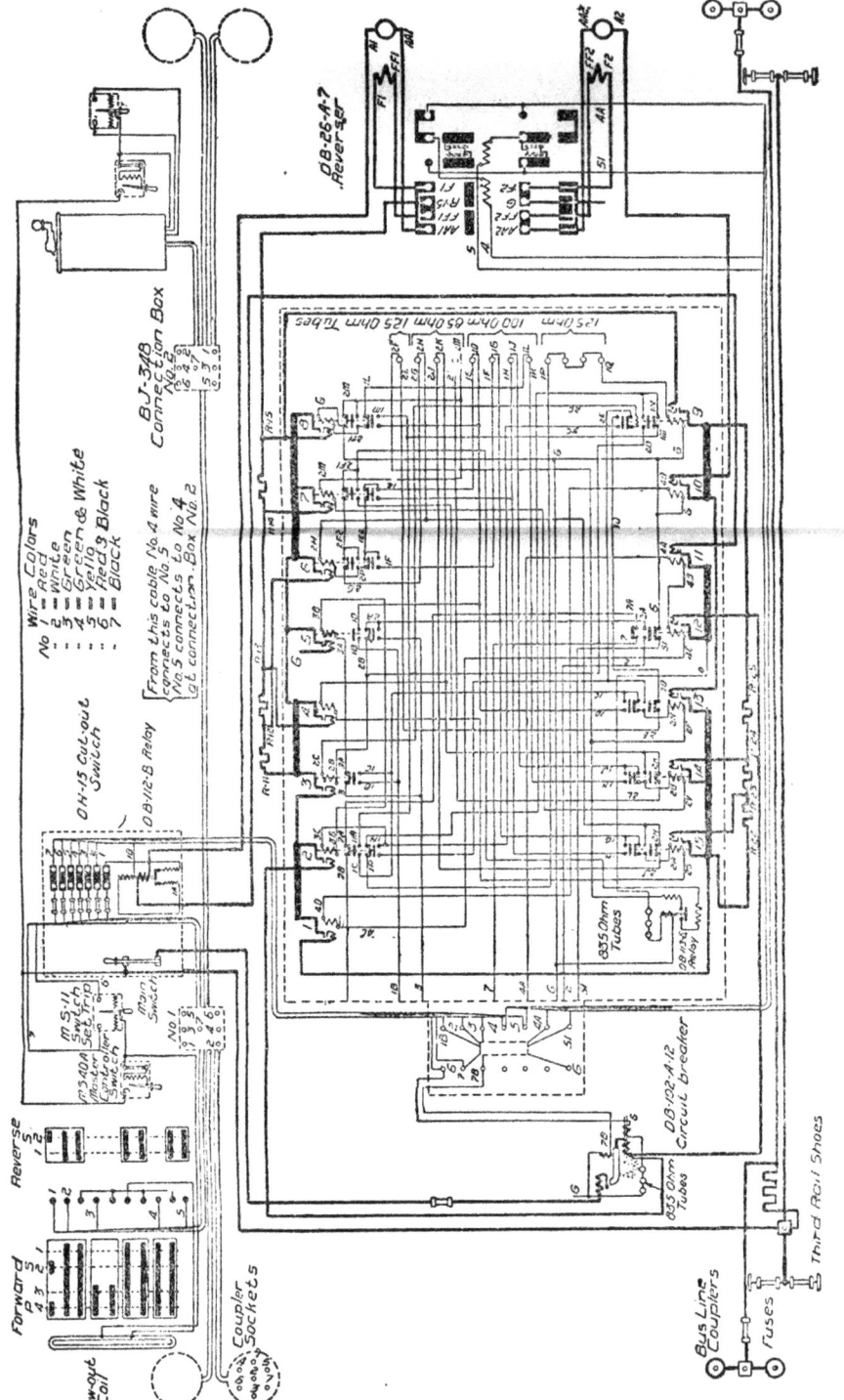

Fig. 537. Wiring Diagram. New York Central Motor Car.

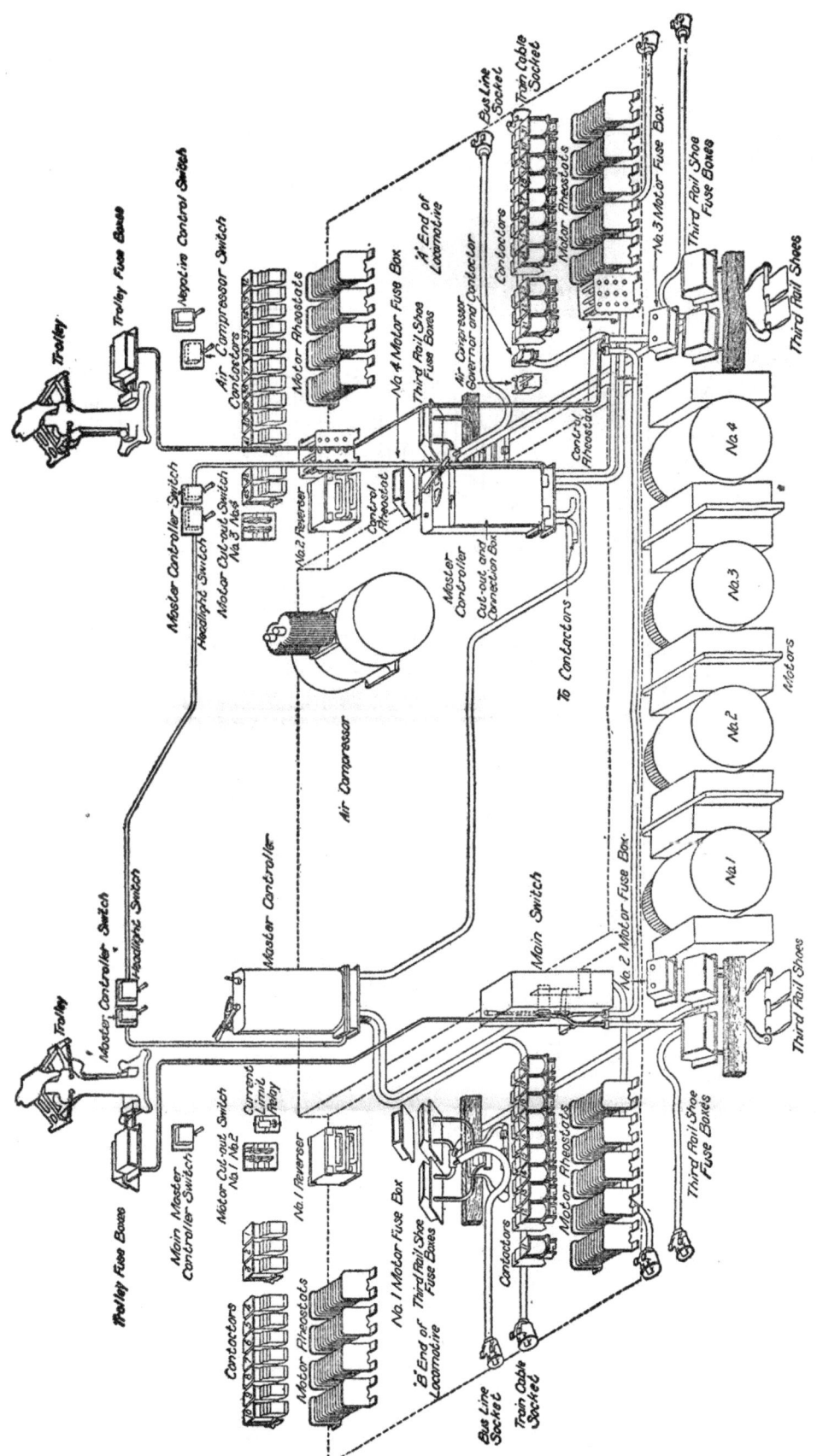

Fig. 538. Arrangement of Apparatus on Locomotive.

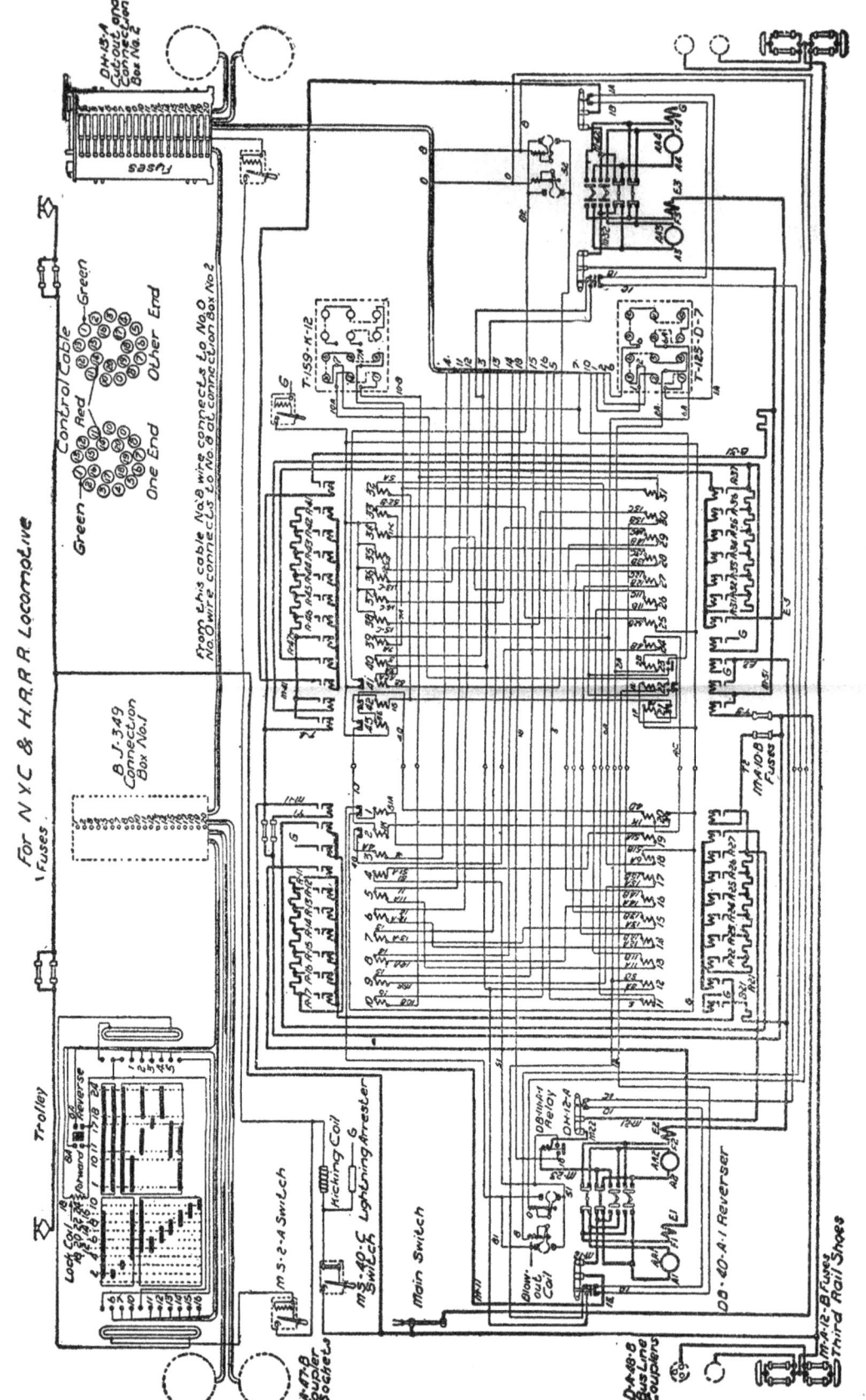

Fig. 539. Wiring Diagram. New York Central Locomotive.

diately ahead of the burst hose and release the brakes back of the burst hose by closing the double cut-out cocks and opening the bleed cocks in the auxiliary reservoirs, leaving them open. The brakes ahead of the fractured hose can be released, provided the brake is still operative upon at least half of the cars in the train. If the motorman has control of less than half of the brakes of the train, the hand brakes on the cut-out cars must be applied to assist in controlling the train.

Question 125. In the event of a control-pipe hose bursting, what should be done?

Answer. Close the round-handled cut-out cocks immediately ahead and behind of the disabled hose, the brakes may then be operated in the usual manner until the train reaches the terminal, when the fractured hose must be replaced.

Question 126. Should the cross-over pipe connecting the brake-pipe and triple valve be broken, what should be done?

Answer. If the break is between the double cut-out cock and the triple valve, the double cut-out cock should be closed and the release valve opened under the disabled car. If the pipe is broken between the double cut-out cock and the brake-pipe, the flat-handled cut-out cock on the front end of the disabled car should be closed, release valves in all auxiliary reservoirs behind disabled car, as well as on that car opened, and the brakes operated the same as with the burst hose.

Question 127. If the brake pipe should be broken or burst, what should be done?

Answer. Close the cut-out cock on the front end of the car and operate brakes as per Answer 124.

Question 128. In setting off cars, what should be done?

Answer. The cut-out cocks should be closed first and the hose parted by hand and hung up properly.

Question 129. Should the hand-brake be set before releasing the air-brake?

Answer. No.

Question 130. What is the proper way to release a brake with a bleed cock?

Answer. The bleed cock should be held open until the exhaust air commences to escape from the triple valve; it should then be closed, as, if it is held open longer, it results in waste of air and has a tendency to set the other brakes.

Question 131. When it is permissible to cut out brakes on cars?

Answer. Only when they are in such condition to render it impossible to operate the brakes on such cars.

Question 132. Are small leaks sufficient cause for cutting out cars?

Answer. No.

In Fig. 535 is given the arrangement of the apparatus on a motor car of the West Jersey and Seashore R. R. Fig. 536 shows a slightly different arrangement of the apparatus on the motor cars of the New York Central.

The wiring of the apparatus is the same in both roads, and is proven by Fig. 537.

The arrangement of apparatus on the locomotives of the New York Central is shown by Fig. 538, and the wiring diagram in Fig. 539.

GENERAL RULES.

1. Employes whose duties are prescribed by these rules must provide themselves with a copy.

2. In addition to these rules, Bulletin Orders and Time Tables will be issued from time to time containing special instructions, as necessity demands. Such special instructions shall be fully observed while in effect, whether in conflict with these rules or not.

3. Employes must be conversant with and obey the rules and special instructions. If in doubt as to their meaning, they must apply to proper authority for an explanation.

4. Employes must pass the required examinations.

5. All persons authorized to transact business or engaged in performing any service at stations or on trains are subject to the rules governing the employes of the Company.

6. Employes must render every assistance in their power in carrying out the rules and special instructions.

7. Any violation of the rules or special instructions must be reported.

8. The use of intoxicants by employes while on duty, or the frequenting of places where they are sold, is prohibited.

9. Smoking by employes when on duty in or about passenger stations, or on passenger cars, is prohibited.

10. Employes on duty must wear the prescribed badge and uniform, and be neat in appearance.

11. Persons authorized to transact business at stations or on trains must be orderly and avoid annoyance to passengers.

12. In case of danger to the Company's property, employes must unite to protect it.

13. Employes are required to look after their own safety, and to exercise the utmost caution to avoid injury to fellow employes.

14. All forms of gambling, including bets and raffles, are forbidden upon the premises of the Company.

15. Reading newspapers, letters, or other printed or written matter, when on duty, except to consult the Rules and Time Tables, is prohibited.

16. Employes, when passengers on a train, are forbidden from occupying seats to the exclusion of other passengers.

17. All articles furnished by the Company for use of employes must, on leaving the service, be returned to the proper officer. The right is reserved to withhold from wages due the value of such articles lost or that are not surrendered on leaving the service.

17a. Employes whose duties require its use will be furnished a switch key, for which they will be required to give receipt, which will be filed in the Office of the Superintendent. Upon leaving the service of the Company, such receipt will be returned upon delivery of key.

18. It is the duty of all employes of the Company to report to the respective heads of their department anything coming under their notice which appears to them to affect the safe and proper working of the Railroad, or which may affect the interest of the Company in any way, or the convenience and accommodation of the public.

19. In all matters not fully covered by these Rules and

Regulations, employes must bear in mind that they are engaged in a public service in which they are constantly called upon to exercise great patience, forbearance, and self control. Politeness and courtesy continually practiced by employes will prevent controversy and complaint, and greatly benefit the service.

20. Employes of every grade will be considered in the line of promotion, dependent therefor upon the faithful discharge of duty, and the qualifications and capacity for assuming increased responsibilities.

21. No person defective in hearing, sight, or color perception, shall be employed in any branch of the service involving the use of signals or the movement of cars and trains. All persons thus employed will be required to pass an examination by one of the authorized examiners for this company as to their hearing, sight, and ability to distinguish colors.

22. Boisterous, profane, or vulgar language by employes, around or on the premises of the Company, is strictly forbidden. Civil, gentlemanly, and quiet deportment toward fellow employes, as well as patrons of the road is required of all employes.

23. Any employe finding any article in cars or stations of this Company will deposit same with the Dispatcher, noting on an envelope attached to the article his name, the number of car, or the name of the station where found, date and time of finding. Articles remaining unclaimed after three months will be returned to the finder.

24. If an employe should be disabled by sickness or other cause, the right to claim compensation will not be recognized. An allowance, if made, will be a gratuity justified by the circumstances of the case and the employe's good conduct.

25. Employes will be liable to discipline or dismissal for incompetency, insubordination, disobedience of orders, negligence, or misconduct. A record of each employe will be kept in the Superintendent's Office.

26. No employe will be allowed to absent himself from duty without special permission from the head of the department in which he is employed, nor will any employe be allowed to engage a substitute to perform his duties.

27. The assignment or attaching of an employe's wages by garnishee process or proceedings in aid of execution will be considered sufficient cause for his dismissal, unless a satisfactory explanation is given.

28. When a person is discharged from the Company's service he will not be re-employed without the consent of the officer who dismissed him, or that of the head of the department from which he was discharged.

DEFINITIONS.

TRAIN—A motor or more than one motor coupled with or without cars, displaying Markers.

REGULAR TRAIN—A train represented on the Time Table. It may consist of sections.

SECTION—One of two or more trains running on the same schedule displaying signals, or for which signals are displayed.

EXTRA TRAIN—A train not represented on the Time Table. It may be designated as

EXTRA—For any extra train, except work extra.

WORK EXTRA—For work train extra.

SUPERIOR TRAIN—A train having precedence over other trains. A train may be made superior to another train by *right, class,* or *direction.*

Right—Is conferred by Train Order; Class and Direction by Time Table.

Right is superior to Class or Direction. Direction is superior as between trains of the same class.

Train of Superior Right—A train given precedence by Train Order.

Train of Superior Class—A train given precedence by a Time Table.

Train of Superior Direction—A train given precedence in the direction specified in the Time Table as between trains of the same class.

Time Table—The authority for the movement of regular trains subject to the rules. It contains the classified schedules of trains with special instructions relating thereto.

Schedule—That part of a Time Table which prescribes the class, direction, number, and movement of a regular train.

Main Track—A principal track upon which trains are operated by Time Table, Train Orders, or Block Signals.

Single Track—A main track upon which trains are operated in both directions.

Double Track—Two main tracks, upon one of which the current of traffic is in a specified direction, and upon the other in the opposite direction.

Current of Traffic—The direction in which trains will move on a main track, under the Rules.

Station—A place designated on the Time Table by name, at which a train may stop for traffic; or to enter or leave the main track; or from which fixed signals are operated.

SIDING—A track auxiliary to a main track for meeting or passing trains.

MEETING POINT—A place where meeting or opposing trains, i. e., trains moving in opposite directions, meet by schedule or Train Order.

PASSING POINT—A place where trains moving in the same direction pass by schedule or Train Order.

FIXED SIGNAL—A signal of fixed location, indicating a condition affecting the movement of a train.

"Fixed Signals" cover such signals as whistle boards, slow boards, stop boards, yard limits, switch, block, semaphore, or other means for indicating whistle, stop, caution, or proceed.

YARD—A system of tracks within defined limits provided for the making up of trains, storing of cars, and other purposes, over which movements not authorized by Time Table or by Train Order may be made, subject to prescribed signals and regulations.

YARD MOTOR—A motor or motors consigned to yard service and working within yard limits.

PILOT—A person assigned to a train when the motorman or conductor, or both, are not fully acquainted with the physical characteristics, or running rules of a road, or portion of a road over which the train is to be moved.

AUTOMATIC BLOCK SYSTEM—A block system in which the signals are operated by electric, pneumatic, or other agency actuated by a train, or by certain conditions affecting the use of a block.

HOME SIGNAL—A fixed signal controlling the entrance to a block governing movements over switches at interlockings.

DISTANT SIGNAL—A fixed signal used in connection with home signals to regulate the approach thereto.

ADVANCE SIGNAL—A fixed signal placed in advance of the home signal or switches at an interlocking to control the entrance to the block ahead.

DWARF SIGNAL—A low fixed signal.

POT SIGNAL—A revolving signal.

TRAIN RULES.

STANDARD TIME.

30. Standard Time obtained from Washington (D. C.). Observatory will be telegraphed to the Dispatcher's Office at 11.00 A. M. week days and at 10.00 A. M. on Sundays.

31. Watches that have been examined and certified to by a designated inspector must be used by Dispatchers, Station Masters, Conductors, Motormen, Flagmen, Yardmen, and Section Foremen.

(FORM OF CERTIFICATE.)

32. This is to certify that on .... 19..
the watch of .... employed
as .... was examined by me.

It is correct and reliable, and in my judgment will, with proper care, run within a variation of thirty seconds per week.

Name of Maker.................Brand...........
No. of Movement..........Metal of Case.........
Stem or Key Winding............................
Open or Hunting Case...........................

Old or New.....................................
If rejected, state reasons........................
      Signed......................
            Watch Inspector.
Address ....

33. Watches of Conductors and Motormen must be compared before starting on each portion of their day's run with a Standard Clock, and register their names, the time at which they compared their watches, and note any variation on the daily registration sheet.

34. If the variation be in excess of thirty (30) seconds per week, they must report the fact immediately to the Superintendent.

35. The clock in the Dispatcher's Office at Wheaton and such others as may be hereafter designated, are Standard Clocks.

36. When station clocks are provided, Station Agents must see that they show correct time; but Trainmen must not take time from such clocks unless they are designated as Standard Clocks.

TIME TABLES.

37. See Definitions, page 245.

38. Copies of Time Tables will be furnished to Trainmen, Yard and Road Masters, and all others concerned. Receipt of same must be acknowledged to the Superintendent on the prescribed form before the Time Table takes effect. These receipts will be filed in the Superintendent's Office. Proposed change of Time Table will be bulletined at least twenty-four (24) hours in advance.

39. Each Time Table, from the moment it takes effect, supersedes the preceding Time Table and all special instructions relating thereto.

40. A train of the preceding Time Table thereupon loses both right and class, and can thereafter proceed only by Train Order.

41. Not more than two times are given for a train at any station; where one is given, it is, unless otherwise indicated, the leaving time; where two, they are the arriving and the leaving times.

42. Unless otherwise indicated, the time applies to the switch; where there is no switch, it applies to the place from which fixed signals are operated; where there is neither siding nor fixed signals, it applies to the place where traffic is received or discharged.

43. Schedule meeting or passing points are indicated by figures in full-faced type.

44. Both the arriving and leaving times of a train are in full-faced type when both are meeting or passing times when one or more trains are to meet or pass it between those times.

45. Attention is called to meeting and passing points by small figures showing numbers of trains to be met or passed.

SIGNAL RULES.

46. Employes whose duties may require them to give signals, must provide themselves with the proper appliances, keep them in good order, and ready for immediate use.

47. Flags of the prescribed color must be used by day, and lamps of the prescribed color by night.

48. Night signals are to be displayed from sunset to sunrise. When weather or other conditions obscure day signals, night signals must be used in addition.

VISIBLE SIGNALS.

49.   MANNER OF USING.   INDICATION.

(a) Swung across the track.   } Stop.

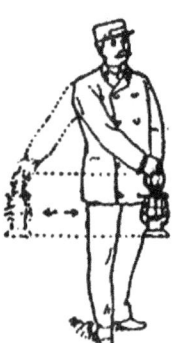

(b) Raised and lowered vertically. } Go ahead.

(c) Swung vertically in a circle across the track when the train is standing. } Back

TRAIN SIGNALS 251

(d) Swung vertically in a circle at arm's length across the track, when the train is running. } Train has parted.

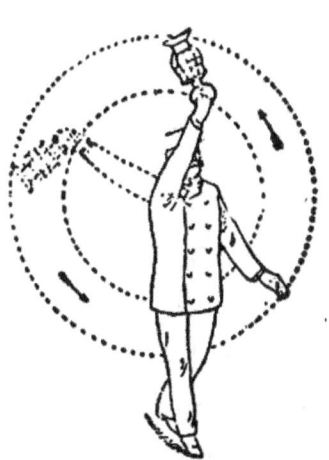

(e) Swung horizontally in a circle, when the train is standing. } Apply air brakes.

(f) Held at arm's length above the head, when train is standing. } Release air brakes.

50. Any object waved violently by anyone on or near the track is a signal to stop.

AUDIBLE SIGNALS.

MOTOR WHISTLE SIGNALS.

51. (Note)—The signals prescribed are illustrated by "o" for short sounds; "——" for longer sounds. The sound of the whistle should be distinct, with intensity and duration proportionate to the distance signal is to be conveyed.

52. SOUND.   INDICATION.

(a) o — Stop. Apply brakes.
(b) ——·—— — Release brakes.
(c) —— o o o — Flagman go back and protect rear of train.
(d) —— —— —— —— — Flagman return from west.
(e) —— —— —— —— —— — Flagman return from east.
(f) —— —— —— — When running, train parted; to be repeated until answered by the signal prescribed by Rule 49-D.
(g) o o — Answer to any signal not otherwise provided for.
(h) o o o — When train is standing, back.
(j) o o o o — Call for signals.
(k) —— o o — To call the attention of the trains of the same or inferior class to signals displayed for a following section.
(l) —— —— o o — Approaching public crossings at grade.

(m) ——————— Approaching stations, junctions, and railroad crossings at grade.

53. A succession of short sounds of the whistle is an alarm for persons or cattle on the track, and calls the attention of trainmen to danger ahead.

54. The explosion of one torpedo is a signal to stop; the explosion of two, not more than 100 feet apart, is a signal to reduce speed, and look out for a stop signal.

55. A fusee on or near the track burning red must not be passed until burned out. When burning green it is a caution signal.

BELL CORD SIGNALS.

CONDUCTOR TO MOTORMAN.

56. SOUND.   INDICATION.

(a) Two bells.   When train is standing, start.

(b) One bell.   When train is running, stop at next station.

(c) Three bells.   When train is standing, back the train.

(d) Three bells.   When train is running, stop at once—emergency.

(e) Four bells.   When train is running, reduce speed.

(f) Five bells.   When train is standing, call in flagman.

MOTORMAN TO CONDUCTOR.

57.

SOUND.	INDICATION.
(a) One bell.	Come to cab.
(b) Two bells.	Watch trolley.
(c) Three bells.	By motorman is signal to conductor that he wishes to back train and must be answered by Conductor before train is backed.
(d) Four bells.	Set rear brakes.
(e) Five bells.	Pull trolley down to roof.

TRAIN SIGNALS.

58. An electric headlight will be displayed to the front of every train by night, but the headlight must be concealed when a train turns out to meet another, and has stopped clear of the main track, or is standing to meet trains at the end of double track, or at junctions, but the opposing train must not assume track is clear until given proper signal with hand lantern by crew of such standing train.

59. When a headlight is out of order and will not light and another can not be procured, a white light must be displayed in the exact place of the headlight.

60. Yard motors will display the headlight to the front and rear by night. When not provided with a headlight at the rear, two white lights must be displayed. Yard motors will not display markers.

61. The following signals will be displayed, one on each side of the rear of every train, as markers, to indi-

cate the rear of the train: By day, two red flags; by night, at least two red lights.

62. All sections of a train, except the last, will display one on each side of the front of the motor, in places provided for that purpose: By day, two green flags; by night, two green lights.

63. Extra trains will display, one on each side of the front of the motor, in places provided for that purpose: By day, two white flags, and by night, two white lights.

64. When two or more motors are coupled, the leading motor only shall display signals as prescribed by Rule 62.

65. One flag or light displayed, where in Rules 61-62-63 two or prescribed, will indicate the same as two; but the proper display of all train signals is required.

66. When cars are pushed by motor (except when shifting or making up trains in yards), a white light must be displayed on the front of the leading car by night.

67. A blue flag by day and a blue light by night, displayed at one or both ends of a motor car, or train, indicates that workmen are under or about it. When thus protected it must not be coupled or moved. Workmen will display the blue signals and the same workmen are alone authorized to remove them. Other cars must not be placed on the same track so as to intercept the view of the blue signals without first notifying the workmen.

USE OF SIGNALS.

68. A signal imperfectly displayed, or the absence of a signal at a place where a signal is usually shown, must be regarded as a stop signal, and the fact reported to the Superintendent.

69. The combined green and white signal is to be used to stop a train only at the flag stations indicated on the schedule of that train. When it is necessary to stop a train at a point that is not a flag station for that train, a red signal must be used.

70. When a signal (except a fixed signal) is given to stop a train, it must be acknowledged as prescribed in Rule 52-G.

71. The foot gong must be rung or whistle sounded when a motor is about to move.

72. The regular crossing whistle signal must be sounded on approaching all public road crossings at grade and at all whistling posts.

73. The unnecessary use of either the whistle or foot gong is prohibited. They will be used as prescribed by rule or law, or to prevent accident.

74. Watchmen stationed at public road and street crossings must use red signals only when necessary to stop trains.

CLASSIFICATION OF TRAINS.

75. Trains of the first class are superior to those of the second; trains of the second class are superior to those of the third; and so on. Extra trains are inferior to regular trains.

76. Trains of the same class, in either direction, have no superior rights over trains in opposite direction, but will meet as per Time Table unless otherwise ordered by the Dispatcher.

77. Regular trains two hours behind their schedule time lose both right and class, and can thereafter proceed only by train order.

MOVEMENT OF TRAINS.

78. A train must not leave its initial station on any division, or a junction, or pass from double to single track without orders, and until it has been ascertained whether all trains due, which are superior, or of the same class, have arrived or left.

79. A train leaving its initial station on each division, or leaving a junction, when a train of the same class in the same direction is overdue, will proceed on its schedule and the overdue train will run as prescribed in Rules 77 and 90.

80. A train must not start until the proper signal is given.

81. An inferior train must keep out of the way of a superior train, and clear its time at least five minutes.

82. A train failing to clear the main track by the time required by rule, must be protected as prescribed by Rule 99.

83. No train shall pass any other train at any point without first coming to a stop, and all crews shall ascertain the number and class of each train before proceeding.

84. At meeting points between trains of the same class the inferior train must clear the main track before leaving time of the superior train, and must pull into siding when practicable.

85. If necessary to back in, the train must be first protected as prescribed in Rule 99, unless otherwise provided.

86. At meeting points between trains of different classes, the inferior train must take the siding and clear the superior train at least three minutes, and must pull into the siding when practicable. If necessary to back

in, the train must first be protected as prescribed by Rule 99, unless otherwise provided.

87. An inferior train must keep at least three minutes off the time of a superior train in the same direction.

88. West bound trains will take siding at single track meeting points, unless train orders otherwise direct.

89. A train must stop at schedule meeting or passing points, if the train to be met or passed is of the same class, unless the switches are right and the track clear. Trains should stop clear of the switch used by the train to be met or passed in going on the siding.

90. Following sections of trains must not leave stations and stops under two minutes after preceding section has left, and unless some form of block signal is used, the trains must keep at least 2,500 feet apart, except when closing up at stations and meeting sidings.

91. A train must not arrive at a station in advance of its schedule arriving time. A train must not leave a station in advance of its schedule leaving time.

92. A train must not display signals for a following section, nor an extra train be run without orders from the dispatcher.

93. When signals displayed for a section are taken down at any point before that section arrives, the Conductor will, if there be no other provisions, arrange with the Operator, with the Switch-tender, or in the absence of both, with a Flagman left there for the purpose, to notify all opposing trains of the same or inferior class leaving such point, that the section for which the signals were displayed has not arrived. If impossible for the Conductor to notify opposing trains as provided herein, then the train displaying the signals shall await the arrival of the section for which signals are displayed be-

94. Messages or orders respecting the movement of trains, or the condition of tracks, or bridges, must be in writing.

95. Work extras will be assigned working limits. Within these limits such trains must move with the current of traffic, unless train orders otherwise direct.

96. Trains must approach the end of double track, junctions, railroad crossings at grade, and drawbridges, prepared to stop, unless the switches and signals are right and the track is clear. Where required by law, trains must stop.

97. If practicable to avoid it, a train must not be allowed to stand on a curve between stations.

98. If a train should part while in motion, Trainmen must, if possible, prevent damage to the detached portions. The signals prescribed by Rules 49D-52F must be given, and the front portion of the train kept in motion until the detached portion is stopped.

99. When a train stops or is delayed, under circumstances in which it may be overtaken by another train, the *conductor or flagman must go back immediately with stop signals a sufficient distance to insure full protection.* When recalled, he may return to his train, first placing two torpedoes on the rail when the conditions require it. The front of a train must be protected in the same way, when necessary, by the Motorman.

100. When the Flagman goes back to protect the rear of his train, the Conductor must assume his duties on the train.

101. When cars are pushed by a motor (except when shifting and making up trains in yards) a Flagman must take conspicuous position on front of the leading car and signal the Motorman in case of need.

102. Switches must be left in proper position after having been used. Conductors are responsible for the position of the switches used by them and their trainmen, except where Switchtenders are stationed.

103. Both Conductors and Motormen are responsible for the safety of their trains and proper fulfillment of all running orders received by them, either from Operators or direct from the Dispatchers governing the operation of their trains. and under conditions not provided for by the rules must take every precaution for their protection.

104. In all cases of doubt or uncertainty the safe course must be taken and no risks run.

105. Trains must be operated with caution when passing a train receiving or discharging passengers.

RULES FOR MOVEMENT BY TRAIN ORDERS.

108. For movements not provided for by Time Table, train orders will be issued by authority and over the signature of the Train Dispatcher. They must contain neither information nor instructions not essential to such movements.

109. They must be brief and clear; in the prescribed forms when applicable; and without erasure, alteration, or interlineation.

110. Each Train Order must be given in the same words to all persons or trains addressed.

111. Train Orders will be numbered consecutively each day, beginning with No. 1 at midnight.

112. Train Orders must be addressed to those who are to execute them, naming the place at which each is to receive his copy. Those for a train must be addressed to

the conductor and Motorman, and also to any one who acts as its Pilot. A copy for each person addressed must be supplied by the Operator.

113. Each Train Order must be written in full in a book provided for the purpose at the office of the Dispatcher, and with it must be recorded; the names of those who have signed for the order; the time and from what Station the order was repeated, and the Train Dispatcher's initials. These records must be made at once, and never from memory or memoranda.

114. Regular trains will be designated in Train Orders by their numbers, as "No. 10," or "2d No. 10," adding car numbers; extra trains by leading car numbers, as "Extra 50," with the direction when necessary, as "East" or "West."

115. To obtain orders at station where there are Operators or Agents, the Operator will call up the Dispatcher upon approach of train, who will give such orders as are necessary, whereupon he will write same plainly and without abbreviations, on a blank provided for that purpose, with three carbon copies and as many additional carbon copies as may be ordered by the Dispatcher, and when the Agent has finished writing the order, he shall repeat it to the Train Dispatcher, who will O. K. same, if correct; the Agent shall sign same and repeat his signature with the number of the order to the Dispatcher, who will then give the time at which the order is O. K.'d, which shall be entered upon the order by the Agent. The Agent will hand the orders to the Conductor of the train, for whom it is intended, who shall sign same with name and train number, and read the order in full, without abbreviation, back to the Dispatcher. The dispatcher will, if the order is correct, complete the order by giving

his initials and the time of completion to the Conductor, who will immediately write same on the order, which will then be in full force and effect. If for any reason the line should fail before the Dispatcher completes the order, it is of no effect and then must be treated as if it had not been sent. In case the line is out of order the Dispatcher will use such other means of communicating with the Agents as may be at his command.

116. If the Agent, or one, or both of the crew, or any of them do not understand the order, or have any doubt concerning its meaning, the Dispatcher shall be notified.

117. In no case shall the agent, nor either, nor both, of the crew attempt to influence the decision of the others as to the meaning of an order, nor shall either attempt to assume the sole responsibility for its interpretation. The slightest disagreement must be referred to the Dispatcher.

118. In no case shall a train leave a siding and run out on the main track before the orders have been received by the Motorman and read back as provided and the Conductor has given the proper signal to proceed.

119. To obtain orders at telephone stations where there are no Operators, the Conductor of a train will call the Dispatcher, who will give such orders as are necessary, whereupon the Conductor will write the same plainly without abbreviations, on a blank with carbon copy provided for that purpose, and when the Conductor has finished writing the order he will repeat it to the Train Dispatcher, who will O. K. same, giving time of such O. K., if correct. The Conductor will thereupon enter the time of such O. K. upon order, signing same with train number, and repeat the order without abbreviation with his signature and train number to the Dispatcher, who will complete the order by giving his initials and

time of completion to the Conductor, which initials and time shall be promptly written on the order by the Conductor. When the order has thus been properly completed, it will be in full force and effect. If for any reason the line should fail before the Dispatcher completes the order, it is of no effect and must be then treated as if it had not been sent.

120. When any train reaches a meeting point and finds that the train or trains to be met have not arrived, the Conductor shall immediately call the Dispatcher for orders as provided in Rule 119.

121. Operators receiving Train Orders must write them in manifold during transmission, and if they cannot at one writing make the requisite number of copies, must trace others from one of the copies first made.

122. In case Conductors or Motormen change off before the completion of their trip, they must carefully exchange and receipt for all special orders they may have, and each must know that his orders are perfectly understood by the other. Changes of this kind, however, must never be made without permission from the Train Dispatcher.

123. When a Train Order has been repeated, and before "complete" has been given, the order must be treated as a holding order for the train addressed, but must not be otherwise acted on until "complete" has been given.

124. If the line fails before an office has repeated an order, the order at that office is of no effect, and must be then treated as if it had not been sent.

125. The Operator who receives and delivers a Train Order must preserve the lowest copy.

126. For Train Orders delivered by the Train Dispatcher, the requirements as to the record and delivery are the same as at other offices.

127. A Train Order to be delivered to a train at a point where the train can not get in communication with the Dispatcher, must be addressed to C. & M. ———— at————care of Conductor or other person in whose care it is addressed. When Telephone Train Order is used, "complete" will be given upon the signature of the person by whom the order is to be delivered, who must be supplied with copies for the Conductor and Motorman addressed, and a copy upon which he shall take the signatures.

128. This copy he must deliver to the first Operator accessible, who must preserve it and at once transmit signatures of the Conductor to Train Dispatcher.

129. Orders so delivered must be acted on as if "complete" had been given in the usual way.

130. When a train is named in a Train Order, all its sections are included unless particular sections are specified, and each section included must have copies addressed and delivered to it.

131. Trainmen must know before passing trains against which they have orders, that the train met or passed is the one specified.

132. Unless otherwise directed, an operator must not repeat a Train Order for a train, the motor of which has passed his Train Order signal or station, until he has ascertained that the Conductor and Motorman have been notified that he has orders for them.

133. Train Orders once in effect continue so until fulfilled, superseded, or annulled. Any part of an order specifying a particular movement may be either superseded or annulled.

134. Operators will promptly record and report to the Dispatcher the time of departure of all trains and the direction of extra trains. They will record the time of arrival of trains and report it when so directed. Operators must have the proper appliances for hand signaling for immediate use, if required.

135. Initials for signature of Dispatcher.

Such office and other signals as are arranged by the Chief Train Dispatcher.

C. & M.   for Conductor and Motorman.
No.   for number.
Sec.   for section.
Psgr.   for passenger.
Frt.   for freight.
Mins.   for minutes.
Jct.   for junction.
Dspr.   for train dispatcher.
Opr.   for operator.

The usual abbreviations for the names of the months and stations.

FORMS OF TRAIN ORDERS.

FORM A—FIXING MEETING POINTS FOR OPPOSING TRAINS.

(1) ——— will meet ——— at ———.
(2) ——— will meet ——— at ——— at ———
(and so on).

EXAMPLES.

(1) *No. 1 will meet No. 2 at Bombay.*
No. 3 will meet No. 2d No. 4 at Siam.
No. 5 will meet Extra 95 at Hong Kong.
Extra 652 North will meet Extra 231 South at Yokohama.

(2) *No. 1 will meet No. 2 at Bombay, 2d No. 4 at Siam, and Extra 95 at Hong Kong.*

Trains receiving these orders will run with respect to each other to the designated points and there meet in the manner provided by the rules.

FORM B—DIRECTING A TRAIN TO PASS OR RUN AHEAD OF ANOTHER TRAIN.

(1) ———will pass———at———.
(2) ———will pass———when overtaken.
(3) ———will run ahead of ——— ——— to ———.
(4) will pass———at———and run ahead of——— ——— to ———.

EXAMPLES.

(1) *No. 1 will pass No. 3 at Khartoum.*

(2) *No. 6 will pass No. 4 when overtaken.*

(3) *Extra 594 will run ahead of No. 6, Bengal to Madras.*

(4) *No. 1 will pass No. 3 at Khartoum and run ahead of No. 7, Madras to Bengal.*

When, under (1), a train is to pass another, both trains will run according to rule to the designated point and arrange for the rear train to pass promptly.

Under (2), both trains will run, according to rule, until the second-named train is overtaken and then arrange for the rear train to pass promptly.

Under (3), the second-named train must not exceed the speed of the first-named train between the points designated.

FORM C—GIVING A TRAIN THE RIGHT OVER AN OPPOSING TRAIN.

——— has right over ——— ——— to ———.

EXAMPLES.

(1) *No. 1 has right over No. 2, Mecca to Mirbat.*

(2) *Extra 37 has right over No. 3, Natal to Ratlam.*

This order gives the train first named the right over the other train between the points named.

If the trains meet at either of the designated points the first-named train must take the siding, unless the order is otherwise prescribed.

Under (1), if the second-named train reaches the point last named before the other arrives, it may proceed, keeping clear of the opposing train as many minutes as such train was before required to clear it under the rules.

If the second-named train, before meeting, reaches a point within or beyond the limits named in the order, the Conductor must stop the other train where it is met and inform it of his arrival.

Under (2), the regular train must not go beyond the point last named until the extra train has arrived.

When the extra train has reached the point last named, the order is fulfilled.

The following modification of this form of order will be applicable for giving a work extra the right over all trains in case of emergency.

(3) Work Extra ——— has a right over all trains between ——— and ——— from ———m. to ——— m.

EXAMPLE.

Work Extra 275 has right over all trains between Stockholm and Edinburgh, from 7 p. m. to 12 midnight.

This gives the Work Extra the exclusive right between the points designated between the times named.

FORM D—GIVING REGULAR TRAINS RIGHT OVER A GIVEN TRAIN.

Regular trains have right over ——— between ——— and ———.

EXAMPLE.

Regular trains have right over No. 1 between Moscow and Berlin.

This order gives to regular trains receiving it the right over the train named in the order, and the latter must clear the schedule times of all regular trains, as if it were an extra.

FORM E—TIME ORDERS.

(1) ——— will run ——— late ——— to ———.
(2) ——— will run ——— late ——— to ———, and ——— late ——— to ———, etc.
(3) ——— will wait at ———, until ——— for ———

EXAMPLES.

(1) *No. 1 will run 20 minutes late, Joppa to Mainz.*
(2) *No. 1 will run 20 minutes late, Joppa to Mainz, and 15 minutes, Mainz to Muscat, etc.*
(3) *No. 1 will wait at Muscat, until 10 a. m., for No. 2.*

(1) and (2) make the schedule time of the train named between the stations mentioned, as much later as stated in the order, and any other train receiving the order is required to run with respect to this later time, as before required to run with respect to the regular schedule time. The time in the order should be such as can be easily added to the schedule time.

Under (3) the train first named must not pass the designated station before the time given, unless the other run with respect to the regular schedule time of the train first named.

FORM F—FOR SECTIONS.

———will display signals———to———for———.

EXAMPLES.

Car 20 will display signals and run as 1st No. 1, London to Paris.

No. 1 will display signals, London to Dover, for Car 80.

2d No. 1 will display signals, London to Dover, for Car 90.

This form may be modified as follows:

Cars 70, 80, and 90 will run as 1st, 2d, and 3d No. 1.

Cars 70, 80, and 90 will run as 1st, 2d, and 3d No. 1, London to Dover.

Under these examples the car last named will not display signals.

For annulling a Section:

Car 80 is annulled as 2d No. 1 from Chatham.

If there are other sections following, add:

Following sections will change numbers accordingly.

The character of a train for which signals are displayed may be stated. Each section affected by the order must have copies, and must arrange signals accordingly

FORM G—EXTRA TRAINS.

(1) Car———will run extra———to———.

(2) Car———will run extra———to——— and return to———.

EXAMPLES.

(1) *Car 99 will run extra Berber to Gaza.*

(2) *Car 99 will run extra Berber to Gaza and return to Cabal.*

A train receiving this order is not required to protect itself against opposing extra trains, unless directed by order to do so, but must keep clear of all regular trains, as required by rule.

(3) Car———will run extra, leaving———on———as follows, with right over all trains, as required by rule:

    Leave ———
      "   ———
    Arrive ———
      "   ———

EXAMPLES.

(3) *Car 77 will run extra, leaving Turin on Thursday, February 17, as follows, with right over all trains:*

    Leave Turin 11:30 P. M.
      "   Pekin 12:25 A. M.
      "   Canton 1:47 A. M.
    Arrive Rome 2:25 A. M.

This order may be varied by specifying the kind of extra and the particular trains over which the extra shall or shall not have the right. Trains over which the extra is thus given the right must clear the time of the extra three minutes.

FORM H—WORK EXTRA.

(1) Work extra ——— will work ——— until ——— between———and———.

EXAMPLES.

(1) *Work extra 292 will work 7 a. m. until 6 p. m. between Berne and Turin.*

TRAIN ORDER RULES

The working limits should be as short as practicable, and to be changed as the progress of the work may require. The above may be combined, thus:

(a) *Work extra 292 will run Berne to Turin and work 7 a. m. until 6 p. m. between Turin and Rome.*

When an order has been given to "work" between designated points, no other extra shall be authorized to run over that part of the track without provision for passing the Work Extra.

When it is anticipated that a work extra may be where it cannot be reached for orders, it may be directed to report for orders at a given time and place, or an order may be given that it shall clear the track for (or protect itself after a certain time against) a designated extra by adding to (1) the following words:

(b) *And will keep clear of (or protect against) Extra 223 south between Antwerp and Brussels after 2:10 p. m.*

In this case Extra 223 must not pass the northernmost point before 2:10 P. M., at which time the Work Extra must be out of the way, or protected (as the order may require) between those points.

When the movements of an extra over the working limits cannot be anticipated by these or other orders to the Work Extra, an order must be given to such extra, to protect itself against the Work Extra, in the following form:

(c) *Extra 76 will protect against Work Extra 90 between Lyons and Paris. This may be added to the order to run extra.*

A Work Extra when met or overtaken by an extra must allow it to pass.

When it is desirable that a Work Extra shall at all

times protect itself while on working limits, it may be done by adding to (1) the following words:

(d) *Protecting itself.*

A train receiving this order must, whether standing or moving, protect itself within the working limits in both directions in the manner prescribed by Rule 99.

Whenever an extra is given orders to run over working limits, it must at the same time be given a copy of the order sent to the Work Extra.

To enable a Work Extra to work upon the time of a regular train, the following form may be used:

(e) *Work Extra 292 will protect against No. 55 between Berne and Turin.*

A train receiving this order will work upon the time of the train mentioned in the order, and protect itself against it as prescribed in Rule 99.

The regular train receiving this order must run, expecting to find the Work Extra protecting itself within the limits named.

FORM J—HOLDING OR CALLING UP ORDER.

Hold ——— at ———.
——— will call for orders at ———.

EXAMPLES.

(1) *Hold No. 2 at Detroit.*
(2) *Hold all east bound trains at Halifax.*
(3) *No. 2 will call for orders at Siding 235.*

This order when transmitted as Examples (1) and (2) will be addressed to the operator and acknowledged in the usual manner.

It must be respected by Conductors and Motormen of trains thereby directed to be held as if addressed to them.

Whenever transmitted as per Example (3), it must be completed in same manner as any other telephone train order.

When a train has been so held or ordered to call for orders at any specified place it must not proceed until the order to "hold" or "call" is annulled, or an order given in the form "———" may go.

Form J will only be used when necessary to hold trains until orders can be given or in case of emergency.

If in case train is ordered to call for orders at any specified place, and train cannot get in communication with the Dispatcher, it must stay until communication is established or orders sent to them.

FORM K—ANNULLING A REGULAR TRAIN.

(1) ———of———is annulled———to———.

(2) ———due to leave———is annulled———to———.

EXAMPLES.

(1) *No. 1 of February 29th is annulled, Alaska to Halifax.*

(2) *No. 2, due to leave Naples Saturday, February 29th, is annulled, Alaska to Halifax.*

The train annulled loses both right and class between the stations named and must not be restored under its original number between those stations.

FORM L—ANNULLING AN ORDER.

Order No. ——— is annulled.

If an order which is to be annulled has not been delivered to a train, the annulling order will be addressed to the Operator, who will destroy all copies of the order annulled but his own, and write on that: "Annulled by Order No. ———."

EXAMPLE.

Order No. 10 is annulled.

An order which has been annulled must not be reissued under its original number.

In the address of an order annulling another's orders the train first named must be that to which right was given by the order annulled, and when the order is not transmitted simultaneously to all concerned, it must be first sent to the point at which that train is to receive it, and the required response made, before the order is sent for other trains.

FORM M—ANNULLING PART OF AN ORDER.

That part of Order No. ———, reading ———, is annulled.

EXAMPLE.

That part of Order No. 10, reading No. 1 will meet No. 2 at Sparta, is annulled.

In the address of an order annulling a part of an order, the train first named must be that to which right was given by the part annulled, and when the order is not transmitted simultaneously to all concerned, it must be first sent to the point at which that train is to receive it and the required response made before the order is sent for other trains.

FORM P—SUPERSEDING AN ORDER OR PART OF AN ORDER.

This order will be given by adding to prescribed forms the words "instead of."

(1) ——— will meet ——— at ———, instead of ———.

(2) —— has right over ——, —— to —— instead of ——.

(3) —— will display signals for —— to —— instead of ——.

(4) —— will pass —— at —— instead of ——.

EXAMPLES.

(1) *No. 1 will meet No. 2 at Hong Kong, instead of Bombay.*

(2) *No. 1 has right over No. 2, Mecca to Medina, instead of Mirbrat.*

(3) *No. 1 will display signals for Car No. 85, Astrakan to Teheran, instead of Cabul.*

(4) *No. 1 will pass No. 3 at Medina instead of Khartoum.*

An order which has been superseded must not be reissued under its original number.

FORM R—PROVIDING FOR A MOVEMENT AGAINST THE CURRENT OF TRAFFIC.

—— has right over opposing trains on —— track —— to ——.

EXAMPLE.

(1) *No. 1 has right over opposing trains on No. 2 (or eastward) track, Mecca to Mirbrat.*

A train must not be moved against the current of traffic until the track on which it is to run has been cleared of opposing trains.

Under this order the first-named train must use the track specified between the two points named and has the right over opposing trains on that track between these points. Opposing trains must not leave the point last named, until the first-named train arrives.

An inferior train between the points named, moving with the current of traffic in the same direction as the first-named train, must receive a copy of the order, and may then proceed on its schedule, or right.

(2) This order may be modified as follows:

After ——— arrives at ——— ——— has right over opposing trains on ——— track ——— to ———.

EXAMPLE.

After No. 4 arrives at Mecca, No. 1 has right over opposing trains on No. 2 (or eastward) track, Mecca to Mirbrat.

Under (2), the train to be moved against the current of traffic must not leave the first-named point, until the arrival of the first-named train.

FORM S—PROVIDING FOR THE USE OF A SECTION OF DOUBLE TRACK AS SINGLE TRACK.

——— track will be used as single track between ——— and ———.

If it is desired to limit the time for such use, add (from ——— until ———).

EXAMPLE.

No. 1 (or westward) track will be used as single track between Mecca and Mirbrat.

Adding, if desired:

From 1 p. m. until 3 p. m.

Under this order all trains must use the track specified between the stations named and will be governed by rules for single track.

Trains running against the current of traffic on the track named must be clear of the track at the expiration of the time named, or protected as prescribed by Rule 99.

TRAIN ORDER RULES

(FORM OF TRAIN ORDER)

Train Order No..............

Chief Dispatcher's Office..........190..

To C. & M. ....Train No........Car No. ....

At...................

....

....

....

....

....

....

Conductor	Train	Made	Time	Dispatcher	Operator
....	....	....	....M	....	....
....	....	....	....M	....	....
....	....	....	....M	....	....
....	....	....	....M	....	....

The Conductor and Motorman must both have a copy of this order.

(FORM OF TRAIN ORDER)

Train Order No............

Chief Dispatcher's Office.........190..

To C. & M........Train No. .... Car No......

At....................

....

....

....

....

....

....

Train No.   O. K. at

Dispr.

Conductor ....M ....

Train No.   Received

Motorman ....M .... Opr.

The Conductor and Motorman must both have a copy

TRAIN ORDER RULES

(FORM OF TELEPHONE TRAIN ORDER)

TRAIN ORDER.

East

....

West

Order No. .... Time .... Date ....190...

To Conductor and Motorman

Train No.......... Car No..........at........

Meet Train No.......... Car No..........at........

Meet train No.......... Car No..........at........

and report at ....

....

....

....

....

..............Conductor   ....Opr.

..............Motorman   ....Dispr.

(FORM OF TRAIN CLEARANCE ORDER)

TRAIN CLEARANCE ORDER.

Order No..........   Station..............

Date ....190..

To Conductor and Motorman of Train No.........

Last Train ahead left at........M.

Delivered by........................Opr.

...............Conductor.

....

(Note.)—Should any train have orders not to pass any station *"without orders,"* the reception of this blank does not release it, but in such cases regular orders must be obtained.

TRAIN ORDER RULES

FIXED SIGNALS.

136. Fixed signals are placed at drawbridges, railroad crossings, junctions, stations, and at other points, as required.

SEMAPHORE SIGNALS.

137. Semaphore signals, except Train Order Signals, will be supported on a separate mast for each track. So far as practicable, they will be placed either over or upon the right of and adjoining the track to which they refer and in the same order, whether supported by a signal bridge over the tracks, by putting a bracket and two or more masts on one post, or by using separate masts from the ground.

If there be more than one arm on a mast, the upper will govern the main line, or fast-running route; the second arm will govern the diverging or slow-speed route.

138. The governing arm is displayed to the right of the signal mast, as seen from an approaching train, and the indications are given by positions.

(a) An arm with square end, in a horizontal position, indicates STOP.

(b) An arm with forked end, in a horizontal position, indicates CAUTION—proceed under control.

(c) An arm inclined at an angle of 60 degrees or more below the horizontal, indicates PROCEED.

(d) At night the positions of signals will, in addition, be shown by colored lights:

Red	STOP.
Green	CAUTION.
White	PROCEED.

139. Dwarf Semaphore signals govern slow movements only, the indications being the same as for the high signals.

140. Semaphore signals used for train orders are located at telephone stations. The arms have square ends, and are attached to the same mast for trains in both directions, the governing arm displayed to the right of the mast, as seen from an approaching train. The indications are the same as for other square-end semaphore signals.

BULLETIN ORDERS.

141. Bulletin orders will be posted on the face of bulletin boards for thirty days, after which those still in force will be placed in a permanent file connected with the bulletins. Rules regulating publication of general orders and general notices will be issued by special instructions.

TRAIN DISPATCHERS.

150. Train Dispatchers report to and receive their instructions from the Superintendent.

151. They will issue telephone orders for the movement of trains; see that they are transmitted and recorded in the manner prescribed in the rules; keep a record showing the time of arrival and departure of trains at all open telephone offices. Such record to be carefully filed for subsequent reference.

152. They must use great care in sending Orders, and not transmit an order faster than receiving Operator can take and plainly write it. They will anticipate the necessity for orders as far as possible and have them ready for trains; compel a prompt performance of duty on the part of the Trainmen, with a view to preventing delay.

CONDUCTORS AND MOTORMEN.

153. Conductors and motormen report to and receive their instructions from the Superintendent. They will comply with the instructions of the Dispatchers.

153a. REPORT FOR DUTY—Regular Conductors and Motormen must report for duty five minutes before leaving time for their first trip, or, if for any good reason unable to report, they must give notice at least thirty minutes before such leaving time.

Extra men must report at such time as ordered, or must give notice at least thirty minutes before such time. They must not absent themselves after answering roll call without permission.

153b. When an extra or regular man who has been marked off sick, desires to return to work, he must report to the Dispatcher at 5 o'clock p. m. the day previous to the one on which he wishes to return to work, so that he may be marked for work for the next day.

153c. Conductors and motormen operating trains of this company over the structure east of 52nd Ave. are subject to, and will be governed by the Rules and Regulations of that Company.

154. Before going out on the road they must have a copy of the latest Time Table, and must examine the bulletin board and be fully informed as to all notices posted for their guidance.

They must compare time, before starting, with standard clock, and also check their watches with each other.

155. They are jointly and equally responsible for the safety of the train and the proper use of all precautions required by the Rules and Regulations, and although the Motormen are under the direction of the Conductors as

regards the management of train, they will not obey instructions which imperil the safety of the train or involve a violation of the rules.

156. On arrival at a terminal station, or where there is an Inspector, or Foreman of Repairs, they must report to him any defects in the condition of the cars, or any imperfect action of the brakes during the trip.

156a. Conductors and motormen are positively forbidden to go to meals or delay their trains or permit other employes on their trains to do so, without first obtaining permission from the Train Dispatcher. When such permission is received, Conductors must report when they are ready to go, and ascertain if there are any further orders for their train.

157. They will report promptly by telephone to the Superintendent, any defective switch, or target lights, switch locks, etc., noticed by them.

158. RAILROAD CROSSINGS—Trains must be brought to a full stop at a safe distance approaching railroad crossings at grade, unless controlled by an interlocking system, and Motorman must not proceed until Conductor has gone ahead to the center of crossing, looking both ways, and given the "Come Ahead" signal. Before starting the Motorman will look back to see that no passengers are getting on or off; and in no case proceed, even after Conductor's signal, until he has also examined the crossing and satisfied himself that cars are not approaching.

When there is more than one track, the Conductor must remain in advance of the car until the last track is reached.

CONDUCTORS.

159. In case Conductors change off before the completion of their trip, they must carefully exchange all special orders which they may have, and each must know that his orders are perfectly understood by the other, and they must then carefully compare the orders they receive with those in the hands of the Motorman of the train to which they have transferred, before proceeding on the trip. But changes of this kind must never be made without permission from the proper officers.

160. In case of accident resulting in the loss of life, injury to persons, or damage to property, Conductors must use the utmost care in making reports, and such record as will enable them to furnish a full and complete statement of all the facts with the names and addresses of all persons who witnessed or may have information concerning the accident. See Rule 190.

161. Each Conductor must know that his train is supplied with proper signals.

162. Conductors of passenger trains will pass entirely through their train after leaving each station where their train stops, for the purpose of collecting tickets and fares; and where stops are made at long intervals, they shall frequently pass through to look after the comfort of the passengers.

163. Conductors will keep themselves thoroughly posted as to the time of arrival and departure of trains of connecting roads at junction stations.

164. Conductors are expected to render to all travelers such aid and information as they may need, bearing in mind that many matters plain to the experienced, need explanation to those who are inexperienced, especially to

the humbler classes, many of whom are ignorant of our customs and our language. Such should command the sympathy of every one.

165. They will, if possible, provide all passengers with seats, not permitting anyone to occupy more seats than tickets entitle to, unless there is room for all.

166. Conductor will see that stations are promptly and properly called in each car in his train, and at junction stations and crossings, where trains leave in different directions, the Conductor of each train must announce distinctly in each car before starting, the principal stations on the route.

167. Conductors must make out promptly at the end of each trip, all reports required of them by the several departments. They will strictly observe any special instructions that may be placed upon the blanks used for reports, and will take proper care that their reports are punctually and safely deposited in the designated places for mail. They should keep a memorandum book in which to note the date and all particulars of any occurrence important to remember.

168. Conductors must collect fares at the earliest moment after train has started and *cancel each ticket or trip pass by punching it as soon as presented.*

Great care must be taken in accepting special tickets and passes to know that they are presented by the proper persons, and to see that persons over limited age do not ride without proper tickets.

168a. Conductors must not refuse to accept any form of transportation or eject passenger on account of same unless they *positively know* that said ticket is not good.

168b. Conductors will use extreme care in issuing cash fare receipts to passengers. They will offer this receipt to passenger and if passenger shows disposition to pay no attention, conductor will state that the slip is a receipt for fare and same should be retained by passenger.

169. Should a person be found upon a train without proper transportation, such person must be required by the conductor to pay fare, and in case of refusal, should be requested to leave the train. If such person refuses to leave the train without force being used for that purpose, after the train has been stopped at a regular station, he or she should be removed therefrom, only such force being used for such removal as is necessary therefor.

When necessary to eject a person from the train ascertain the name and address of such person, and the names and addresses of a number of passengers who witnessed the removal, and report the occurrence to the proper officer in writing. But it should not be at such place, in such weather, or at such an unreasonable hour of the night as would be likely to injure the health or safety of the person removed. In no case should a person be removed who is a child of tender years, a person of unsound mind, or a person in such feeble or helpless condition as to be unable to take care of himself or herself at the place of removal.

169a. It is the duty of Conductors to protect passengers who are lawfully on their trains, from rudeness, threatened violence, abusive or obscene language; and any person acting in a disorderly manner, or that annoys passengers as stated above, may be removed from the train at the next station whether provided with a ticket or not. If a ticket or fare has been taken from such person, Conductors should return the ticket properly endorsed for the balance of the journey, or should tender back to such person the regular fare for the uncompleted portion of the journey. Each Conductor will be held responsible for the exercise of reasonable discretion in the performance of this duty, maintaining self control, and being careful to use no unnecessary force that might subject the company to litigation or annoyance.

MOTORMEN.

170. Motormen are required to observe the position of all switches and must know that such switches are right before passing over them.

They will be held responsible for the detection and careful interpretation of all signals given while on the road, when such signals are visible from any position in the vestibule.

171. When approaching switches which they are to use, they must know positively that they are in proper position and that no portion of their train or car is allowed to stand where it will obstruct other tracks improperly.

When switches are being turned ahead of approaching cars, Motormen must know that their train is under control, so as to avoid derailment in case of the imperfect working of the switch.

They will report the absence of lights at switches where lights should be shown, and in approaching such switches they will reduce speed, with the train under control, until the position of the switch is determined.

172. They will exercise caution and good judgment in moving and coupling cars, and in stopping and starting trains, and must avoid all unnecessary jerking, so as to prevent disturbance to passengers, or injury to persons or property.

173. When a passenger train runs by a station or other stopping place, they must always give the back-up signal (See Rules 49-C, 52h, or 56c, or 57c) and receive a response from the Conductor before starting back. Great care must be exercised in backing a train to avoid injury to passengers or others by sudden or unexpected movement.

174. They must not move any train or car at night without a light in front and rear. If any accident should happen to the headlight, a lantern must be used in its place.

175. Motormen will, under no circumstances, allow any one, no matter what rank, to operate any of the machinery on the car, unless they have a letter directed to them personally and signed by the Superintendent; in which case they will be held accountable for the safety of the train.

175a. Motormen must not allow, under any circumstances, any person to ride in his vestibule, unless such person presents a proper permit, or pass, or is entitled to ride therein under a rule or order of the Company.

175b. Under no circumstances shall the Conductor remain in the Motorman's vestibule longer than is necessary to properly receive or deliver Train Orders.

176. STOPPING FOR PASSENGERS—Keep a careful lookout on both sides of the track and bring the car to a full stop for every person who signals at a regular stopping point for such train.

177. REVERSING CAR—Never use the reversing lever to stop car, except to avoid a collision or the injuring of a person or animal, or when the brake rigging is disabled.

Do not reverse the power when the brakes are set, but release the brake and reverse the power simultaneously, and when the reverse lever is thrown in position, apply the current one point at a time; otherwise the fuse will melt.

178. PASSING CARS—Never run against the switch point of crossover when meeting a train or car, but slacken speed sufficiently to allow the train moving in the opposite direction to pass before striking switch point.

This rule refers particularly to all crossovers having switch points facing opposite to the direction in which the train is moving.

179. ECONOMICAL USE OF CURRENT—In order to effect an economical use of the electric current, it is necessary that the continuous movements of starting and increasing speed should be made gradually. An economical start does not jerk a car or train.

In starting a car or train, let it run until the maximum speed of each notch has been obtained before moving the handle to the next notch.

Do not apply brakes when the current is on.

Do not apply current when the brakes are applied.

A great amount of power can be saved by using judgment and discretion in approaching stopping places and switches by shutting off the power so as to allow the train to drift to the stopping place or switch without a too vigorous use of the brake, but time must not be sacrificed to save power.

180. POWER OFF LINE—When the power leaves the line, the controller must be shut off, the light switch turned on, and the car started only when the lamps burn brightly.

181. SANDED RAILS—Never run on freshly sanded rails with brakes full on, except to prevent an accident, as the wheels are liable to be flattened when this is done.

182. DO NOT SLIDE WHEELS—On a slippery rail do not allow wheels to slide; as soon as wheels commence to slide, the brake must be released and reset.

183. "SPINNING OF WHEELS"—Care must be taken, particularly during snow storms, to avoid "spinning" of the wheels with no forward or back movement of the car.

184. If wheels "spin," throw off power and build up one notch at a time, repeating the operation as often as wheels "spin."

185. WATER ON TRACK—When there is water on the track, run the car very slowly, drifting without use of power whenever possible; otherwise there is danger of burning out the motors.

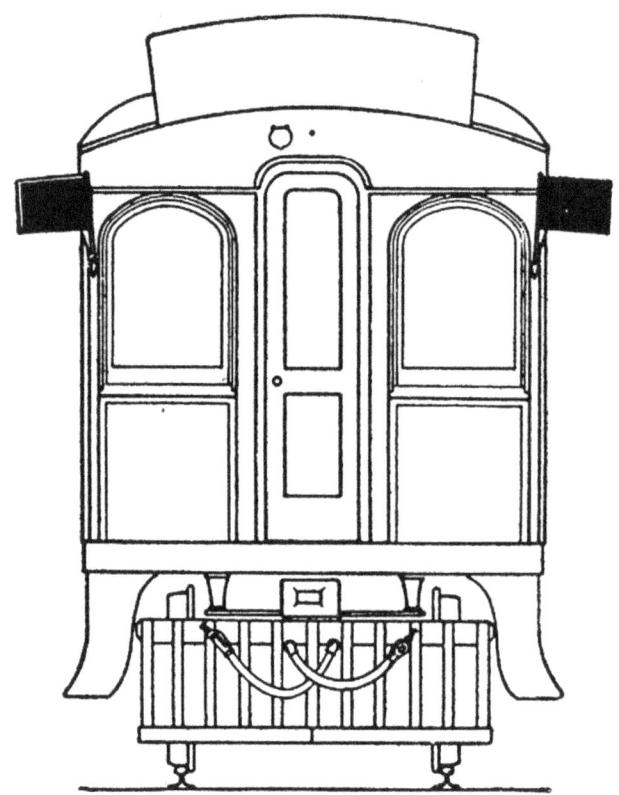

Rear of train by day.
(Red Flags, See Rule 61)

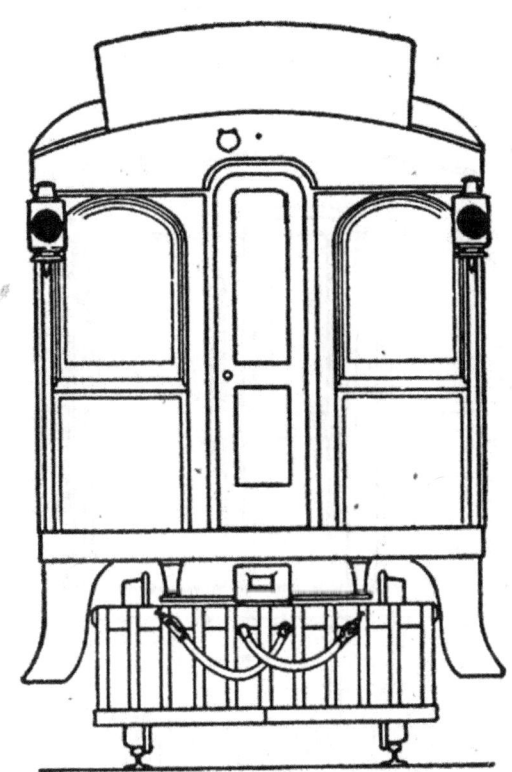

Rear of train running at night.
(Red Lights, See Rule 61)

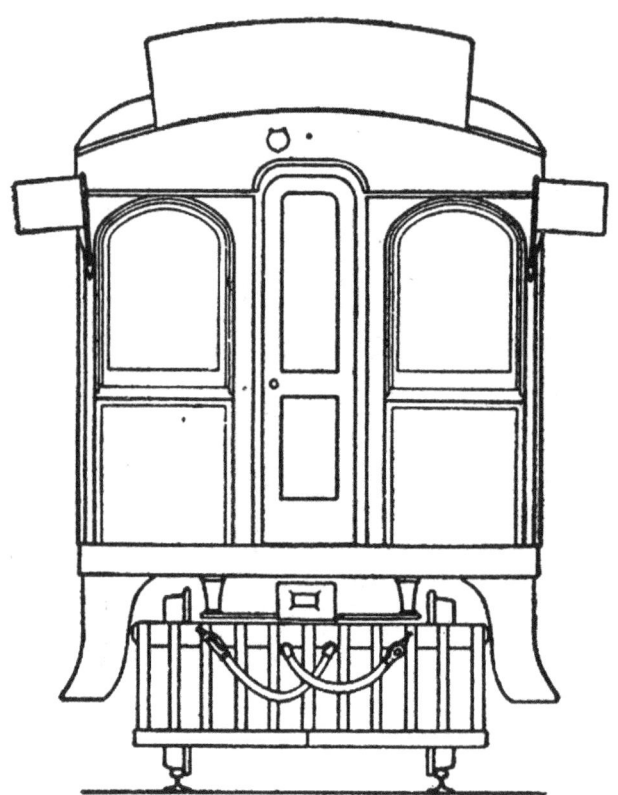

Motor running forward by day as an extra train.
(White Flags, See Rule 63)

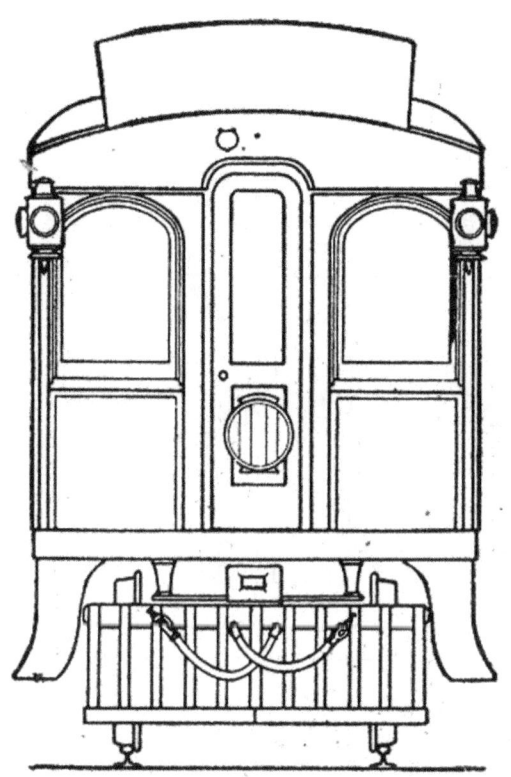

Motor running forward by night as an extra train.
(White Lights, See Rule 63)

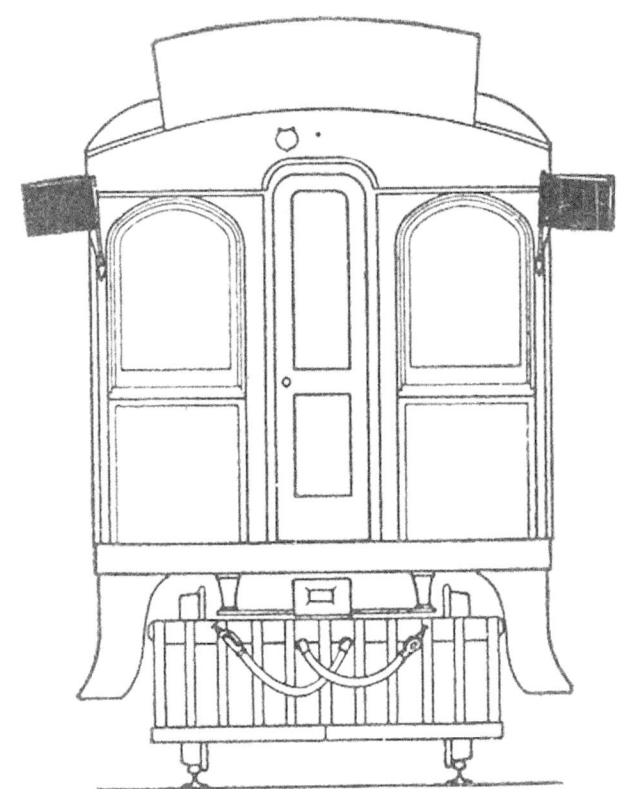

Motor running forward by day displaying signals
for a following section.
(Green Flags, See Rule 62)

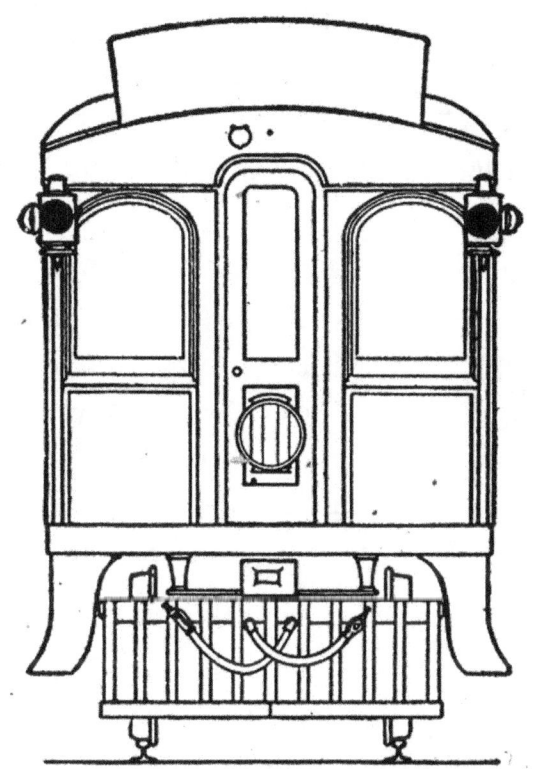

Motor running forward by night displaying signals
for a following section.
(Green Lights, See Rule 62)

EXAMINATION QUESTIONS.

1. Have you read the rules and regulations of this company governing the employes of the operating department, and do you fully understand the provisions that relate to your particular duties?

2. Do you understand that you are required to have a copy of these rules and the current time table with you when on duty?

3. Where are the special instructions to be found?

4. Where are bulletin boards to be consulted?

5. Are special instructions, whether in conflict with these rules or not, to be fully observed while in force?

6. What is expected of you when you know of an infringement of any rule or special instruction?

7. What is expected of you when the meaning of any rule or special instruction is not clear to you?

8. Do you understand that in accepting employment with this company you are required to absolutely obey its rules and assume its risks?

9. Do you understand that you are required to familiarize yourself with the location of all structures or obstructions along the line that will not clear you when on the top or sides of cars? Also as to the condition of equipment or track?

10. Do you understand that you are required to know all brake wheels, dogs, grab irons, hand holds, steps and all other appliances are in safe condition before using same?

11. Who are required to wear uniforms and badges when on duty?

STANDARD TIME.

12. At what points are time-pieces designated as standard, located?

13. Have you a reliable watch, and has it passed inspection?

14. How often should employes' watches be inspected?

15. How often are conductors and motormen required to compare their time-pieces with standard time?

16. When you have not had access to standard time for eight or more hours, what are you required to do before starting on a trip?

TIME TABLE.

17. What is a time table?

18. When a new time table takes effect what does it supersede?

19. When two times are shown for a train at a station, what are they?

20. How are regular meeting and passing points indicated on the table?

21. When there are more trains than one to be met or passed at a given point, how may attention be called to it?

22. How are trains designated and classed on the time table?

SIGNAL RULES.

23. With what appliances must employes, whose duty it is to give signals, be provided and when should they be ready for use?

24. What signals are used by day?

25. What signals are used by night or in foggy weather?

26. What does red signify?

27. What does green signify?

28. What does white signify?

29. What does green and white shown together signify?

30. What does blue signify?

31. What is a torpedo and when should it be used?

32. The explosion of one torpedo indicates what?

33. The explosion of two torpedoes indicates what?

34. What are fusees used for, and what is required when one is found burning on the track?

35. What does a flag, lamp, hat, or any object waved violently across the track indicate?

TRAIN SIGNALS.

36. What are markers? Where displayed? What do they indicate?

37. Are yard motors required to display markers?

38. If while at a meeting or passing point, a train meets or passes you without displaying markers, how would you act?

39. What signals must be provided on the front of a train after sunset or in a fog?

40. What signals are carried on the rear of a train after sunset or in a fog?

41. What do two green flags by day and in addition to green lights by night, carried on the front of a motor, indicate?

42. What do two white flags by day and in addition to white lights by night, carried on the front end of a motor, indicate?

EXAMINATION QUESTIONS

43. When two or more motors are coupled together and carrying signals, as per rules Nos. 20 and 21, should each motor display the signals?

44. If only one flag or light is displayed as a classification signal, how must it be regarded?

45. Who are responsible for the proper display of all train signals?

46. Whose particular duty is it to know that a train is properly equipped with the necessary signal appliances before starting on a trip?

47. When a blue signal is shown on the end of a car, motor or train, what must be done before coupling to, moving or placing other cars in front of car, motor or train so protected?

STEAM WHISTLE SIGNALS.

48. What is the signal for approaching stations, railroad crossing and junctions?

49. What is the signal to apply brakes?

50. What is the signal to throw off brakes?

51. What is the signal from motor that train has parted?

52. Should the signal be repeated and how often?

53. What is the signal to back when the train is standing?

54. What is the signal to call in flagmen from west?

55. What is the signal to call in flagmen from the east?

56. What is the motorman's call for signals from switch tenders, watchmen, trainmen and others?

57. What is the motorman's signal for the flagman to go back and protect the rear of the trains?

58. What signal is used to call attention of trains

being met or passed, to signals that are being carried for a following train? In case signal is not answered, what is required?

59. What is the signal for road crossings at grade?

60. What is the meaning of a succession of short blasts of the whistle?

BELL CORD SIGNALS.

61. What does one tap of the bell indicate when train is running?

62. What do two taps of the bell indicate when train is standing?

63. What do three taps of bell indicate when train is running?

64. What do three taps of bell indicate when train is standing?

65. What do four taps of bell indicate when train is running?

66. What do five taps of bell indicate when train is standing?

67. What does one tap of bell indicate when given by the motorman?

68. What does two taps of bell indicate when given by the motorman?

69. What does five taps of bell indicate when given by motorman?

HAND AND LAMP SIGNALS.

70. What is the signal to stop?

71. What is the signal to move ahead?

72. What is the signal to move back?

73. What is the signal that the train has parted?

74. May these signals be given any other way?

FIXED SIGNALS.

75. What are fixed signals?
76. Where are rules regarding use of fixed signals found?

RULES GOVERNING THE USE OF SIGNALS.

77. How shall a signal imperfectly displayed or the absence of a customary fixed or block signal be regarded, and what is your duty in regard to it?
78. How should a danger signal, other than a fixed signal, be acknowledged by the motorman?
79. When a train is being pushed by a motor at night or when the train is obscured by fog or other causes, what signals must be displayed, and where?
80. Is there any exception to this rule, and where?
81. When should head lights on motors be covered?
82. At what points are torpedoes not to be placed?
83. What is your duty in reference to looking for signals?
84. Is the unnecessary use of the whistle prohibited?
85. What do whistle posts indicate?

TRAIN RULES.

86. What is a regular train?
87. How are regular trains designated on time tables?
88. What is a section of a train?
89. What is an extra train?
90. Is a motor without cars in service on the road considered to be a train?
91. Where and how are trains classified?
92. State the relative rights of tracks of each class of train?

93. How may extra trains be distinguished?

94. Extra trains are of what class compared with regular trains?

95. What is required of a train of inferior class with respect to a train of superior class?

96. What train should take the switch in meeting?

97. If you are obliged to run by a siding and back in, how would you proceed?

98. How long must a train clear the time of a train of a superior class at a meeting point?

99. How long must a train wait at a station before starting, after the departure of a passenger train in the same direction, and how far apart should passenger trains keep when going in the same direction if no form of block system is used?

100. In case you fail to get your train entirely clear of main track by the time required to clear a train of superior right, what must be done?

101. May a train arrive at a station in advance of its schedule arriving time, when shown? If so, under what circumstances?

102. May a train leave a station in advance of its schedule time?

103. What must all trains do in meeting or passing each other?

104. In case a train, to be met, is not at the schedule meeting point, what should you do?

105. How should all trains approach the end of double track, junctions, railroad crossings at grade, and draw bridges?

106. What must be ascertained before leaving a junction, terminal or other starting point, or passing from double to single track?

EXAMINATION QUESTIONS

107. How would you ascertain this?

108. Name the terminals or starting points and ends of double track.

109. When a train has occasion to stop on the road, should care be used to stop where the view is long and clear?

110. When a train is stopped by accident or obstruction or detained at a station or fails to make running time, how should it be protected?

111. How long should flagman wait before going back with signal?

112. How far must flagman go back, and where should he place torpedoes?

113. Under what circumstances may flagman return to his train?

114. When flagman is recalled to his train what should he do before returning?

115. Should flagman return to his train, even if recalled, if an approaching train is within sight or hearing?

116. When flagman goes back to protect train, who should take his place?

117. State in detail what you would do in case your train parted?

118. In case you overtake a train that is parted, how would you proceed?

119. When a train is being pushed by a motor what precautions must be taken to insure safety?

120. Does a delayed train that falls back on the time of another train of the same class thereby lose its rights?

121. Is a train that is unable to keep out of the way of a following train of the same class required to allow the following train to pass it?

122. When do regular trains lose all their rights?

123. In case you overtake a train of the same or superior class that is disabled so it cannot move, how would you proceed?

124. By whose authority shall trains display signals for a following train?

125. What authority is required for running an extra train?

126. How shall work trains run?

127. What precautions are necessary when approaching a station where a train is receiving or discharging passengers?

128. What is the duty of motormen in respect to trains following too closely on the opposite track?

129. What persons are permitted to ride in a motor vestibule?

130. Who are responsible for the switches when there are no switch tenders?

131. May you leave a switch open for train or section that is following you?

132. How must all accidents, detentions to trains, and defects in track, bridges and third rail and overhead lines be reported?

133. May a train leave a station without a signal from its conductor?

134. Are conductors and motormen equally responsible for the safety of their trains and for an observance of the rules relating thereto?

135. What course should be pursued in case of doubt or uncertainty?

136. When for any reason motormen on the road desire to change motors, from whom should they receive authority?

EXAMINATION QUESTIONS

137. Should time be made up in thick and foggy weather?

138. What is required of motormen in regard to air brakes before approaching railroad, crossings at grade, junctions, drawbridges and terminal.

139. What is the maximum speed of all trains through ———— and ————?

140. What precautions must all trains take through yards?

141. Are flying switches prohibited?

142. What precautions must extra trains take in approaching yard limits?

143. Do yard motors have to protect against extra trains?

RULES FOR THE MOVEMENT OF TRAINS BY TELEPHONE ORDERS.

144. By whom are special orders given?

145. In what manner must special orders be given to all sections of trains directly affected by them?

146. How are orders numbered.

147. To whom are orders for a train addressed?

148. Are telephone orders bearing erasures, alterations or interlineations to be accepted?

149. How must each order be recorded at the dispatcher's office?

150. When are these records required to be made?

151. Would a train be required to remain at a meeting point until all sections had arrived?

152. How are orders transmitted?

153. How does a train receive an order at a siding or any place where there is no operator? Explain the procedure fully?

154. How must receiving operators write the orders, and if necessary to make additional copies, how it is to be done?

155. After the order has been repeated correctly by the operator, how will the train dispatcher be governed and what is required of each operator receiving it?

156. How is the order to be handled by those to whom addressed and how is the operator to handle it?

157. What is required of those to whom the order is delivered?

158. After "O. K." has been given and acknowledged, how shall the order be treated by a train addressed?

159. If the line fails before an office has received and acknowledged "O. K." to an order, how it is to be treated?

160. What is a "train clearance" order?

161. When should a "train clearance" order be used?

162. What should O. K. be preceded by?

163. What order must the operator preserve and what should appear thereon?

164. To whom must these orders be sent?

165. Orders used by conductors must be sent to whom?

166. To whom should the conductors and motormen show their orders?

167. Where will motormen place their orders until executed?

168. What is required of orders delivered at superintendent's office?

169. How are orders to be handled when addressed to persons in charge of work requiring the use of the track?

170. What should be done with the copy of order upon which conductors takes signatures of trainmen?

171. How are orders so delivered to be handled by train to which it is delivered?

172. When a train is named does the order include all sections, and should each have a copy of the order?

173. What should an operator do before acknowledging receipt of an order for a train, the motor of which has passed his office?

174. When should an order for a train at a station where it has much work to do be delivered?

175. Can any rights be assumed except those conveyed by the terms of the order?

176. In other respects how should trains be governed?

177. How long does an order remain in effect?

178. What is required of all trains when red is displayed?

179. What is the meaning of semaphore arm, when horizontal and also in an inclined position?

180. What do the rules require of operators in regard to reporting trains?

181. How are regular trains designated in orders?

182. How are extra trains designated?

183. Is the direction of extra trains specified in orders?

184. When you receive an order to meet or pass a train or trains, how do you determine whether the train or trains you meet or pass are those covered by the order?

185. Do you understand that an order to call the dispatcher at any given siding is a holding order at such siding?

TRAIN ORDERS.

186. "1st No. 10 will call for orders at Bushnell's Basin." Siding 9. If you were on 1st No. 10 and could not get in telephone communication at Bushnell's Basin with the dispatcher, what would you do?

187. Suppose 2nd No. 10 did not have above order and arrived at Bushnell's Basin with 1st No. 10 what would she do?

188. No. 3, Car 4, and No. 6, Car 8, will meet at Gary siding. How would you be governed if in charge of No. 3?

189. 1st No. 10, Car 5, will meet extra 100 East at Pleasant Hill, Extra 32 at Ingalton siding, and Extra 4 at Smith's siding. What would you do under this order?

190. No. 5, Car 1, and Extra 8 West, will meet at Gary's siding. Extra 8 West and Extra 31 East will meet at Warrenville. Explain this order.

191. No. 10, Car 6, will carry signals, Wheaton to Eola Junction, for Car 30. Explain this order and say how it may be modified?

192. Car 31 will run extra Wheaton to Elgin. Explain what you would do if in charge of this train?

193. Car 9 will work extra, 7 a. m. to 6 p. m., between College Ave. and Glen Ellyn, protecting itself against all trains. Explain this order?

QUESTIONS ON AIR BRAKE.

194. What is the power used to operate an air brake?
195. What form is used on this road?
196. How does it apply the brake?
197. Why is it called automatic brake?
198. How is the brake released?

199. Where is the pressure stored that supplies the brake cylinder?

200. What parts compose the automatic brake on a motor car?

201. On a trailer?

202. From the pump, where does the air go?

203. Where are the main reservoirs located?

204. What is the duty of the triple valve?

205. What is the brake valve used for?

206. What pressure should be carried in the main reservoir?

207. What pressure should be carried in the auxiliary reservoir?

208. What is main reservoir pressure used for?

209. Where does main reservoir pressure end?

210. What is the duty of the feed valve?

211. Where does the air go after leaving main reservoir?

212. How many pipe lines through car, and what are they?

213. To what is control pipe connected?

214. How many positions has the brake valve and what are they?

215. What is release position used for?

216. What is lap position used for?

217. What is service application position used for?

218. What is emergency position and when should it be used?

219. What is the purpose of the brake pipe?

220. How great a reduction of brake pipe pressure is needed to fully apply brake?

221. Why does this fully apply brakes?

222. What bad feature would result in a greater reduction of pressure?

223. How many applications should be made for ordinary service stops?

224. What do you understand by an application?

225. Why should brake cylinder pressure gradually be released as speed decreases?

226. In case of bursting hose or conductors' valve being operated on train, what should be done? Why?

227. How should conductors' valves be operated?

228. How would you release a brake?

229. How would you cut out a brake?

230. If pipe should burst at main reservoir in train of two or more motor cars, what should be done?

231. If supply line hose burst between two motor cars, what should be done?

232. If supply line hose burst between motor and trailer, what should be done?

233. If brakes should become disconnected on forward car in a two motor car train and also broken pipe at main reservoir, what should be done?

234. In case of feed valve sticking and allowing auxiliary reservoir pressure to equalize with main reservoir pressure, how can feed valve be cleaned temporarily?

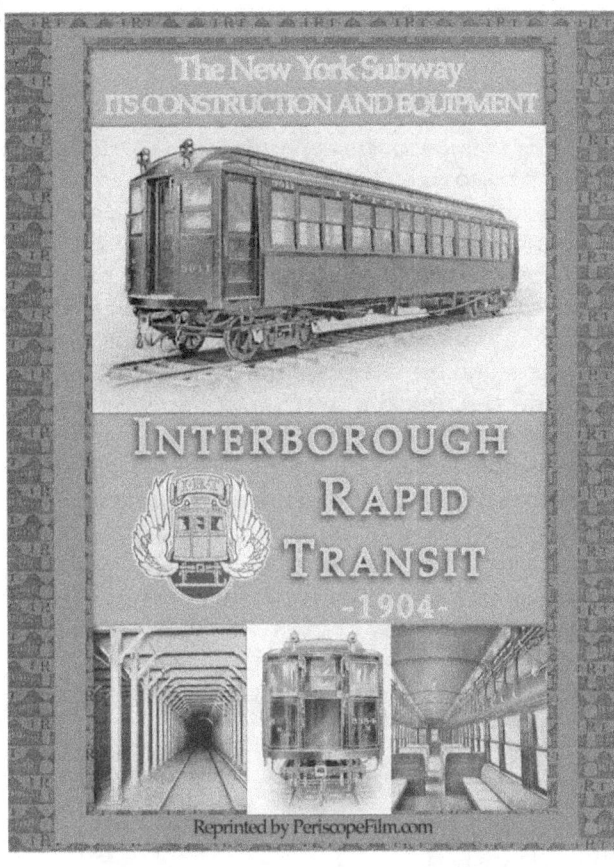

On October 27, 1904, the Interborough Rapid Transit Company opened the first subway in New York City. Running between City Hall and 145th Street at Broadway, the line was greeted with enthusiasm and, in some circles, trepidation. Created under the supervision of Chief Engineer S.L.F. Deyo, the arrival of the IRT foreshadowed the end of the "elevated" transit era on the island of Manhattan. The subway proved such a success that the IRT Co. soon achieved a monopoly on New York public transit. In 1940 the IRT and its rival the BMT were taken over by the City of New York. Today, the IRT subway lines still exist, primarily in Manhattan where they are operated as the "A Division" of the subway. Reprinted here is a special book created by the IRT, recounting the design and construction of the fledgling subway system. Originally created in 1904, it presents the IRT story with a flourish, and with numerous fascinating illustrations and rare photographs.

Originally written in the late 1900's and then periodically revised, A History of the Baldwin Locomotive Works chronicles the origins and growth of one of America's greatest industrial-era corporations. Founded in the early 1830's by Philadelphia jeweler Matthais Baldwin, the company built a huge number of steam locomotives before ceasing production in 1949. These included the 4-4-0 American type, 2-8-2 Mikado and 2-8-0 Consolidation. Hit hard by the loss of the steam engine market, Baldwin soldiered on for a brief while, producing electric and diesel engines. General Electric's dominance of the market proved too much, and Baldwin finally closed its doors in 1956. By that time over 70,500 Baldwin locomotives had been produced. This high quality reprint of the official company history dates from 1920. The book has been slightly reformatted, but care has been taken to preserve the integrity of the text.

NOW AVAILABLE AT
WWW.PERISCOPEFILM.COM

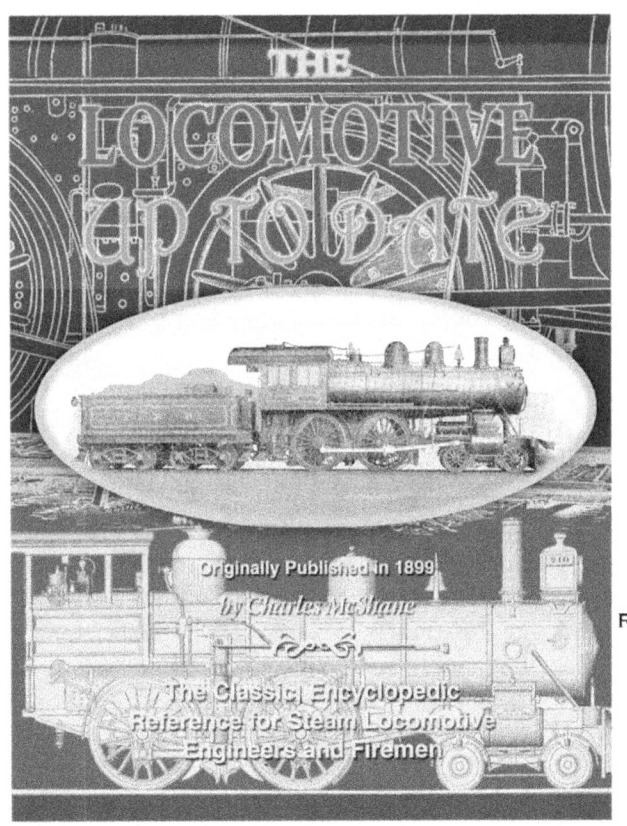

When it was originally published in 1899, **The Locomotive Up to Date** was hailed as "...the most definitive work ever published concerning the mechanism that has transformed the American nation: the steam locomotive." Filled with over 700 pages of text, diagrams and photos, this remains one of the most important railroading books ever written. From steam valves to sanders, trucks to side rods, it's a treasure trove of information, explaining in easy-to-understand language how the most sophisticated machines of the 19th century were operated and maintained. This new edition is an exact duplicate of the original. Reformatted as an easy-to-read 8.5x11 volume, it's delightful for railroad enthusiasts of all ages.

Originally printed in 1898 and then periodically revised, **The Motorman...and His Duties** served as the definitive training text for a generation of streetcar operators. A must-have for the trolley or train enthusiast, it is also an important source of information for museum staff and docents. Lavishly illustrated with numerous photos and black and white line drawings, this affordable reprint contains all of the original text. Includes chapters on trolley car types and equipment, troubleshooting, brakes, controllers, electricity and principles, electric traction, multi-car control and has a convenient glossary in the back. If you've ever operated a trolley car, or just had an electric train set, this is a terrific book for your shelf!

ALSO NOW AVAILABLE FROM PERISCOPEFILM.COM!

THE CLASSIC 1911 TROLLEY CAR BUILDER'S REFERENCE BOOK

ELECTRIC RAILWAY DICTIONARY

By Rodney Hitt
Associate Editor, Electric Railway Journal

REPRINTED BY PERISCOPEFILM.COM

©2008-2010 Periscope Film LLC
All Rights Reserved
ISBN #978-1-935700-24-1
www.PeriscopeFilm.com

www.ingramcontent.com/pod-product-compliance
Lightning Source LLC
Chambersburg PA
CBHW082034230426
43670CB00016B/2656